D1621271

READERS AND AUTHORSHIP IN EARLY MODERN ENGLAND

While authors in early modern England were gaining new authority – legally, economically, and symbolically – Renaissance readers also were expected to participate in and make use of an author's writings. In this book, Stephen B. Dobranski examines how the seventeenth-century phenomenon of printing apparently unfinished works ushered in a new emphasis on authors' responsibility for written texts while it simultaneously reinforced Renaissance practices of active reading. Bringing together textual studies, literary criticism, and book trade history, Dobranski provides fresh insight into Renaissance constructions of authorship and offers new, discerning interpretations of publications by Sir Philip Sidney, Ben Jonson, John Donne, Robert Herrick, and John Milton. The omissions in all these writers' works provide a unique window into English literary history: through these blank spaces we glimpse the tension between implication and inference, between writers' intentions and readers' responses, and between an individual author and a collaborative community.

STEPHEN B. DOBRANSKI is Associate Professor of English at Georgia State University. He is the author of *Milton, Authorship and the Book Trade* (Cambridge, 1999), and co-editor of *Milton and Heresy* (Cambridge, 1998).

READERS AND AUTHORSHIP IN EARLY MODERN ENGLAND

STEPHEN B. DOBRANSKI

CAMBRIDGE
UNIVERSITY PRESS

CAMBRIDGE UNIVERSITY PRESS

Cambridge, New York, Melbourne, Madrid, Cape Town, Singapore, São Paulo

Cambridge University Press
The Edinburgh Building, Cambridge CB2 2RU, UK

Published in the United States of America by Cambridge University Press, New York

www.cambridge.org
Information on this title: www.cambridge.org/9780521842969

First published 2005

Printed in the United Kingdom at the University Press, Cambridge

A catalogue record for this book is available from the British Library

Library of Congress Cataloguing in Publication data
Dobranski, Stephen B.
Readers and authorship in early modern England / by Stephen B. Dobranski.
Includes bibliographical references and index.
1. English literature – Early modern, 1500–1700 – History and criticism.
2. Authorship – History – 16th century.   3. Literature publishing – England – History – 16th century.
4. Literature publishing – England – History – 17th century.   5. Authors and readers – England –
History – 16th century.   6. Authors and readers – England – History – 17th century.   7. Books and
reading – England – History – 16th century.   8. Books and reading – England – History – 17th
century.   9. Authorship – History – 17th century.   10. Reader-response criticism.   1. Title.
PR428.A8D63   2004
820.9′003 – dc22   2004048198

ISBN-13 978-0-521-84296-9 hardback
ISBN-10 0-521-84296-4 hardback

For Shannon

Contents

List of illustrations

Acknowledgments

This book has benefited from the suggestions and encouragement of many readers during the years it was in progress. Stephen M. Fallon, Dayton Haskin, and Leah S. Marcus read and commented on parts of an earlier manuscript; their thoughtful advice and questions helped me to revise individual sections and to elaborate the book's larger argument. The late D. F. McKenzie also responded kindly to an earlier version of one chapter, and, with characteristic generosity, he shared with me parts of his unpublished lectures. I am indebted as well to Ray Ryan, Jackie Warren, and the astute readers at Cambridge University Press. Ray and Jackie have guided this project through each stage of the publication process, and the readers' thorough comments helped me to fine-tune parts of several chapters and to re-shape the overarching organization.

For their contributions to my writing and thinking, my students and colleagues at Georgia State University deserve my warm thanks. In particular, I am grateful to Michael Galchinsky, Pitt Harding, Scott Lightsey, Pearl McHaney, Mary Ramsey, LeeAnne Richardson, Marilynn Richtarik, Robert Sattelmeyer, Renée Schatteman, and Paul Schmidt. Their responses to sections of the work in progress improved the book as a whole, and their enthusiasm for the project revived my sometimes flagging spirits. James Hirsh deserves special thanks for his detailed comments that helped me polish the prose and logic in two chapters. I am also grateful for the generous encouragement I have received from a wide community of Renaissance and textual scholars, especially Sharon Achinstein, Thomas L. Berger, Dennis Danielson, Charles W. Durham, Achsah Guibbory, Charles A. Huttar, William Kerrigan, Albert C. Labriola, Michael Lieb, Kristin A. Pruitt, Stella Revard, Elizabeth Sauer, John T. Shawcross, Michael Winship, and Joseph Wittreich. Directly and indirectly, their own work on bibliography and the seventeenth century has improved much of what follows.

The research for this book was facilitated by the helpful staffs at the Bodleian Library, the British Library, the New York Public Library, and the Rare Book and Special Collections Library at the University of Illinois at Urbana-Champaign. Most of the research, however, was conducted at the Harry Ransom Humanities Research Center at the University of Texas at Austin, and I remain grateful to past and present members of the staff for their friendly assistance. Two of my trips to the Ransom Center were funded in part by grants from the Department of English at Georgia State University, and, during the final summer of revision, the department generously awarded me an additional grant that helped me to complete the manuscript.

I am also indebted to the editors and conference organizers who first allowed me to make public some of my findings about seventeenth-century readers and authorship. Briefer versions of chapters 3 and 6 were published, respectively, as "Jonson's Poetry Lost," *English Literary Renaissance* 30 (Winter 2000): 77–94, and "Text and Context for *Paradise Regain'd* and *Samson Agonistes*," in *Altering Eyes: New Perspectives on* Samson Agonistes, ed. Joseph Wittreich and Mark R. Kelley (Newark: University of Delaware Press, 2002), pp. 30–53; sections of chapter 1 and 6 appear in a condensed form as part of "Milton's Ideal Readers," in *Milton's Legacy*, ed. Charles W. Durham and Kristin A. Pruitt, forthcoming from Susquehanna University Press. I am pleased to acknowledge the Massachusetts Center for Renaissance Studies, the University of Delaware Press, and Susquehanna University Press for their permission to build on these materials.

Finally, I wish to thank John P. Rumrich for his inestimable acumen and kindness. His keen insights improved parts of this book, and he was never too busy to send me some reassuring lines via email. My parents and sisters have also helped to make this book possible – in more ways than I can express and more ways than they realize. My first readers and teachers, they early on instilled in me the rewards of hard work and have never stopped teaching me the value of family. My wife Shannon also deserves my warmest thanks; without her good sense and wise counsel, this book would not exist. Shannon challenged me again and again to write more clearly and argue more incisively. From beginning to end, she has graced this project with her unbounded support and unwavering confidence. Any faults that remain are my own.

Note on the texts

When quoting from seventeenth-century texts, I have tried to preserve the spelling, pointing, capitalization, elision, and use of roman and italic case. However, ſ and u/v have been silently modernized; most small capitals have been treated as upper case letters; and ligatures and swash letters have been ignored. I have retained ſ only when it affects the content of a title page or errata list. Translations from Latin, unless otherwise indicated, are my own.

Abbreviations

CP	*The Complete Prose Works of John Milton*, gen. ed. Don M. Wolfe, 8 vols. (New Haven, 1953–82).
Herford and Simpson	*Works of Benjamin Jonson*, ed. C. H. Herford, Percy Simpson, and Evelyn Simpson, 11 vols. (Oxford, 1925–52).
OED	*Oxford English Dictionary*, 2nd edn.
Pforz	Carl H. Pforzheimer Library, English Literature 1475–1700, held at the Harry Ransom Humanities Research Center, the University of Texas at Austin.
STC	A. W. Pollard and G. R. Redgrave, comps., *A Short-Title Catalogue of Books Printed in England, Scotland, and Ireland, and of English Books Printed Abroad, 1475–1640*, rev. W. A. Jackson, F. S. Ferguson, and Katharine F. Pantzer, 2nd edn., 3 vols. (London, 1976–91).
Wing	Donald Wing, comp., *Short-Title Catalogue of Books Printed in England, Scotland, Ireland, and British America and of English Books Printed in Other Countries, 1641–1700*, 2nd edn., 4 vols. (New York, 1982–88).

Introduction: Renaissance omissions

> I have said somewhere it is the unwritten part of books that would be
> the most interesting.
> – William M. Thackeray[1]

When Lady Anne Bacon observed in 1613, "that the old proverbis be not
alwaies trewe, for I do fynde that the absence of my Nath. doth brede in
me the more continuall remembrance of hym," she was presumably challenging two popular contemporary aphorisms, "out of sight, out of mind"
and "long absent, soon forgotten."[2] This conventional wisdom reached
back at least to 1250 and the medieval manuscript the *Proverbs of Alfred*,
but Bacon's contrary observation, that "absence sharpens love," began to
appear more often during the sixteenth and seventeenth centuries as various
writers noted the perverse rewards of missing something or someone.[3] Thus
Milton's Adam agrees to work apart from his insistent consort because, as he
rationalizes, "short retirement urges sweet returne," and Ariosto in *Orlando
Furioso* accepts that "Long absence grieves," but notes that when lovers
"meet againe / Absence delights, & doth more pleasant make it."[4] Probably
Shakespeare's sonnet 39 most fully addresses the benefits of missing someone. While the speaker acknowledges that a young man's absence could feel
"sour" and "a torment . . . prove," he also desires such "sweet leave" so that

---

[1] William M. Thackeray, "To Paul Émile Daurand Forgues, 16 September 1854," in *The Letters and
Private Papers of William Makepeace Thackeray*, ed. Gordon N. Ray, 4 vols. (Cambridge, MA, 1946),
3: 389–91.

[2] Lady Anne Bacon, "Letter to Lady Jane Cornwallis (1613)," in *The Private Correspondence of Lady Jane
Cornwallis*, ed. Lord Braybrooke (London, 1842), pp. 11–12; and Morris Palmer Tilley, *A Dictionary of
the Proverbs in England in the Sixteenth and Seventeenth Centuries* (Ann Arbor, 1950), S438 and F596.
Tilley also notes the related proverb, "seldom seen, soon forgotten" (S208).

[3] See *The Proverbs of Alfred*, ed. Hellen Pennock South (New York, 1931), p. 122; and *The Oxford
Dictionary of English Proverbs*, 3rd edn., rev. F. P. Wilson (Oxford, 1970), p. 602.

[4] John Milton, *Paradise Lost*, ed. Alastair Fowler, 2nd edn. (London, 1998), book IX, line 250; and
Ludovico Ariosto, *Orlando Furioso in English Heroical Verse*, trans. John Harrington (1591; New
York, 1970), XXXI.1–3 (p. 250). Subsequent quotations from *Paradise Lost* are taken from Fowler's
edition.

he can "entertain the time with thoughts of love."[5] Absence, traditionally associated with loss, in this poem gives the speaker something: his heart not only grows fonder, but, as the speaker retreats to create and think, he discovers he can imaginatively summon his friend.

In this book I am examining various ways that the paradoxical effects of absence found expression in Renaissance literature. But rather than addressing the absent beloved or separation as a general concept, I am interested in the interpretive implications of works with actual missing pieces. The seventeenth-century phenomenon of printing apparently unfinished works ushered in a new emphasis on authors' responsibility for written texts while it simultaneously reinforced Renaissance practices of active reading. In terms of the conflicting logic in the above proverbs, readers might not mind certain elements that an author removes from a text, or, as I show in the following case studies, readers might find the pieces an author omits especially provocative and meaningful. This book's overarching premise is that authors, like all speakers, can convey ideas by saying almost nothing; the best writers can create moments of audible silence, or as Milton envisions in *Paradise Lost*, of "darkness visible" (book I, line 63).

I have thus tried, borrowing Wallace Stevens' eloquent distinction, to differentiate between the "Nothing that is not there and the nothing that is."[6] By "Renaissance omissions" I mean the nothing that is there – Renaissance texts that look incomplete but whose deliberate holes establish an author's authority and enhance rather than diminish meaning. In a 1655 edition of Sir Philip Sidney's *Arcadia*, for example, an anonymous poet pretends to restore a previously omitted verse so as to cement Sidney's contemporary reputation; in Ben Jonson's 1616 *Workes*, Jonson himself has removed part of a poem to demonstrate his control over his book and his patrons; in John Donne's posthumous *Poems* (1633), the printer and publisher use the collection's verse fragments to authorize Donne and create the illusion of his direct involvement; in Robert Herrick's *Hesperides* (1648), the poet includes two incomplete poems to illustrate the reader's role in establishing his fame after death; and in John Milton's *Paradise Regain'd . . . Samson Agonistes* (1671), the poet asserts his own authority by strategically leaving out ten lines that appear at the back of the book as an *Omissa*. Publications such as these differ from other unfinished or censored Renaissance works because their authors and/or publishers seem to want

---

[5] *Shakespeare's Sonnets*, ed. Katherine Duncan-Jones (Nashville, TN, 1997), lines 5, 9–14. Shakespeare would elsewhere write about separation less optimistically. See sonnets 57, 58, and 109.

[6] Wallace Stevens, "The Snow Man," in *The Collected Poems of Wallace Stevens* (New York, 1995), pp. 9–10, line 15.

readers to notice the imperfections. Like Lady Anne Bacon's "Nath." or the companion in Shakespeare's sonnet, all these omissions remain evocatively present; something may be missing, but its absence is palpable.

The publishing of genuinely incomplete literary works began in the fifteenth century with the introduction of printing to England: William Caxton published two editions of Geoffrey Chaucer's unfinished *Canterbury Tales*, in 1478 and 1484, which were followed by a series of black-letter folios by various Renaissance publishers. The raggedness of Chaucer's medieval canon also prompted some contemporary readers to try to complete his works. Caxton himself composed a brief envoi to Chaucer's unfinished *House of Fame* (1483) in which the speaker "*sodeynly awoke anon*" and "*remembryd what I had seen / And how hye and ferre I had been*" (lines 2–4).[7] But whereas Caxton carefully separated his words from Chaucer's – he labeled the added verse "Caxton" and announced "I fynde nomore of this werke to fore sayd" – later publishers and writers proved less scrupulous. So much spurious Chauceriana sprang up and cleaved to subsequent printed texts that readers had difficulty distinguishing imitations from Chaucer's genuine writings.[8] By 1602 the approximately 34,000 lines of Chaucer's medieval canon had swelled to almost 55,000 lines in more than forty works.[9] These addenda, including two spurious *Canterbury Tales*, were presented as omissions, works by Chaucer that previous editions had mistakenly excluded.

Probably the most well-known Renaissance response to Chaucer's incomplete works remains Edmund Spenser's attempt in the fourth book of *The Faerie Queene* to "revive" Chaucer's "labours lost" from the *Squire's Tale*.[10] Unlike those writers who tried to pass off their works as Chaucer's, Spenser openly appeals to his "renowmed [*sic*]" predecessor to help him "follow . . . the footing of thy feete, / That with thy meaning so I may the rather meete" (IV.2.32, 34). Spenser distinguishes himself from contemporary pretenders by laying claim to the "infusion sweete" of Chaucer's "owne spirit," which, he believes, "doth in me survive" (IV.2.34). Spenser's own *Faerie Queene* was also published as an incomplete text – the first two editions containing only

[7] Geoffrey Chaucer, *The Book of Fame* ([Westminster], 1483; STC 5087), d3r.
[8] Chaucer, *The Book of Fame*, d3r. As Caxton complained in his second edition of the *Canterbury Tales*, "many of the sayd bookes / whyche wryters have abrydgyd it and many thynges left out / And in so*mm*e [sic] place haue sette certayn varsys / that he neuer made ne sette in hys booke." See W. J. B. Crotch, ed., *The Prologues and Epilogues of William Caxton* (London, 1956), pp. 90–91.
[9] Alice S. Miskimin, *The Renaissance Chaucer* (New Haven, 1975), p. 257.
[10] Edmund Spenser, *The Faerie Queene*, ed. Thomas P. Roche, Jr. with C. Patrick O'Donnell, Jr. (New York, 1978), book IV, canto 2, stanza 34. Subsequent quotations from the poem are also taken from this edition and are cited by book, canto, and stanza number.

half of the twelve books overconfidently predicted on the first title page –
and in 1609 there appeared three additional fragments that the printer
introduced as "CANTOS OF *MUTABILITIE*: Which, both for Forme
and Matter, appeare to be parcell of some following Booke of the *FAERIE
QUEENE*."[11]

That England's two greatest poetic sons had never finished their greatest
poetic works presumably provided sufficient precedent for later Renaissance
stationers and writers who wanted to take incomplete works to press. Given,
too, that classical texts such as Ovid's *Metamorphoses* had come down to the
Renaissance unfinished and that the ongoing practice of manuscript publication accommodated the circulation of works in progress, we should not be
surprised to find that so many incomplete literary texts were printed during
the seventeenth century. Christopher Marlowe's *Hero and Leander* (1598)
appeared as an "unfinished tragedy" that George Chapman attempted to
supplement;[12] Lady Mary Wroth had *The Countess of Montgomery's Urania*
(1621) published before it was complete;[13] John Davies' *Orchestra* (1622)
was printed "*Not finished*" and "*wanting some Stanzaes describing Queene
Elizabeth*";[14] William Rawley had Francis Bacon's *New Atlantis* (1626) published posthumously as "A Work Unfinished";[15] Milton's incomplete "The
Passion" was printed in his *Poems* (1645, 1673) with the explanation that
the verse was "*above the yeers he had, when he wrote it*";[16] John Hall had an
incomplete "Hymne" published in his *Divine Poems* (1647), "though other
occasions suffer him onley to present it in the habit of a Fragment";[17] Sir
William Davenant published a preface (1650), then only the first three books
(1651) of his epic *Gondibert*;[18] Abraham Cowley had his *Davideis* printed

[11] Spenser, *The Faerie Queene* (London, 1609; STC 23083), Hh4r.
[12] *Hero and Leander. Begun by C. Marloe; and finished by G. Chapman* (London, 1598; STC 17414).
    Marion Campbell, "'*Desunt Nonnulla*': The Construction of Marlowe's *Hero and Leander* as an
    Unfinished Poem," *ELH* 51.2 (1984): 241–68, has challenged the status of *Hero and Leander* as an
    incomplete text.
[13] See Lady Mary Wroth, *The Countesse of Mountgomeries Urania* (London, 1621; STC 26051), Zzz6v.
    The *Urania* ends abruptly in mid-sentence with the word "And", which may have been included
    deliberately to emulate Sidney's incomplete *Arcadia*, or may have resulted from the printer's mis-
    reading the manuscript's catchword as part of the text. See Wroth, *The First Part of the Countess of
    Montgomery's Urania*, ed. Josephine A. Roberts (Binghamton, NY, 1995), pp. cx–cxi.
[14] John Davies, *Nosce Teipsum* (London, 1622; STC 6359), H3r, L2r. *Orchestra* is printed at the back of
    the book, H3r–L3r.
[15] See Francis Bacon, *Sylva Sylvarum or A Naturall History* (London, 1626; STC 1168). *New Atlantis* is
    printed at the back of the book, ²A–G3.
[16] *Poems of Mr. John Milton, both English and Latin, Compos'd at Several Times* (London, 1645; Wing
    M2160), B2r.
[17] John Hall, *Poems*, 2nd edn. (Cambridge, 1647; Wing H355). The collection is printed as a double
    book with a separate title page and imprint for *Divine Poems* (London, 1647). "A Hymne" appears
    in this second half, G7v–H1r.
[18] Sir William Davenant, *The Preface to Gondibert, An Heroick Poem* (Paris, 1650; Wing D334A), and
    Davenant, *Gondibert: An Heroick Poem* (London, 1651; Wing D324), especially Kkk1r.

(1656), never having found "*Leisure*" nor "*Appetite*" to "finish the work" or "revise that part which is done";[19] Katherine Philips' translation of the French play *Horace* appeared as a fragment at the end of her posthumous *Poems* (1667);[20] and Charles Cotton's two incomplete poems, "An Essay upon Buchanan's First Book of Sphæra" and "Philoxipes and Policrite," were printed in his *Poems on Several Occasions* (1689), each with the tag "*Caetera desunt.*"[21]

Writing in the 1690s, Jonathan Swift made satiric hay out of such omissions and what they signify. As the writer in *A Tale of a Tub* turns to the subject of religious factions, he inserts a faux "*Hiatus in MS*," and Swift playfully adopts the guise of editor in a footnote:

Here is pretended a defect in the manuscript; and this is very frequent with our author either when he thinks he cannot say anything worth reading, or when he has no mind to enter on the subject, or when it is a matter of little moment; or perhaps to amuse his reader (whereof he is frequently very fond) or lastly, with some satirical intention.[22]

Although the Renaissance writers I am examining did not share *A Tale's* "satirical intention," they, like Swift, still appreciated the rhetorical effect of genuine or feigned hiatuses. These writers and publishers wanted "defects" in their texts not because they "cannot say anything worth reading" but because they had something to say that required, as we will see, special emphasis.

In this book I am recommending, in other words, that we take Swift seriously: during the early modern period, astute authors could communicate with astute readers through a text's omissions. While I am not proposing that the appearance of these omissions characterizes seventeenth-century literature in general, or even that they occur more frequently during the Renaissance than during other periods, a careful analysis of such missing pieces offers us more than fresh insight into the meaning of individual literary works. Scrutinizing the blank spaces in publications by Sidney, Jonson, Donne, Herrick, and Milton helps us better understand the changing conditions of authorship in early modern England: while the notion of an

[19] Abraham Cowley, *Poems* (London, 1656; Wing C6682), b2r. Cowley's *A Poem on the Late Civil War* (London, 1679; Wing C6679) was also published posthumously as a fragment. The publisher concludes the text with the evocative explanation, "*The Author went no further*" (E4v).
[20] Katherine Philips, *Poems* (London, 1667; Wing P2033), Aaaa1r–Mmmm1v. Sir John Denham completed Philips' translation of *Horace* for its first performance in 1668; this composite text was then printed in the second and third editions of Philips' *Poems*.
[21] Charles Cotton, *Poems on Several Occasions* (London, 1689; Wing C6389), KK1r–KK8r, Pp8v–Qq1v.
[22] Jonathan Swift, *A Tale of a Tub*, ed. Angus Ross and David Woolley (Oxford, 1986), p. 29.

autonomous author was emerging, an equally empowering concept of active readers was also taking shape. The omissions I examine pull in both directions. When viewed as moments of exquisite authorial control, omissions seem to suggest that a text was created by an "author," a single individual who oversaw the production and could finesse even the most subtle poetic nuances. But, if early modern readers were then expected to make something meaningful out of a text's missing pieces, Renaissance omissions seem to imply that readers shared responsibility for the author's work. Simultaneously authorizing both writers and readers, the omissions that I address provide a unique window into English literary history: through these blank spaces we glimpse the tension between implication and inference, and between an individual author and a collaborative community.

At the core of this book thus lie two related questions, "How much authority did authors have during the Renaissance?" and "How much interpretive activity were Renaissance readers willing or expected to undertake?" Authors, we need to remember, traditionally had little power within the Renaissance book trade. W. W. Greg has located only one acknowledgment by the Stationers' Company of an author having any rights during this period, a terse stipulation that seems to require that a book's owner inform the author before having an item reprinted.[23] Prior to the Copyright Act of 1709, a member of the Stationers' Company who obtained a text by any means could secure legal ownership by publishing it in print or entering it in the Stationers' *Register* – with or without the author's approval.[24] Authors had little recourse: they could provide the printer with a good copy so as to prevent the circulation of a poorly made edition, or they could compensate the unscrupulous stationer so that a corrected version could be later printed. Thus when a "false Edition" of Katherine Philips' *Poems* was published without "*any manner of* [her] *knowledge, much less connivance,*" she arranged to publish a competing version, restoring her works, she hoped, to "their native Shape and Beauty."[25] In like manner, when Sir Thomas Browne discovered that his private religious exercises had been "*most imperfectly and surreptitiously*" printed, he worked with

---

[23] The exact wording is that "the author of any such copy be no hindrance thereunto." See W. W. Greg, *Some Aspects and Problems of London Publishing between 1550 and 1650* (Oxford, 1956), p. 16; and *A Transcript of the Registers of the Company of Stationers of London, 1554–1660*, ed. Edward Arber, 5 vols. (London, 1877), 4: 421 (4 June 1638).

[24] For a fuller description of authors' legal, economic, and practical authority during the seventeenth century, see Dobranski, *Milton, Authorship and the Book Trade* (Cambridge, 1999), pp. 14–26.

[25] Philips, *Poems*, A1r, A2r, a2v.

the volume's unscrupulous publisher – aptly named Andrew Crooke – to produce "*A true and full coppy*" under the same title, *Religio Medici*.[26]

That a few Renaissance authors were nevertheless compensated for their works suggests that authorial rights emerged gradually with the demise of patronage and the rise of a market system. As early as 1593, for example, Edwin Sandys paid Richard Hooker £10 for *Of the Lawes of Ecclesiastical Politie*, Books I–IV, adding £20 in 1597 for Book V, along with an unspecified number of complimentary copies of each installment.[27] The surviving evidence is insufficient, however, for charting a steady increase in the author's economic authority during the Renaissance, in part because publishing terms depended on the type of work and its potential marketability. Forty years after Hooker's publication, William Prynne was paid in kind, with thirty-five or thirty-six copies of *Histrio-mastix* (1633), while in the last part of the century Henry More received only twenty-five copies of his Folio *Opera theologica* (1675) but had the option of purchasing either 100 additional copies at the publisher's price of fifteen shillings apiece, or fewer copies at the bookseller's price of sixteen shillings.[28] Whereas Annie Parent-Charron has located thirty Parisian contracts between authors and booksellers for the years 1535 through 1560, the author's authority developed more slowly in England.[29] The earliest surviving formal agreement of this kind remains Milton's 1667 contract with Samuel Simmons for the publication of *Paradise Lost*.[30] Perhaps most notably, this agreement seems to treat the author as the work's owner: rather than assume the publisher's perpetual right to print Milton's poem, the contract stipulates that Simmons had to compensate the poet for the epic's two subsequent editions.

Likely fueling the author's growing economic authority was the name recognition that came with the spread of print culture. In practical terms,

---

[26] Thomas Browne, *Religio Medici* (London, 1643; Wing B5169), πIr, AIv.

[27] According to contemporary accounts, Sandys agreed to pay Hooker a total of £40 or £50 for the complete work of eight books. See W. Speed Hill, *Richard Hooker: A Descriptive Bibliography of the Early Editions: 1593–1724* (Cleveland, 1970), pp. 1–17; and Charles J. Sisson, *The Judicious Marriage of Mr. Hooker and the Birth of* The Laws of Ecclesiastical Polity (Cambridge, 1940), pp. 49–60.

[28] R. B. McKerrow, "A Publishing Agreement of the Late Seventeenth Century," *The Library*, 4th series 13 (1932): 184–87.

[29] See Roger Chartier, *The Order of Books*, trans. Lydia G. Cochrane (Stanford, 1994), pp. 47–50. On the terms and conditions of publishing in Italy, see Craig Kallendorf, "In Search of a Patron: Anguillara's Vernacular Virgil and the Print Culture of Renaissance Italy," *The Papers of the Bibliographical Society of America* 91 (1997): 294–325; as well as M. D. Feld, "A Theory of the Early Italian Printing Firm. Part II: The Political Economy of Patronage," *Harvard Library Bulletin* 34.3 (1986): 294–332.

[30] I discuss Milton's contract more fully in *Milton, Authorship and the Book Trade*, pp. 35–36, 78, 208 n.50.

printers continued to make the essential decisions for transforming authors' ideas into their printed, public forms, but publishers began to include authors' portraits in some editions. And, as Kevin Pask has observed, composing biographical accounts of poets supplanted the medieval tradition of writing saints' lives.[31] While more than half of the items published in the 1600s were still printed anonymously, other title pages advertised books as the creation of a particular person, such as "POEMS. *By* THOMAS CAREW Esquire" (1640); "POEMS, AND FANCIES: WRITTEN *By the Right HONOURABLE, the Lady* MARGARET Countesse [sic] of NEW-CASTLE" (1653); or, most famously, "Mr WILLIAM SHAKESPEARES COMEDIES, HISTORIES, & TRAGEDIES" (1623).[32] A few writers also attempted to forge distinct authorial personae within their writings. Richard Helgerson has described this urge as characteristic of a generation of Renaissance writers who, aspiring to emulate the Italian model of the laureate poet, tried to "maintain an ethically normative and unchanging self."[33] Whereas early Renaissance poets had modeled themselves as gentleman amateurs disdaining print, the courtly tradition of authorship disappeared during the ensuing decades; by the early 1700s, as Roger Chartier has observed, the originality and thus value of a work would be predicated on the existence of a visible writer.[34]

In this book, I am examining how the publication of incomplete works contributed to the Renaissance author's emerging status. By focusing readers' attention on what writers left unsaid, these unfinished works paradoxically helped to make writers more visible: through a text's omissions, readers seemed to witness firsthand an author's poetic development. Here were works in their ore, before they had been molded and polished, before they had been readied for publication. Readers could also infer that a specific author's writings must be worth perusing if the publishers bothered to print even the unfinished fragments. As the printer Miles Flesher explains in John Donne's 1633 collection, "a scattered limbe of this Author, hath

[31] Kevin Pask, *The Emergence of the English Author* (Cambridge, 1996), pp. 10–13.

[32] The statistic in the first part of this sentence is based on D. F. McKenzie's study of the items published in 1644 and 1688. I am indebted to Don McKenzie for sharing with me parts of his unpublished Lyell Lectures, 1988, from which these numbers are taken. See also McKenzie, "The London Book Trade in 1644," in *Bibliographia: Lectures 1975–1988 by Recipients of the March Fitch Prize for Bibliography*, ed. John Horden (Oxford, 1992), pp. 131–51.

[33] Richard Helgerson, *Self-Crowned Laureates: Spenser, Jonson, Milton, and the Literary System* (Berkeley, 1983), p. 9.

[34] Chartier, *The Order of Books*, pp. 37–39. See also Elizabeth L. Eisenstein, *The Printing Press as an Agent of Change*, 2 vols. (Cambridge, 1979), as well as her abridged version, *The Printing Revolution in Early Modern Europe* (Cambridge, 1983).

more amiablenesse in it, in the eye of a discerner, then a whole body of some other [poet]."[35]

This latter premise in particular reached beyond literary authorship and can also be found, for example, in the visual arts, where artists' increasing authority was similarly associated with the Renaissance cult of the *non-finito*. When sculptors and painters left their works incomplete, it was interpreted as a deliberate decision, testifying to – rather than diminishing – the artist's genius. Despite a painter's tremendous skill, in other words, his imagination defied material realization. Thus Leonardo left many of his works unfinished because, he believed, "the hand could never give its due perfection to the object or purpose which he had in his thoughts, or beheld in his imagination."[36]

Yet, if the visual cult of the *non-finito* paid tribute to the artist's fore conceit, it simultaneously presumed an active, resourceful audience, capable of inferring information that the artist had withheld. Audiences were at least expected to look beyond an artwork's missing pieces and, in trying to imagine the original idea, confirm for themselves the work's and the artist's greatness. If we glance back at Flesher's introduction to Donne's 1633 *Poems*, the phrase "in the eye of a discerner" similarly indicates the reader's active participation in establishing Donne's authority: only a discerning reader, the printer suggests, can grant that the poet's parts are greater than other writers' wholes.

The Renaissance omissions that I analyze in this book accordingly represent sites of authorial *and* readerly authority. Just as changing cultural conditions granted authors increased importance during the early modern period, so a convergence of conventions and circumstances encouraged readers to interact with printed texts. Renaissance omissions were only one way that such an interaction was possible. In extreme cases, as with Chaucer's fragmented canon, readers became writers and published supplements to the works that they perused. But readers, as I will show in chapter 1, could also interact with a text through such protocols as marginalia, commonplace books, and errata lists. Based on these rigorous reading practices, I argue that omissions would have similarly prompted Renaissance readers to participate in their books – to read more carefully, to review the text for possible clues to seal a rift, or perhaps to come up with their own original ideas for how to fill a text's blanks.

[35] *Poems, By J. D.* (London, 1633; STC 7045), πA1v.
[36] Giorgio Vasari, *Lives of Seventy of the Most Eminent Painters, Sculptors and Architects*, ed. E. H. Blashfield, E. W. Blashfield, and A. A. Hopkins, 4 vols. (New York, 1926), 2: 376.

All reading, as reception theory has taught us, naturally depends on such speculation and inference; without an actively interpreting reader, a literary work remains a mere collection of symbols. According to some reader-response critics, most notably Roman Ingarden and Wolfgang Iser, reading requires us to "concretize" a text so as to make it internally coherent.[37] Iser specifically distinguishes between two types of omissions: *blanks*, which mark a text's "missing links," and *negations*, which invalidate a reader's aesthetic expectations. Both of these signals stimulate the audience, he explains, "whereby the hollow form of the text is filled by the mental images of the reader."[38] But for Iser these "mental images" are always determined by the text's underlying structure, not the reader's own imagination. We do not freely fill in the blanks between apparently disconnected utterances; we must fill them in and must follow the instructions that a text provides for doing so.[39]

Other reception theories instead emphasize each reader's own power to render a text meaningful. Whereas approaches such as Iser's privilege a text's strategies and conventions as fundamentally regulating readers' interpretations, this second type of reader-response criticism assumes that texts inherently contain nothing determinate. Stanley Fish, for example, suggests that readers supply meaning themselves by applying what he has identified as shared "interpretive strategies." All communication occurs in a situation, already informed by assumptions, practices, and goals – "so habitual as to be unthinking" – which pre-determine how we will hear any utterance.[40]

---

[37] This specific term is introduced by Roman Ingarden, *The Cognition of the Literary Work of Art*, trans. Ruth Ann Crowley and Kenneth R. Olson (Evanston, IL, 1973).

[38] Wolfgang Iser, *The Act of Reading: A Theory of Aesthetic Response* (Baltimore, 1978), pp. 184, 212–13, 225; and his earlier essay, "Indeterminacy and the Reader's Response in Prose Fiction," in *Aspects of Narrative: Selected Papers from the English Institute*, ed. J. Hillis Miller (New York, 1971), pp. 1–45, especially pp. 11, 13 n. 8. In *The Act of Reading* Iser introduces a third, more amorphous category of omission, *negativity*, which he describes as the latent "double" to which almost all "formulations of the text refer" and of which "blanks and negations are the abstract manifestations" (pp. 225–26). In terms of representation, negativity signifies a text's "unformulated background" (p. 225); in terms of reception, it represents "that which has not yet been comprehended" (p. 229). As readers begin to comprehend a text, the previously hidden elements come to the fore: "negativity traces out what is not given and enables it to be communicated" (p. 226). See Iser, *The Act of Reading*, pp. 225–31, as well as the fuller discussion in Sanford Budick and Wolfgang Iser, eds., *Languages of the Unsayable: The Play of Negativity in Literature and Literary Theory* (New York, 1989), especially pp. xi–xvii.

[39] In like manner, Iser argues, a literary text uses negation for a prearranged effect: the text subverts our aesthetic expectations so that we are drawn in and forced to reassess habitual ways of perception. Only by temporarily shedding our familiar frame of reference can we discover a new belief system and arrive at what Iser calls a text's "virtual theme," namely, the meaning of the text that is "outlined but concealed." See Iser, *The Act of Reading*, pp. 217–21.

[40] Stanley Fish, *Is There a Text in This Class?* (Cambridge, MA, 1980), p. 320.

For Fish, then, the text itself represents an omission because everything in it must be created through interpretation.

Rather than proceeding deductively from either of these theoretical models (for Iser, text-centered; for Fish, reader-centered), I devote the next chapter to an inductive, historical analysis of seventeenth-century conditions of reading and writing.[41] We will see that Renaissance readers sometimes assumed an author's importance in interpreting a literary work and that Renaissance writers sometimes attempted to direct readers' responses by providing instructions within accompanying prefaces and epistles.[42] But in emphasizing early modern authors' authority, I am not suggesting that writers had the last word. On the contrary, some Renaissance readers, not thinking themselves constrained by an author's goals, might have overlooked or dismissed an omission in a poem; or a blank space might have arisen, independent of the author, because of a text's complex provenance. An author's intentions, regardless of the literary period, always remain limited by and reliant on the circumstances of reading, writing, and publishing – not to mention the culturally constructed values and beliefs an author may internalize without realizing. Never fully knowable, the author's plans, as Chartier has discussed, "are not necessarily imposed either on those who turn his text into a book (bookseller–publishers or print workers) or on those who appropriate it by reading it."[43]

Instead, Renaissance writing conditions suggest a cooperative relationship between writers and readers. Writers commonly wanted readers to collaborate in their texts – that is, to share responsibility for the texts' meanings. Thus Ben Jonson in his *Discoveries* looks beyond his detailed

[41] In practice, I think, Iser and Fish are not too far from each other's perspective. Iser may refer to the text itself as a type of "consciousness," but, if readers are not free to fill in blanks and must follow a text's instructions, he still seems to privilege the author who writes such instructions. And Fish's groundbreaking work on Milton sometimes belies his own reader-response theory: Fish is not unwilling to attribute subtle – almost supernatural – control to Milton when it suits his rhetorical purposes. See Iser, *The Implied Reader: Patterns of Communication in Prose Fiction from Bunyan to Beckett* (Baltimore, 1974), p. 293; and Fish, *Surprised by Sin: The Reader in* Paradise Lost, 2nd edn. (Cambridge, MA, 1999).

[42] Writing on Renaissance literature, John T. Shawcross has similarly emphasized the value of talking about "authorial presence" (p. 13). Shawcross distinguishes among the "'text' . . . the specific words as they appear on the page; the 'reader's text' . . . the understanding the reader derives from reading that text; [and] the 'author's text' . . . the text the author has provided for the reader to read, with all its potentialities" (p. 4). But Shawcross believes that "the important text is the reader's text" (p. 9), whereas I am instead privileging the "potentialities" that an author – always operating within a social process of literary production – can create. See Shawcross, *Intentionality and the New Traditionalism: Some Liminal Means to Literary Revisionism* (University Park, PA, 1991).

[43] Chartier, *The Order of Books*, pp. 28–29.

scheme for becoming a good poet ("by nature, by exercise, by imitation, by Studie") and demands that readers work equally hard: "things, wrote with labour, deserve to be so read."[44] My argument is that both authors and readers gained considerable authority during the early modern period – and that the two phenomena were reciprocal. Early modern authors who developed individual identities did so by envisioning and, in some cases, trying to train active readers. Throughout the seventeenth century, as Raymond Williams observes, "'individual' was rarely used without explicit relation to the group of which it was, so to say, the ultimate indivisible division."[45] While sociologists and psychologists have suggested that all human beings attain a sense of "personal autonomy" only in relation to a larger community, this process became especially important with the advent of print publication: to develop their individual authority, authors not only had to work with members of the book trade, but also had to allow unseen readers to join what Cecile Jagodzinski has described as a "gigantic coterie."[46]

Such a cooperative relationship between authors and readers stemmed in part from the traditionally collaborative practices of Renaissance writing. Although the authority of authors was increasing during the early modern period, writing in practice remained a deeply entrenched social enterprise; during both the imaginative and material stages of creation, writers depended on other people to help them produce their works. Occasional poems and masques, for example, were shaped by the specific circumstances of their creation, and sometimes by the specific people or patrons who commissioned or inspired them. Other popular types of writing, such as plays, group-writings, and verse competitions, depended on a more directly cooperative process, and some literary works, we will see in chapter 2, prompted readers to take up their pens and compose their own answer poems.[47] Although we ought to distinguish loose collaborations from co-authorship, these varying degrees of socializing suggest that Renaissance authors would have been receptive to outside influences, such

---

[44] Ben Jonson, *Discoveries*, lines 2404–5, 2465–66 in Herford and Simpson, 8: 636, 638.

[45] Raymond Williams, *Keywords*, rev. edn. (New York, 1983), p. 163.

[46] Cecile M. Jagodzinski, *Privacy and Print: Reading and Writing in Seventeenth-Century England* (Charlottesville, 1999), p. 11.

[47] On collaborative practices of Renaissance writing, see Dobranski, *Milton, Authorship and the Book Trade*, especially pp. 14–31; on collaborative play-writing during the Renaissance, see Gerald Eades Bentley, *The Profession of Dramatist in Shakespeare's Time, 1590–1642* (Princeton, 1971), pp. 197–234; and Jeffrey Masten, *Textual Intercourse: Collaboration, Authorship, and Sexualities in Renaissance Drama* (Cambridge, 1997), pp. 12–20.

as readers' active engagement with their texts. To write publicly, Milton explains in *Areopagitica* (1644), an author "searches, meditats, is industrious, and likely consults and conferrs with his judicious friends" (*CP* 2: 532). Milton describes writing as a relational practice that requires an author "to be inform'd in what he writes, as well as any that writ before him" (*CP* 2: 532). To arrive at truth, "there of necessity will be much arguing, much writing, many opinions" (*CP* 2: 554).

This collaborative context is crucial for understanding how contemporary readers may have approached the type of omissions I am addressing. As an extension of this process, early modern readers were encouraged to intervene in their books to make them meaningful. Social practices of authorship, along with, as I show in the next chapter, Protestant hermeneutics, printing conventions, education theories, and the cultural upheaval associated with the Civil War – all helped to foreground the reader's presence in what Kevin Sharpe has called the early modern "republic of letters."[48] These active readers could analyze the implications of a text's omissions by assuming the author's expertise, just as authors could confidently include subtle poetic effects because they expected discerning readers.

Returning to Donne's 1633 *Poems*, we can borrow his conceit of "stiffe twin compasses" from "A Valediction Forbidding Mourning" to describe the interdependent relationship that authors and readers formed.[49] Like the hinged feet of a rotating compass (which Donne uses to depict the lovers' coactive souls), so Renaissance authors and readers exerted a mutual, though not equal force on each other: one foot enabled the motion, the other ran obliquely; when one foot leaned, the other hearkened after it. This complementary motion neatly captures the interactive processes of writing and reading during the seventeenth century, and suggests how authors and readers remained simultaneously separated and connected. While forging a link through the text, they could never achieve complete mutual knowledge.[50]

---

[48] Kevin Sharpe, *Reading Revolutions: The Politics of Reading in Early Modern England* (New Haven, 2000), p. 41.

[49] John Donne, "A Valediction Forbidding Mourning," in *Poems, By J. D.*, Ccir–Cciv, line 26.

[50] Dan Sperber and Deirdre Wilson, *Relevance: Communication and Cognition*, 2nd edn. (Oxford, 1995), helpfully compare the relationship between speaker and hearer to the relationship between two ballroom dancers; one partner leads, and the other "has merely to follow" (p. 43). John P. Rumrich brilliantly develops this analogy in *Milton Unbound* (Cambridge, 1996): writers attempt to lead readers, who, though "*relatively* passive and restricted," can initiate a dance of their own (pp. 26–27).

In "Of Experience" (1587–88), Montaigne prefers a metaphor of two tennis players to depict the writer's and reader's mutual participation:

Speech belongs half to the speaker, half to the listener. The latter must prepare to receive it according to the motion it takes. As among tennis players, the receiver moves and makes ready according to the motion of the striker and the nature of the stroke.[51]

Whereas classical and some medieval theorists emphasized reading as a relatively passive exercise, Montaigne's diction effectively conveys the type of cooperative relationship that shaped writing and reading during the seventeenth century. Authors might serve, but readers then had the opportunity to return and redirect the author's best strokes. Tracing the development of Montaigne's concept of reading, Cathleen Bauschatz discovers that in *The Essays* he played his own game of back-and-forth, oscillating "between a belief in the text or author as dominant in the reading process and a view of the reader himself as the creator of it."[52] I am pursuing the same idea in this book: through moments of omission we discover that both of these perceptions hold true.

In maintaining the author's and reader's reciprocal status, however, I am not pursuing E. D. Hirsch's distinction between a text's absolute, authorial "meaning" and the subjective, shifting "significance" that individual readers can contrive.[53] Instead, if we apply Dan Sperber and Deirdre Wilson's theory of inferential communication, Renaissance omissions represent a type of *ostensive stimuli* – that is, language or behavior "which makes manifest an intention to make something manifest."[54] The conspicuous omissions in these Renaissance texts subtly draw our attention to things that, authors seem to believe, we will find worthy of attention. As Sperber and Wilson explain, "Inferential communication and ostension are one and the same process, but seen from two different points of view: that of the communicator who is involved in ostension and that of the audience who is involved

[51] Michel de Montaigne, "Of Experience," in *The Complete Essays of Montaigne*, trans. Donald M. Frame (Stanford, 1958), pp. 815–57, this quotation, p. 834. Although this passage focuses attention on oral communication, Montaigne applies the same metaphor when exclusively addressing books. Describing the writers he likes to read, he observes, for example, that "The historians come right to my forehand." See Montaigne, "Of Books," in *The Complete Essays of Montaigne*, pp. 296–306, this quotation, p. 303.
[52] Cathleen M. Bauschatz, "Montaigne's Conception of Reading in the Context of Renaissance Poetics and Modern Criticism," in *The Reader in the Text: Essays on Audience and Interpretation*, ed. Susan R. Suleiman and Inge Crosman (Princeton, 1980), pp. 264–91, this quotation, p. 289.
[53] See E. D. Hirsch, Jr., *Validity in Interpretation* (New Haven, 1967), especially pp. 8, 38, 57, 62.
[54] Sperber and Wilson, *Relevance*, p. 49.

in inference."⁵⁵ When a writer or any communicator makes it apparent that she intends to inform the audience of something, she is in effect indicating that the audience is responsible for fulfilling that intention.

But by specifically choosing omissions as ostensive stimuli, Renaissance poets also shaped what they were trying to convey. A literary omission not only indicates the poet's intention for the reader to infer something (what Sperber and Wilson call the speaker's "communicative intention"); it importantly affects what the reader infers (what they call the speaker's "informative intention"). Following Sperber and Wilson, I would argue that no communicative act offers a clear "cut-off point" between meanings "strongly backed by the speaker" and inferences that are "the hearer's sole responsibility."⁵⁶ Instead, all utterances can express a range of meanings, from those specifically encouraged by the communicator to those entirely supplied by the audience. Between these two extremes fall strong or weak contextually produced assumptions, without an obvious indication whether communicator or audience is responsible for them.

In the case of omissions, this set of assumptions is especially broad, and the distinction between intended and unintended inferences especially murky. The omissions described in this book deserve attention precisely for this reason: they represent distinct sites where the authors' intentions and readers' responses meet. Such blank spaces require that we confront the relative significance of authors' implications and readers' inferences during the Renaissance. The authors discussed here may have had specific ideas in mind for us to infer, or may have left open various possibilities from which we can choose. But because parts of the text are finally unwritten, contemporary readers appear to have had ultimate authority over how – or even if – such omissions were filled. The paradox of an omission arises from its dearth of textual detail. We may suspect that the less information an author provides at a given moment, the more freedom the reader has to make that part of a text meaningful. Yet the reader may also feel less engaged with instances of omission because the diminution of data recommends fewer plausible inferences.⁵⁷ The reader is both liberated and limited, in other words, by the author's reticence – although so is the author, who

---

⁵⁵ Sperber and Wilson, *Relevance*, p. 54, and see p. 62.
⁵⁶ Sperber and Wilson, *Relevance*, p. 199.
⁵⁷ Specifically discussing prose narratives, Iser offers the corollary argument that the more detail an author provides in a text, the more interpretations individual readers can generate, and the more ambiguous a text in effect becomes. In *Ulysses* and *Finnegans Wake*, Iser accordingly observes, "the overprecision of the presentation gives rise to a proportionate increase in indeterminacy." See Iser, "Indeterminacy and the Reader's Response in Prose Fiction," p. 12.

asserts authority by choosing to be quiet and at the same time is giving up authority by ceding the floor.

Such a reciprocal exchange also recalls Annabel Patterson's related concept of "functional ambiguity." This theory, she explains,

does not privilege either writer or reader, or eliminate either. It is hospitable to, and indeed dependent upon, a belief in authorial intention; yet it is incapable of reduction to a positivist belief in meanings that authors can fix. Indeed . . . authors who build ambiguity into their works have no control over what happens to them later.[58]

Whereas Patterson focuses attention on textual indeterminacy as a response to political censorship – which she identifies as "the central problem of consciousness and communication" in early modern England – I am interested in the ways that Renaissance authors chose to make omissions, sometimes for political reasons, but independently of such repressive structures.[59] The value of Patterson's argument lies in the implication that the degree of a reader's and author's authority can be directly proportional. As opposed to post-structuralists who have declared the death of the author, Patterson seems to establish Renaissance writers as masters of both the said and unsaid in their works.[60] But as she acknowledges in the above passage, and as subsequent critics have also emphasized, her hermeneutic simultaneously author-izes the politically minded reader. By appealing to "a principle of inexact analogy" and a "scattershot approach" instead of "the tight system of equivalences we call allegory," Patterson cuts a wide path for

---

[58] Annabel Patterson, *Censorship and Interpretation: The Conditions of Writing and Reading in Early Modern England* (Madison, WI, 1984), p. 18.

[59] Patterson, *Censorship and Interpretation*, p. 17. A fundamental problem with Patterson's argument for an all-pervasive, repressive political culture is that historians have largely disproved it. As Sheila Lambert has shown, economic and practical considerations played at least an equally important role in the types of books produced during the reigns of James I and Charles I. Under the Tudor and Stuart system for the regulation of printing, a text had to be "licensed" by an appointed official; afterwards, an agent of the Stationers' Company also had to approve the text before having the clerk enter it in the *Register*. But this system of regulation was not carried out consistently nor its penalties executed systematically. In most cases of unlawful publication, the government seems to have tried to punish only repeat offenders. Focusing attention on Renaissance drama and "the breadth of political exploration which did secure untroubled presentation," A. B. Worden has concluded that "the government lacked not merely the power, but the inclination, to impose conditions of writing that can helpfully be called 'repressive'" (p. 48). If the government censored a play, Worden argues, it was because of an individual expressing a personal complaint against a dramatist or the pressures of international diplomacy. See Lambert, "The Printers and the Government, 1604–1637," in *Aspects of Printing from 1600*, ed. Robin Myers and Michael Harris (Oxford, 1987), pp. 1–29; and Worden, "Literature and Political Censorship in Early Modern England," in *Too Mighty to Be Free: Censorship and the Press in Britain and the Netherlands* (Zutphen, 1987), pp. 45–62.

[60] For a post-structuralist notion of authorship, see Roland Barthes, "The Death of the Author," *Image, Music, Text*, trans. Stephen Heath (New York, 1977), pp. 142–48.

herself as recoverer of lost wit; by arguing for deceitful writers capable of subverting government censorship, she posits equally adept readers, expert enough to discover a text's deepest secrets.[61] The more control we grant an author, in other words, the more interpretation we warrant a reader to perform.[62]

Seventeenth-century practices of reading and writing, we will see in the next chapter, recommend exactly this double emphasis. While the five traditionally canonical figures I have chosen for this book – Sidney, Jonson, Donne, Herrick, and Milton – represent especially powerful creators of meaning during the Renaissance, I will show that readers were expected, through various printed protocols, to participate actively in the literary works they perused. We can, of course, never fully know any author's intentions nor any reader's predisposition and assumptions. But by bringing together textual studies, book trade history, and literary criticism, I am attempting to reconstruct the milieu out of which Renaissance works arose and, through the window of their omissions, examine the complex, interdependent relationship between writers and readers.

This book begins with an overview of seventeenth-century reading practices. When I describe readers during the seventeenth century as "active" or "collaborative," I mean that the act of reading was literally a *co-laboring*: writers invoked readers who had to participate in various ways to determine a text's meaning. Briefly tracing the reader's evolution from antiquity to the early modern period, I examine theories of biblical exegesis, conventions of printed books, and the cultural upheaval associated with the Civil War period. All these forces – along with, as we have seen, the ongoing practice of social authorship – helped to establish reading during the Renaissance as an active rather than passive endeavor. Readers were encouraged not only to peruse books but also to interact with some texts and read beyond the

---

[61] Patterson, *Censorship and Interpretation*, pp. 81, 63, 31.

[62] Writing specifically on Milton's allusion to Bellerophon in *Paradise Lost*, Stephen M. Fallon has similarly charted the latitude and limit of an author's conscious control over a text. In the invocation in book VII, Milton borrows the myth of Bellerophon to describe himself and "exorcise the specter of presumption" (p. 176). But, as Fallon convincingly reveals, this carefully calibrated allusion also conveys meanings that Milton could not have intended. Because the language Milton uses to describe Bellerophon echoes his earlier description of Satan and the fallen angels, the poet seems to undermine his own self-representation. Fallon is showing how we can find evidence of Milton's doubt even at those moments when he most confidently asserts his authority as a vatic poet. But Fallon's analysis also suggests that it is "precisely at this moment of exquisite control" that "meanings apparently unintended by the author flood back into the text" (p. 176). See Fallon, "Intention and Its Limits in *Paradise Lost*: The Case of Bellerophon," in *Literary Milton: Text, Pretext, Context*, ed. Diana Treviño Benet and Michael Lieb (Pittsburgh, 1994), pp. 161–79.

author's apparent intentions. The missing pieces in some Renaissance books represent one specific way that writers and readers could work together.

Organized in a rough chronology, the subsequent chapters offer five case studies, each focusing attention on a different author and a different use of omission. We can plot these uses along two axes: "real" or "feigned," and "particular" or "open-ended." The first two terms describe the authenticity of an apparently unfinished text, while the second pair describes whether the author hints at a particular piece that is missing or leaves open various possible ways to fill a blank.[63] Thus, an anonymous seventeenth-century poet first pretends that Sidney's *Arcadia* is missing a poem about Mopsa (a "feigned" omission) and then composes the allegedly absent verse himself (so that it is also "particular"). Herrick, by comparison, included two unfinished poems in *Hesperides* (apparently "real" omissions), but in one poem he implies a specific conclusion ("particular"), while in the other he invites readers to devise their own solutions ("open-ended").

Rather than impose a strict taxonomy, however, I am primarily interested in Renaissance omissions as simultaneously moments of ostension and inference; these blank spaces allowed early modern authors to assert their authority but only by requiring readers' intervention. The poet can assert his authority through omission (Jonson), can collaborate with the book's publisher to do so (Milton), can appeal to future readers to do so (Herrick), or, if the poet is already deceased, a reader (as with Sidney) or a publisher (as with Donne) can use omission to establish the poet's authority posthumously. It is by examining these various negotiations that we then can trace the emergence of the author in seventeenth-century England.

In the first case study, I examine how one reader used omission to enhance Sir Philip Sidney's poetic authority. I am specifically interested in seventeenth-century editions of *The Countess of Pembroke's Arcadia* and the satiric verse "A Remedie for Love," printed, beginning in 1655, as a newly discovered omission from Sidney's romance. Although presented as an error, something that previous publishers had overlooked, the "Remedie" is actually a new poem that uses the pretence of omission to re-calibrate Sidney's reputation and romance for a seventeenth-century audience. The "Remedie" that this anonymous poet prescribes exposes the

---

[63] Balachandra Rajan, by comparison, has differentiated between "incomplete poems," which he defines as literary fragments that invite completion, and, of more interest to Rajan, "unfinished poems," which are works that reject or avoid closure. The omissions that I discuss in this book will straddle these two categories, sometimes implying and sometimes defying their own completion. See Rajan, *The Form of the Unfinished: English Poetics from Spenser to Pound* (Princeton, 1985).

tension between the emerging cult of the author and the collaborative practices of early modern reading, which allowed readers to become writers and borrow freely from one another's works.

Whereas Sidney had nothing to do with the publication of his collected works and the image of a heroic author that they promulgated, Ben Jonson consciously helped to construct his own image by overseeing the design and printing of his 1616 *Workes*. Because Jonson actively participated in his book, the missing envoi in the Folio version of his "Epistle to Elizabeth Countesse of Rutland" appears to mark an authorial error: Jonson presumably removed this passage when his prediction that the Countess would have a male heir proved impossible. But, as I show in chapter 3, Jonson's omission of the envoi complements and complicates the poem, subtly allowing the poet not just to save face but to adapt the poem to fit its new situational context. As the book trade threatened to demote authors to publishers' employees, Jonson expresses his ambivalence about the prospect of producing a printed edition, and in a rhetorical maneuver that he would repeat throughout his career, he uses omission to remind us that he still wielded the ultimate control over his writings.

John Donne's first collection of poetry, *Poems, By J. D.* (1633), seems, by contrast, to illustrate a writer's relative lack of authority during the Renaissance. While Jonson in his Folio *Workes* was self-consciously attempting to defend his primacy within the rapidly expanding print economy, Donne characteristically avoided printing his poetry. We might accordingly assume that Donne's posthumous *Poems* would represent a creation of the printing house. But chapter 4 shows how a book's material creators helped to "author" the author: attempting to forge the poet's presence in the volume, the printer and publisher cast Donne as an autonomous author whose least works are worthy of readers' attention. The volume's unfinished and censored poems – which should especially demonstrate Donne's lack of control over the collection – instead reinforce his ethos. Calling attention to the *Poems*' missing pieces, the book's creators appeal to a select group of understanding readers whose participation helps both to perfect Donne's poems and, ironically, to amplify his authority.

In *Hesperides* and *His Noble Numbers* (1648) Robert Herrick frets aloud about his lack of authority. He worries in particular that his printed poems will fall into the hands of unappreciative readers. Challenging the recent, critical exaggeration of Herrick's control over his book's design and printing, I emphasize in chapter 5 the volume's collaborative process of production. With *Hesperides*' two incomplete poems, Herrick expands that process dramatically to include readers. These omissions allow the author to acknowledge his limitations while he simultaneously attempts to train his audience to participate in his publication: he calls upon active readers not only to complete his works but also to end England's political strife and to protect his posthumous reputation.

Also using omission to engage readers and assert his authority, Milton fittingly concludes this book by harking back to the feigned omission in Sidney's *Arcadia*. Just as the anonymous poet of "A Remedie for Love" presented his work as an omission while adapting Sidney's romance for a seventeenth-century audience, Milton pretends that a passage is missing from *Paradise Regain'd . . . Samson Agonistes* (1671) so as to highlight the contemporary relevance of his biblical source-texts. The ten lines printed at the end of Milton's two poems look like a compositor's error but a bibliographical examination reveals that they are an important authorial addendum. Milton uses this passage, labeled *Omissa*, to emphasize his poems' interdependence and dramatize the need for readers to follow Jesus' and Samson's examples of active obedience. As a final expression of the paradox at the core of this book, Milton and the book's publisher adroitly manipulate their audience, but the lesson they want to teach readers in the *Omissa* is to act on their own, in both their reading and their world.

Each of these chapters has a relatively narrow focus – one author, one text – and, collectively, the publications I examine span a little less than sixty years. Yet this period and these writers, I contend, are especially significant for the new mode of comprehension they inaugurated and the collaborative mode of communication that they put into service. If we agree that the publication of a writer's complete *works* became one way of establishing authorial authority during the seventeenth century, then we ought to examine also the implications of publishing a writer's incomplete works. Sometimes what an author does not say, as I show in the following case studies, is just as important as what he does.

CHAPTER I

Reading and writing

Then in your reading mend each mis-plac'd letter,
And by your iudgement make bad words sound better.
Where you may hurt, heale; where you can afflict,
There helpe and cure, or else be not too strict.
Looke through your fingers, wink, connive at mee,
And (as you meet with faults) see, and not see.
                                          – John Taylor[1]

That Arthur Kinney introduces *The Cambridge Companion to English Literature, 1500–1600* with a discussion of reading suggests how important the history of reading has become for early modern studies. Kinney infers from the "premium" that English artists placed on a text's "potential multiplicity of perspective" that Tudor readers could appreciate books only by actively "intervening" in them.[2] He speculates that this aesthetic, which "opens things up rather than closes them down," not only "demanded even more active and deeper engagement" than during earlier periods, but also helps to explain why Renaissance literature remains relevant for modern readers – "so alive, so varied, so popular."[3]

Much of the scholarship on the history of reading in early modern England has, like Kinney's, focused attention on the demands of Elizabethan reading practices. In a groundbreaking essay on Gabriel Harvey's copious marginal notations, Lisa Jardine and Anthony Grafton have documented the "strenuous attentiveness" of sixteenth-century scholarly reading, "an active, rather than a passive pursuit" that "was always goal-oriented."[4] William Sherman, analyzing the reading habits of the

[1] John Taylor, "Errata, or Faults to the Reader," in *All the Workes of Iohn Taylor the Water Poet* (London, 1630; STC 23725), A4v. The verse is printed in italics.
[2] Arthur F. Kinney, Introduction, *The Cambridge Companion to English Literature, 1500–1600*, ed. Arthur F. Kinney (Cambridge, 2000), pp. 1–10, this quotation, p. 5.
[3] Kinney, Introduction, pp. 5, 9.
[4] Lisa Jardine and Anthony Grafton, "'Studied for Action': How Gabriel Harvey Read His Livy," *Past and Present* 129 (1990): 30–78, these quotations, p. 30.

polymath John Dee, has similarly concluded that for all types of contemporary reading – scholarly, educational, and practical – the text represented a "site of an active and biased appropriation of the author's material."[5] And Eugene Kintgen, reconstructing the method of interpretation instilled in part through formal education and church services, has also emphasized that Elizabethan reading was above all utilitarian and "radically analytical."[6]

Rather than accepting active reading as a specifically Elizabethan practice, I would argue that a similar style of readerly intervention remained important during the seventeenth century. The emergence of the author did not, as traditional narratives have suggested, coincide with the development of private and passive reading habits; instead, authors established their authority by invoking readers who would participate directly in their texts. These "active readers," as I call them, were not always classically trained scholars, like John Dee and Gabriel Harvey, but still they had to intervene in a text to make it meaningful and in some cases, we will see, they then appropriated that text for their own purposes.[7] Briefly tracing the reader's changing function prior to the early modern period, I then examine contemporary conventions and circumstances that encouraged active reading. Whereas Sharon Achinstein has shown that pamphlet writers during the Civil War imagined "a new kind of public" in their tracts – "active, rational, and deserving of a place in political decision making" – I use readers' prefaces and contemporary descriptions of poetic writing to argue that seventeenth-century authors also wanted active readers.[8] The demanding subtlety of Renaissance omissions reflects this labor and points up the interdependent relationship that authors and readers forged. Writing and reading were collaborative during the seventeenth century – by which I mean that authors and readers had to labor together consciously to produce meaning. Participating in this creative process, readers helped to establish authors' authority, while authors, leaving various kinds of blank spaces in their works, reciprocally empowered early modern readers.

[5] William H. Sherman, *John Dee: The Politics of Reading and Writing in the English Renaissance* (Amherst, MA, 1995), p. 65.

[6] Eugene R. Kintgen, *Reading in Tudor England* (Pittsburgh, 1996), p. 182. See also Kintgen's earlier essay, "Reconstructing Elizabethan Reading," *Studies in English Literature, 1500–1900* 30 (1990): 1–18.

[7] D. R. Woolf notes that Dee and Harvey's scholarly or "intensive" style of reading continued well into the seventeenth century but "diminished in relative importance as the Renaissance petered out." Woolf instead examines a less formal or "extensive" style of reading that "follows little pattern beyond the individual reader's tastes, personal concerns, and daily whims." See Woolf, *Reading History in Early Modern England* (Cambridge, 2000), these quotations, p. 9. My own category of "active readers" is in part an attempt to identify practices and conventions applicable to both of these styles.

[8] Sharon Achinstein, *Milton and the Revolutionary Reader* (Princeton, 1994), p. 224.

THE READER'S CHANGING FUNCTION

The notion of an active reader, while not unique to the Renaissance, helps to distinguish early modern conditions of writing from classical and some medieval theories. Reading during these earlier periods was treated as a relatively passive experience; writers emphasized how the effects of a text moved an audience, with or without readers' participation or even approval. Aristotle describes a tragedy's *catharsis*, for example, as something that the audience undergoes rather than achieves.[9] Anyone who merely hears the plot of a well-constructed tragedy, he argues, cannot help but "[shudder] with fear and pity as a result of what occurs."[10] Later, Italian commentators of Aristotle amplified this sense of the audience's inactivity by likening the effect of tragedy to that of medicinal purgatives: while the artist resembles a healing physician, the audience resembles a patient, passively waiting to be cured.[11] We may also recall the classical myths of Amphion, who charmed stones with his harp, or Orpheus, who enchanted trees and streams with his singing. These stories not only illustrate the artist's potency but also imply an audience's submissiveness. The artist defies the laws of nature, but the audience is allied with inanimate objects, as if the appreciation of Amphion's music or Orpheus' lyrics required neither intellect nor will.

Even the classical rhetorical tradition, which, in contrast, had foregrounded the audience in the act of communication, still subordinated listeners to the writer or speaker. Although Aristotle in *The Art of Rhetoric* catalogues three types of speeches according to three types of auditors, secular rhetorical theory provided little instruction for readers or hearers.[12] Audience members asserted themselves primarily through a type of passive resistance: it was the possibility that an audience might *not* be persuaded by a speech that could influence a speaker's rhetoric.

We detect a similar assumption of passivity behind some medieval and early Renaissance depictions of reading. Perhaps most famously, Dante's Francesca and Paolo are undone by reading a romance. "One particular

---

[9] Aristotle, *Poetics*, trans. W. Hamilton Fyfe (Cambridge, MA, 1953), vi.2–3 (1449b).

[10] Aristotle, *Poetics*, xiv.2 (1453b). Elsewhere, writing about music, Aristotle describes more fully the overpowering effect of *catharsis*: when "emotional people" hear "tunes that violently arouse the soul," the listeners are "thrown into a state as if they received medicinal treatment and taken a purge." See Aristotle, *Politics*, trans. H. Rackham (Cambridge, MA, 1950), VIII.vii.5 (1342a 5–11).

[11] See Joel E. Spingarn, ed., *Critical Essays of the Seventeenth Century*, 3 vols. (Bloomington, 1908), 1: 251.

[12] Aristotle, *The Art of Rhetoric*, trans. John Henry Freese (Cambridge, MA, 1994), I.ii.22–I.iii.4 (1358b).

passage it was / Defeated us," Francesca explains, blaming their sinful act on the book's pandering author (*Galeotto*).[13] In like manner, Boccaccio addresses *The Decameron* to "ladies . . . in love" – although in this case, he promises, the book will heal rather than corrupt. When lovesick women read these tales, Boccaccio boasts, it "can only lead . . . to the removal of their affliction."[14]

Augustine in his *Confessions* had laid the groundwork for this emphasis on a book's effects; he models his own reading experiences after St. Anthony's sudden conversion upon hearing a sentence from Scripture.[15] Thus, in explaining the impact that Cicero's *Hortensius* had on his intellectual development, Augustine gives over all agency to the treatise: "The book changed my feelings. It altered my prayers, Lord, to be towards you yourself. It gave me different values and priorities."[16] Later, when Augustine takes up the Bible and reads the first passage he spies, the book again acts on Augustine instead of his interacting with the text: "At once, with the last words of this sentence, it was as if a light of relief from all anxiety flooded into my heart. All the shadows of doubt were dispelled."[17] Here Augustine's specific syntax (*omnes dubitationis tenebrae diffugerunt*) suggests his lack of activity while the suddenness of this transformation implies his reading's effortlessness.

Not until the late Middle Ages, with the advancement of allegory, did writers fully address how a reader's interpretive activity could alter a text's meaning. Building on the work of early Latin exegetes – including Augustine, as well as Jerome and Origen – medieval theorists generated a series of rules to describe the act of reading. These methods developed in part as a response to the more arbitrary practices of scholastic interpreters; readers of texts were now expected to follow a fourfold interpretive approach – literal, typological, moral, and mystical – to achieve a complete and correct understanding. Thus, Jerusalem, according to one medieval commonplace, represented, literally, the city; typologically, the Church of

---

[13] The Italian reads, "*Quando leggemmo il disïato riso*," and "*Galeotto fu 'l libro e chi lo scrisse.*" See *The Inferno of Dante*, trans. Robert Pinsky (New York, 1994), V.133, 137.

[14] Giovanni Boccaccio, *The Decameron*, trans. G. H. McWilliam, 2nd edn. (London, 1995), p. 3. For the Italian, see Boccaccio, *Decameron*, ed. Vittore Branca (Turin, 1980), pp. 8–10.

[15] St. Augustine, *Confessions*, trans. and ed. Henry Chadwick (Oxford, 1998), VIII.xii (29). For a detailed discussion of Augustine's evolving theory of reading, see Brian Stock, *Augustine the Reader: Meditation, Self-Knowledge, and the Ethics of Interpretation* (Cambridge, MA, 1996).

[16] Augustine, *Confessions*, III.iv (7). The Latin here reads, "*ille vero liber mutavit affectum meum et ad te ipsum, domine, mutavit preces meas et vota ac desideria mea fecit alia.*" See *Confessionum libri XIII, editit Martinus Skutella (1934)*, ed. Heiko Jürgens and W. Schaub (Stuttgart, 1969).

[17] Augustine, *Confessions*, VIII.xii (29). The Latin here reads, "*statim quippe cum fine huiusce sententiae quasi luce securitatis infusa cordi meo omnes dubitationis tenebrae diffugerunt.*"

Christ; morally, the human soul; and anagogically, God's heavenly city.[18]
Although these four interpretive modes were often then simplified into
the more general categories of "literal" and "non-literal," the practice of
allegory remained rigidly structured. Because Virgil's *Aeneid*, for example,
was thought to depict both the story of a hero's mission (literally) and the
phases of human life (non-literally), each episode in the epic had to be
interpreted to fit both levels of meaning.[19]

Later, during the fifteenth century, humanist scholars also wanted readers to approach their texts systematically, but now the emphasis fell on
a work's situational context instead of a multi-part hermeneutic. Some
humanist satires indicted the pedantry of medieval allegorists – "speaking
in their slovenly and barbarous idiom and jabber," as Erasmus complained,
"so that no one except a jabberer can understand them" – but humanists, like medieval theorists, still demanded active readers.[20] The humanist
method in particular required the training of skilled readers, students of
language who would read both comparatively and historically, analyzing
similarities and differences between texts, and examining how an author's
circumstances may have influenced the meaning.[21] As opposed to the sudden transformations that Aristotle and Augustine claimed a text produced
within its audience, the audience was now thought responsible for transforming the text into its proper configuration; a true reading, as philologists
such as Lorenzo Valla attempted to show, could only be arrived at through
a grammatical, contextual, and paleographical scrutiny.[22] Thus, in the case
of the *Aeneid*, humanists did not, like allegorists, try to piece together
multiple levels of meaning; instead, they studied different manuscripts of
Virgil's text and arrived at a coherent and moral interpretation.[23]

I do not mean to suggest, however, that either humanist or medieval
theorists collectively agreed about how texts should be read. Allegorists,
for example, might dispute how many levels of significance readers were
to uncover – two, three, or four – while humanist instructors devised
competing rules for the proper training of readers – whether to work with
a tutor, say, or whether to take long or brief notes.[24] Among the individual

---

[18] Stephen L. Wailes, *Medieval Allegories of Jesus' Parables* (Berkeley, 1987), p. 10.

[19] See C. S. Lewis, *The Allegory of Love*, rev. edn. (London, 1959), pp. 84–85.

[20] Erasmus, *The Praise of Folly*, trans. Hoyt Hopewell Hudson (Princeton, 1969), p. 84. On the persis-
tence of allegorical exegesis during the Renaissance, see Anthony Grafton, *Defenders of the Text: The
Traditions of Scholarship in an Age of Science, 1450–1800* (Cambridge, MA, 1991), pp. 31–32.

[21] See Anthony Grafton, *Commerce with the Classics: Ancient Books and Renaissance Readers*, Jerome
Lecture Series 20 (Ann Arbor, 1997).

[22] John F. D'Amico, *Theory and Practice in Renaissance Textual Criticism* (Berkeley, 1988), p. 17.

[23] Grafton, *Commerce with the Classics*, pp. 46–47.

[24] Wailes, *Medieval Allegories of Jesus' Parables*, p. 10; and Grafton, *Commerce with the Classics*, p. 6.

philological theories and techniques that also arose during the fifteenth century, Angelo Poliziano proposed a genealogical method of organizing manuscripts to arrive at a textual archetype, while Jean Bodin created a list of general rules for evaluating the reliability of ancient historians.[25]

Yet because all these methods, whether allegorical or humanist, posited a set of instructions and emphasized the pursuit of a text's authentic meaning, medieval and early Renaissance readers still had only limited authority. As Terrence Cave observes, "the very fact that the reader's activity is prescribed in advance means that reading is assigned a subordinate status."[26] Allegorical and humanist techniques were performed in the service of a text whose priority remained unquestioned; readers were meant to decode the meaning that was always–already present, not intervene in a text and move beyond the author's intentions. And while the sea of philological commentary that overflowed the margins of early printed texts may have elevated the act of interpretation, it simultaneously threatened to drown out the possibility of future readers' contributions.

In the specific case of Christian exegesis, medieval and humanist theorists expected readers to proceed actively – in both preparing to read the Bible and applying it to their lives afterwards – but Scripture necessarily subordinated the reader's interpretive activity to the text's authorial intentions. While a full discussion of Christian rhetorical theory exceeds the scope of this chapter, we need to understand how this hermeneutic developed and came to influence early modern reading habits. Returning to Augustine's works reveals that medieval readers sometimes had to struggle to understand the divine text. Although in the *Confessions* Augustine had depicted reading as an ultimately passive experience, he admits in *De doctrina christiana* that Scripture contains "problems and ambiguities of many kinds," which can be traced to the fall of language in Babel; to discover the will of God, readers must first analyze the Bible and "find out the thoughts and wishes of those by whom it was written down."[27] Augustine argues that such active readers will be "rewarded" for their efforts, whereas "those who read casually" (*temere*) will surely be "misled . . . mistaking one thing for another. In some passages they find no meaning at all that

[25] D'Amico, *Theory and Practice in Renaissance Textual Criticism*, pp. 21–27; Anthony Grafton, *Defenders of the Text*, pp. 47–75; and Julian H. Franklin, *Jean Bodin and the Sixteenth-Century Revolution in the Methodology of Law and History* (New York, 1963), pp. 140–41.

[26] Terrence Cave, "The Mimesis of Reading in the Renaissance," in *Mimesis: From Mirror to Method, Augustine to Descartes*, ed. John D. Lyons and Stephen G. Nichols, Jr. (Hanover, 1982), pp. 149–65, this quotation, p. 149.

[27] Augustine, *De doctrina christiana*, ed. and trans. R. P. H. Green (Oxford, 1995), II.vi (7), II.v (6).

they can grasp at, even falsely, so thick is the fog created by some obscure phrases."[28]

Following Origen's precedent, Augustine specifically recommends that readers clarify ambiguous passages with plain ones, an interpretive method adopted and developed in the 1500s by writers such as Erasmus.[29] In this way, Erasmus explains, "a person does not, in fact, only attain the advantage of perceiving an otherwise incomprehensible meaning, but he will also have authority for his interpretation added on."[30] While this method seems to elevate the reader's status – that is, individual interpretations become more authoritative through a reader's efforts – we need to remember that both Augustine and Erasmus limited readers' willful activity by emphasizing divine grace. Augustine opened his Bible and was moved by the first passage he spied because he received a divine command to do so, while Erasmus more generally was describing an interpretive method for priests and bishops, representatives of the church who had received the charismatic gift of the Holy Spirit and could thus fathom Scripture's dark matters.[31] Such readers, according to Erasmus, should repeatedly peruse a biblical passage but ideally come to absorb its significance "automatically and spontaneously."[32]

This concept of Scripture's and the ordained reader's shared authority also reaches back to the medieval writings of Thomas Aquinas and Duns Scotus, both of whom accepted the authority of the church's teachings but still insisted on the material sufficiency of Scripture – that is, readers could find everything necessary for their salvation in the divine text.[33] What came to distinguish the Reformation tradition during the sixteenth century was the complementary notion of Scripture's formal sufficiency: readers could also find in Scripture its correct interpretation, or, in Luther's famous phrase, "Scriptures are their own interpreters" (*sacra scriptura sui ipsius*

---

[28] Augustine, *De doctrina christiana*, II.vi (7, 8).

[29] For Erasmus' dependence on Augustine's works, see Terrence Cave, *The Cornucopian Text: Problems of Writing in the French Resistance* (Oxford, 1979), pp. 82–85.

[30] Erasmus, *Ratio seu methodus compendio perveniendi ad veram theologiam*, in Donald Bernard Morrison Conroy, *The Ecumenical Theology of Erasmus of Rotterdam: A Study of the* Ratio verae theologiae, *Translated into English and Annotated, with a Brief Account of His Ecumenical Writings and Activities within His Lifetime*, diss., University of Pittsburgh, 1974 (Pittsburgh, 1974), p. 335.

[31] Augustine, *Confessions*, VIII.xii (29); and Erasmus, *The Free Will* [*De libero arbitrio*], in *Erasmus-Luther: Discourse on Free Will*, trans. and ed. Ernst F. Winter (New York, 1961), II.9.

[32] According to Erasmus, as readers' hearts are transformed through such exercise into "a library of Christ," their fallen state can no longer taint correct scriptural interpretations: identifying with the divine Logos, readers submit to the text, which then, in effect, explains itself. See Erasmus, *Ratio verae theologiae*, pp. 340, 341; and Cave, *The Cornucopian Text*, pp. 84 n.12, 85–86.

[33] Timothy Ward, *Word and Supplement: Speech Acts, Biblical Texts, and the Sufficiency of Scripture* (Oxford, 2002), pp. 29–31, 34–5.

interpres).[34] This theory paradoxically enhanced and restricted the authority of Renaissance readers, for they no longer had to be authorized by the church, but the biblical text was now deemed virtually self-explanatory. Whereas Augustine's and Erasmus' methods seemed to put the Spirit's authoritative work within the hearts of individuals and thus outside Scripture itself, orthodox Reformers claimed that the Word in Scripture received its authority from God alone. As the Second Helvetic Confession (1566) announces,

> . . . we hold that interpretation of the Scripture to be orthodox and genuine which is gleaned from the Scriptures themselves (from the nature of the language in which they were written, likewise according to the circumstances in which they were set down, and expounded in the light of like and unlike passages and of many and clearer passages) and which agree with the rule of faith and love, and contributes much to the glory of God and man's salvation.[35]

While the specific reference to "the light of like and unlike passages and of many and clearer passages" echoes Augustine's and Erasmus' methods, Reformers instead argued for the "clarity" of Scripture's literal meaning (both its *sinceritas* and *simplicitas*). In the past, as Augustine had argued, God's Word was thought to be purposefully unclear in places, "so that pride may be subdued by hard work and intellects which tend to despise things that are easily discovered may be rescued from boredom and reinvigorated."[36] Erasmus, too, had insisted that both the Old and New Testaments contain "contradictory" passages – "the Eternal Wisdom speaks to us, as it were, in stammering language" – which readers, "with the aid of the study of allegory," must work to understand: "Sometimes the literal meaning is obviously false; occasionally it is even ridiculous and absurd, if it is accepted on face value."[37] For Luther, by comparison, "everything there is in the Scriptures has been brought out by the Word into the most definite light, and published to all the world."[38] Luther believed in a God whose glory and virtue are revealed in the divine text *pro nobis*.

---

[34] See Bernard Lohse, *Martin Luther's Theology: Its Historical and Systematic Development*, trans. and ed. Roy A. Harrisville (Minneapolis, 1999), p. 190. Luther did not, however, utterly reject the church's role; as Lohse notes, Luther "was . . . convinced that Scripture and the church belong together" (p. 188).

[35] *Reformed Confessions of the Sixteenth Century*, ed. Arthur C. Cochrane (Philadelphia, 1966), p. 226.

[36] Augustine, *De doctrina christiana*, II.vi (7).

[37] Erasmus, *Ratio verae theologiae*, pp. 296–307. Erasmus nevertheless warns against overzealous allegorists: "whoever wishes to deal with Sacred Literature in a serious manner should observe moderation in such things" (p. 309).

[38] *Luther's Works*, gen. eds. Jaroslav Pelikan and Helmut T. Lehmann, 55 vols. (Saint Louis, 1955–86), 33: 28.

But, as the above passage from the Second Helvetic Confession suggests, Reformers did not entirely abandon the humanists' methods of interpretation. Luther, for example, developed his own practices of active reading by borrowing from medieval and humanist techniques and theories. Whereas Augustine was surprised and converted by the first passage he read upon opening the Bible at random, Luther, reading the same letter from St. Paul to the Romans, achieved a spiritual conversion only after months of arduous effort: "I raged with a fierce and troubled conscience . . . I beat importunately upon Paul at that point, most ardently desiring to know what St. Paul wanted."[39] Luther's method of reading, as Brian Cummings has shown, relied on the "routine discipline of examining standard texts . . . commenting on them for the benefit of students" – and then urging his own readers "to test his conclusions according to principles of practical exegesis."[40]

Presumably, it was the combined influence of all these methods and traditions – allegorical, humanist, and Reformist – that underpinned active reading practices during the seventeenth century. The almost three centuries of writings about reading that preceded the early modern period at least helped to emphasize the *act* of interpretation over a text's *effects*. Whereas the Reformists, in challenging the church's authority, chipped away at the notion of external textual control, allegorical and humanist methods continued to demonstrate the benefits of reading as hard work. In the particular case of biblical exegesis, because God's Word no longer required, say, a papal council or church father for its proper interpretation, Protestant readers could now turn inward and work hard to understand religious texts. Scriptural ambiguity, rather than empowering priests and bishops, provided lay readers with an opportunity for their own interpretive interventions.

But while neither Luther nor Erasmus nor Augustine ever went so far as to recommend private, individual interpretations, readers during the early modern period started to move away from prescribed methods and to exercise more freedom in how they read the divine text. In the middle of the seventeenth century, the Westminster Confession of Faith (1646) may have still insisted that Scripture represents "the Supreme Judge by which all Controversies of Religion are to be determined," but other evidence suggests that in practice readers had already become more active, their style

---

[39] *Luther's Works*, 34: 337. This comparison is discussed by both Lohse, *Martin Luther's Theology: Its Historical and Systematic Development*, pp. 90–92, and Brian Cummings, *The Literary Culture of the Reformation* (Oxford, 2002), p. 62.
[40] Cummings, *The Literary Culture of the Reformation*, p. 69.

of reading influenced no doubt by the impact of the new print technology on Reformation thinking.[41] Writing at the end of the seventeenth century, John Locke noted that printing the Bible in chapter and verse – "chopped and minced" – had led to the splintering of faith and encouraged individual interpretations of Scripture. Readers, he observed, were no longer "bring[ing] their opinions to the sacred Scripture, to be tried by that infallible rule"; instead, they were "bring[ing] the sacred Scripture to their opinions, to bend it to them, to make it, as they can."[42] Just the act of translating the Bible into the vernacular and putting it into the hands of more readers transferred the authority of the Word from the pulpit to members of the laity: readers could now experience the Bible outside of the church, in the privacy of their studies. As Elizabeth Eisenstein neatly summarizes, printed Bibles were "more portable than pulpits, more numerous than priests, and the messages they contain[ed] . . . more easily internalized."[43]

Thus, in introducing a translation of the Pentateuch, William Tyndale invites his sixteenth-century readers to "suck out the pith of the scripture" and "think that every syllable pertaineth to thine own self."[44] By requesting such an introspective approach, Tyndale, following Augustine's and Luther's precedent, was not only calling for active readers who would personally apply Scripture to their own lives; he also seems to create a community of readers who would now be responsible for determining what Scripture meant. He accordingly instructs his audience "to add no interpretations" that contradict "the plain and manifest places of the scriptures," but he acknowledges that his translation remains incomplete without his readers' contributions.[45] He hopes that "learned" readers will "amend if ought were found amiss" and looks forward to collaborating with them: "*we* will give it his full shape, and put out, if ought be added superfluously, and add to, if ought be overseen through negligence" (my emphasis).[46] Tyndale's translation, in other words, would not just facilitate readers' understanding of Scripture; he wanted his readers to participate in this project.

[41] *The Humble Advice of the Assembly of Divines, Now by Authority of Parliament Sitting at Westminster, concerning Part of a Confession of Faith* (London, 1646; Wing W1442), I.10 (A3v).

[42] John Locke, "An Essay for the Understanding of St. Paul's Epistles," in *The Works of John Locke*, 10 vols. (London, 1823; rpt. Germany, 1963), 8: 7–10.

[43] Elizabeth L. Eisenstein, *The Printing Press as an Agent of Change*, 2 vols. (Cambridge, 1979), 1: 428, as well as in her abridged version, *The Printing Revolution in Early Modern Europe* (Cambridge, 1983), p. 169.

[44] William Tyndale, *Doctrinal Treatises and Introductions to Different Portions of the Holy Scriptures*, ed. Henry Walter (Cambridge, 1848), p. 400. I am also influenced here by the discussion of Protestant hermeneutics in Dayton Haskin, *Milton's Burden of Interpretation* (Philadelphia, 1994).

[45] Tyndale, *Doctrinal Treatises and Introductions*, p. 389.

[46] Tyndale, *Doctrinal Treatises and Introductions*, pp. 392, 390.

Without their combined efforts, he suggests, Scripture would remain incomplete.

The King James Bible anticipates the need for readers' even greater intervention. We are told in the preface that "the Scriptures are plain" in all "doctrinal points that concern salvation," but, when an ambiguity does occur, the translators will not presume to provide authoritative glosses in the margins. Instead, readers must interpret the text themselves: "They that are wise, had rather have their iudgements at libertie in differences of readings, then to be captivated to one, when it may be the other."[47] The preface goes on to explain that God deliberately left some biblical passages difficult to interpret,

partly to exercise and whet our wits, partly to weane the curious from loathing of them for their every-where-plainnesse, partly also to stirre up our devotion to crave the assistance of Gods spirit by prayer, and lastly, that we might be forward to seeke ayd of our brethren by conference, and never scorne those [brethren] that be not in all respects so complete as they should bee . . .[48]

While the phrase "to exercise and whet our wits" once again echoes Augustine's and Erasmus' methods, the promotion "of our brethren by conference" suggests a collaborative process. In contrast to Erasmus, who had posited that priests and bishops could accomplish this labor only through the Holy Spirit's inspiration, the language here implies that also by working together readers and translators can understand the Bible's difficult passages. With the spread of the Reformation to England, the sacred text's authority was now vested in all authors and readers who accepted divine guidance.

This new, collaborative function helps to measure the early modern reader's increased authority – especially when such language is compared with the emphasis on a text's effects that characterized, as we have seen, some classical and medieval writings. If for most seventeenth-century believers Scripture and prayer remained the basis of spiritual guidance, other readers began to interpret the divine text more confidently, a few even questioning the Bible's status as God's word.[49] Individual, often creative interpretations of Scripture led to schisms within the church and the growth of diverse sects, each with its own take on questions of faith and theology. John Milton, for example, could defend divorce in cases other than adultery

---

[47] *The Holy Bible, Conteyning the Old Testament and the New* (London, 1611; STC 2216), B2r.
[48] *The Holy Bible*, B2r.
[49] Christopher Hill, *The World Turned Upside Down: Radical Ideas during the English Revolution* (London, 1972), pp. 261–68.

through a dexterous reading of Christ's apparent prohibition, while other lay readers took the more radical tack of interpreting Christ's resurrection and virgin birth as mere allegories.[50] But, unlike medieval allegory, in which priests and bishops analyzed the divine text by following a rigid hermeneutic, this new type of interpretation allowed early modern readers to claim for themselves more authority: now lay readers could devise their own allegorical interpretations, and they did so selectively, without submitting to a set of prescribed formulae.

In 1638, the Anglican William Chillingworth still argued for Scripture's material and formal sufficiency, but, in describing the Bible as "not a Iudge of Controversies, but *a Rule, only*," Chillingworth seemed to validate individual readers' interpretations: "Every man is to judge for himselfe with the *Iudgement of Discretion*."[51] That Chillingworth then attempts to apply his interpretive method more broadly suggests that the license granted Protestant readers was not confined to the Gospels. Chillingworth briefly equates the way readers interpret the Bible with the method used to "understand what I, or any man else saies" (O4r) – an echo of Erasmus' earlier comparison of reading sacred and secular texts. Erasmus had specifically recommended that, "as the scripture is not moche fruytful if thou stande and stycke styll in the lettre: In lyke maner the poetry of Homere, and Virgyll shal not profyte a lytell if thou remember that it must be understande in the sence allegory."[52] By the early seventeenth century, with neither the church nor the divine text in charge of biblical meaning, early modern readers also tried to interpret their other books more actively – a shift that put new pressures, we will see in the next section, on readers as well as authors.

THE READER IN THE PREFACE

Writing specifically about the interpretation of classical literature, Anthony Grafton has helpfully compared reading to dancing: both are activities that "moderns consider free and natural but that the intellectuals of early modern Europe saw as a complex and rule-bound pursuit that must be learned and

[50] See Milton, *Doctrine and Discipline of Divorce*, in *CP* 2: 328–37; and Hill, *The World Turned Upside Down*, pp. 139–50. For an excellent account of Milton's method of scriptural reading, see Haskin, *Milton's Burden of Interpretation*.

[51] William Chillingworth, *The Religion of Protestants: A Safe Way to Salvation* (Oxford, 1638; STC 5138), H1r.

[52] Erasmus, Enchiridion militis christiani: *An English Version* [1534], ed. Anne M. O'Donnell, Early English Texts Series 282 (Oxford, 1981), pp. 46–47. Compare Augustine, *De doctrina christiana*, III.vii (11), for a related argument of applying methods of reading Scripture to literary texts.

practiced with meticulous care."[53] In this and the next sections, I would like to show how reading practices were in flux during the seventeenth century: authors may have tried to lead their audiences, as Grafton's analogy suggests, but readers were discovering that they no longer needed to follow. In *Orbis sensualium pictus* (1659), the educational reformer Johan Comenius thus builds on humanist techniques and theories in describing the proper reading method: a student should lay his books "open upon a Desk and picketh all the best things out of them into his own Manual, or marketh them . . . with a dash, or a little star, in the Margent."[54] Comenius' method of reading is certainly active; the reader creates a new text in his manual by splicing together various passages by various writers. But, with the spread of print culture, who would now determine what were "the best things"? As printed books became more widely available than manuscript publications had been in preceding generations, would the views of scholars and theorists hold the same sway?

In this section, I begin with prefaces to printed books to illustrate how early modern authors sometimes attempted to guide readers' responses and how readers, recognizing both their own authority and the author's newfound prominence, came to participate more actively in various types of texts. While the legacy of Christian rhetorical theory, as we have seen, warranted readerly intervention, other, more immediate conventions and circumstances also contributed to seventeenth-century practices of active reading.

Scripture, we need to remember, still represented for most Renaissance readers a unique text. Because the ultimate Author's intentions presumably lay behind the Gospels, the Bible more than other printed books required an especially vigilant perusal. Renaissance readers had to guard themselves against misleading commentaries, intentional forgeries, and any other perceived contamination that the imperfect medium of print presented for the perfect word of God. Some readerly distrust probably also stemmed from Protestant concerns about the unreliability of images. As Adrian Johns has argued, "typography effectively fused into illustration" and posed "analogous problems" for Protestant readers "avowing emancipation from the imaginative manipulation allegedly facilitated by Catholic iconography and emblems."[55]

[53] Grafton, *Commerce with the Classics*, p. 6.
[54] Jan Amos Comenius, *Orbis sensualium pictus*, trans. Charles Hoole, London, 1659, facsim. (Menston, 1970), O4v–O5r.
[55] Adrian Johns, *The Nature of the Book* (Chicago, 1998), p. 434.

Yet, if early modern readers applied different approaches to, say, the Bible, a political pamphlet, or a collection of poems, we will see that the Reformation tradition of introspective reading still suggests the active labor commonly expected during this period. I have chosen "expected" because we cannot know how many contemporary readers actually accepted recommendations such as Comenius' or Tyndale's for perusing a publication. As Eugene Kintgen observes, "The very fact that an author recommends a particular strategy for reading indicates that someone was capable of reading that way; but the fact that he has to recommend it also suggests that many people, perhaps most, were not already reading that way."[56] To any discussion of the history of reading, we need to add other, important qualifications: all readers probably do not use the same reading strategy in any period, nor does any one reader always read the same way.[57] We should also recall Francis Bacon's distinction, that

some books are to be tasted, others to be swallowed, and some few to be chewed and digested; that is, some books are to be read only in parts; others to be read, but not curiously; and some few to be read wholly, and with diligence and attention.[58]

How a person reads during any period remains contingent on situational constraints as well as such changing and often difficult to determine variables as a reader's ability, inclination, and background. We especially should not assume, as Robert Darnton cautions, "that seventeenth-century Englishmen read Milton and Bunyan as if they were twentieth-century college professors."[59] In "The Author's Apology for his Book" in *The Pilgrim's Progress* (1678), Bunyan himself includes various reasons contemporary readers might turn to his work, from improving their memories to treating melancholy and curing listlessness.[60]

We can nevertheless chart some apparently general tendencies among the expectations of early modern authors – foremost perhaps, this emphasis on

---

[56] Kintgen, "Reconstructing Elizabethan Reading," p. 13. Roger Chartier similarly reminds us "that reading is not simply submission to textual machinery." See Chartier, "Texts, Printing, Readings," in *The New Cultural History*, ed. Lynn Hunt (Berkeley, 1989), pp. 154–75, this quotation, p. 156.

[57] On the specific reading habits of women, see Suzanne W. Hull, *Chaste, Silent, and Obedient: English Books for Women, 1475–1640* (San Marino, 1982), and Brian Richardson, *Printing, Writers and Readers in Renaissance Italy* (Cambridge, 1999), pp. 144–49. D. R. Woolf, *Reading History in Early Modern England*, pp. 108–25, offers a few compelling cases studies of individual reading habits based on readers' notebooks and diaries.

[58] Francis Bacon, "Of Studies," in *Francis Bacon*, ed. Brian Vickers (Oxford, 1996), pp. 439–40.

[59] Robert Darnton, "First Steps toward a History of Reading," *Australian Journal of French Studies* 23.1 (1986): 5–30, this quotation, p. 22.

[60] John Bunyan, *The Pilgrim's Progress*, 2nd edn. (London, 1678; Wing B5558), A2r–A6r.

readers' diversity.[61] As John Kerrigan has argued, the "recurrent stress" on a text's many readers became "almost a condition of authorship in the expanding market for print."[62] Just as John Heminge and Henry Condell in the First Folio (1623) address the "great Variety" of Shakespeare's readers, "From the most able, to him that can but spell," Jonson in *Cataline* (1611) addresses separately "THE READER IN *ORDINARY*" and "the *Reader* extraordinary," and the theologian Laurence Sarson singles out the "less skilfull Reader[s]" of his *Analysis* (1650), advising them to "omit what is contained between page twenty five, and page sixty nine" so that they can concentrate on those parts that are "both more practical and facile."[63] Thomas Dekker, comparing *"He that writes"* with a *"skilfull Cooke,"* complains about the difficulty of satisfying such a diverse audience: *"A thousand palats must bee pleased with a thousand sawces: and one hundred lines must content five hundred dispositions. A hard taske."*[64] More often Renaissance books posit a range of readers from the generous to the malicious. In Sidney's *An Apologie for Poetry* (1595), for example, the publisher Henry Olney imagines three groups of readers: some will "condemne me as a detractor from their Deities," while others will "not onely defend, but praise mee," and still others, he hopes, will become his "Champions."[65] In like manner, Thomas Heywood begins *Troia Britanica* (1609) with a note "TO the two-fold Readers: *the Courteous, and the Criticke,*" and John Guillim concludes *A Display of Heraldrie* (1610), by contrasting *"th'ungentle* Broode *of Envies Groomes"* with those *"gentle* Spirits" who *"will quite"* his efforts with the appropriate *"regard."*[66]

We can trace some of this rhetoric to such classical writers as Persius, who imagined a diverse group of readers in his satires; Plutarch, who compared different reading styles to the different ways that animals

---

[61] I am following Kintgen's method here in trying "to present a relatively unified picture of reading processes" based on the "general agreement" of contemporary sources and the "notion of apparent conflicts . . . being homogenized in actual practice" (*Reading in Tudor England*, pp. 13–14). Kintgen adopts this latter concept from Frank Whigham's study of Renaissance guidebooks in *Ambition and Privilege: The Social Tropes of Elizabethan Courtesy Theory* (Berkeley, 1984), p. 27.

[62] Kerrigan, "The Editor as Reader: Constructing Renaissance Texts," in *The Practice and Representation of Reading in England*, ed. James Raven, Helen Small, and Naomi Tadmor (Cambridge, 1996), pp. 102–24, this quotation, p. 112.

[63] William Shakespeare, *Comedies, Histories, & Tragedies* (London, 1623; STC 22273), A3r; Ben Jonson, *Cataline* (London, 1611; STC 14759), A3r; and Laurence Sarson, *An Analysis of the 1. Timoth[y] 1.15 and an Appendix* (London, 1650; Wing S703), A2v.

[64] Thomas Dekker, *A Strange Horse-Race* (London, 1613; STC 6528), A3r.

[65] Sir Philip Sidney, *An Apologie for Poetrie* (London, 1595; STC 22534), A3v.

[66] Thomas Heywood, *Troia Britanica: Or, Great Britaines Troy* (London, 1609; STC 13366), A4r; and John Guillim, *A Display of Heraldrie* (London, 1610; STC 12500), Oo1v. Guillim's book was published eight times between 1610 and 1724.

feed; and Horace, who urged writers to consider audience expectations and accommodate various types of readers.[67] Renaissance writers, however, sound especially anxious about the reception of their works, an anxiety surely influenced by the spread of print culture, which brought an author's works to unseen, distant audiences. The immediate rhetorical purpose of including an address to the reader was presumably to help sell books; as Nathaniel Field remarked in 1612, "Reader, the Sale-man sweares youle take it very ill, if I say not somewhat to you too."[68] But because prefaces and dedications so often suggest how readers ought to respond to a text, we may infer that authors and stationers were concerned about the interpretive liberty that their audiences might take. The surviving sixteenth-century treatises on writing explicitly acknowledge the reader's authority.[69] Although George Gascoigne's *Certaine Notes of Instruction Concerning the Making of Verse or Rhyme in English* (1575) and George Puttenham's *The Arte of English Poesie* (1589) present detailed instructions for creating effective poetry, both works also recognize that readers ultimately will determine a writer's success. As Puttenham succinctly puts it, "the election is the writers, the judgement is the worlds."[70]

In *A Free and Offenceles Ivstification, of Andromeda Liberata* (1614), George Chapman similarly acknowledges that an author can "meane what he list" but "his writing notwithstanding must be construed *in mentem Legentis . . .* to the intendment of the Reader." Responding to the "violent hoobub" prompted by his poem *Andromeda Liberata* (1614), Chapman had hoped that "at least, in mine owne wrighting, I might be reasonablie & conscionablie master of mine owne meaning." He has discovered he cannot and wonders aloud whether "any rule of reason make it good" that authors have so little control over readers' inferences.[71]

---

[67] Persius, "Satire I," in *The Satires of Persius*, trans. W. S. Merwin (Port Washington, NY, 1973), pp. 55–62; Plutarch, "How A Yoong Man Ought to Heare Poets, and How He May Take Profit by Reading Poems," in *The Philosophie, Commonlie Called, the Morals*, trans. Philemon Holland (London, 1603; STC 20063), D2r; and Horace, *Ars Poetica*, in *Satires, Epistles, and Ars Poetica*, trans. H. Rushton Fairclough (Cambridge, MA, 1966), pp. 450–89. Kevin Dunn discusses the ancient tradition of distrusting prefatory rhetoric in *Pretexts of Authority: The Rhetoric of Authorship in the Renaissance Preface* (Stanford, 1994), pp. 1–7.

[68] Nathaniel Field, *A Woman Is a Weathercock* (London, 1612; STC 10854), qtd. in *An Anthology of Elizabethan Dedications and Prefaces*, ed. Clara Gebert (Philadelphia, 1933), p. 205.

[69] See Kintgen, *Reading in Tudor England*, pp. 149–72, as well as his earlier essay, "Reconstructing Elizabethan Reading," pp. 9–13.

[70] George Puttenham, *The Arte of English Poesie*, ed. Gladys Doidge Willcock and Alice Walker (Cambridge, 1936), p. 263.

[71] George Chapman, *A Free and Offenceles Ivstification, of Andromeda Liberata* (1614; STC 4977), in *The Poems of George Chapman*, ed. Phyllis Brooks Bartlett (New York, 1962), pp. 327–35.

We hear the same concern in the opening of Ben Jonson's *Epigrammes* (1616) as he implores the reader to "Pray thee take care, that tak'st my book in hand, / To reade it well: that is, to understand."[72] Jonson has based this poem on a similar verse in Martial's first book of *Epigrams*, but there Martial specifically addresses the "devoted" or "eager" reader ("*lector studiose*").[73] Whereas Martial thanks his audience for "the glory you have given the author while he lives" ("*quod dedisti / viventi decus atque sentienti*"), Jonson sounds less confident as he begins his *Epigrammes* with an imperative, "Pray thee take care." He is suggesting up front that he depends on an understanding audience and that he feels uneasy about his readers' license.

Faced with this potential lack of control, Renaissance authors – and stationers – commonly ask their readers to examine their works actively; the assumption seems to have been, following the allegorical and humanist traditions, that only through such *directed* effort could readers accurately gauge a book's and author's merits. Jonson's readerly exhortations accordingly reverberate in various dedications and introductory epistles throughout the seventeenth century. Heminge and Condell in Shakespeare's First Folio, for example, urge readers to "Reade him . . . and againe, and againe" before making an assessment (A3r), and Thomas Nabbes concludes his "*Proeme* to the Reader" in *The Unfortunate Mother* (1640) with a similarly direct request, "Read it with observation then, and be / My Judge from reason" (lines 25–26).[74] Sometimes authors or stationers request a reader's "perusal," a term during the seventeenth century that could loosely mean "to read" but, as it does today, more precisely conveyed "to read thoroughly or carefully" or "to survey, inspect, examine, or consider in detail."[75] The bookseller John Benson invites his readers' "*perusall*" of Shakespeare's *Poems* (1640); Richard Brome asks the readers of his comedy *The Antipodes* (1640) for "*thy perusal*"; and the bookseller Humphrey Moseley invites "Eagle-eied" readers to give Milton's *Poems* (1645) "*thy exactest perusal*."[76]

More often authors or stationers wishfully insert formal, prefatory appeals to specific kinds of readers – "the Christian Reader," "the courteous Reader," "the discreete Reader," "the Impartial Reader," "the Iudiciall

[72] Jonson, "To the Reader," *Epigrammes*, in *The Workes of Benjamin Jonson* (London, 1616; STC 14751), Ttt1r.

[73] Martial, *Epigrams*, ed. and trans. D. R. Shackleton Bailey, 3 vols. (Cambridge, MA, 1993), I: 42–43.

[74] Thomas Nabbes, *The Unfortunate Mother* (London, 1640; STC 18346), A3r.

[75] *OED* II.5.a and II.2.c.

[76] Shakespeare, *Poems* (London, 1640; STC 22344), *2v; Richard Brome, *The Antipodes* (London, 1640; STC 3818), L4v; Milton, *Poems* (London, 1645; Wing M2160), a4v.

Reader," "the knowing Reader."[77] By invoking a type of generic reader at the start, these texts set the bar by which authors wanted readers to measure their reactions – are they discreet, impartial, or knowing enough? But this rhetoric also called attention to the importance of the audience's interpretive function. Writing about the structure of Renaissance fiction, Ullrich Langer notes that such prescriptive gestures may appear "to foreclose any reaction . . . other than the one foreseen," when in fact

> this staging of foreknowledge forces the reader to realize his ontological difference, as a being whose substance cannot be captured by *any* text . . . His favorable opinion represented in the text that he then chooses to praise only demonstrates his distinctness as a being precisely not determined by the text.[78]

Authors, in other words, seem to possess a god-like foreknowledge of readers' responses but individual readers can still exercise their interpretive free will. The supposition of readers' reactions only highlights that all such reactions are a choice that can never be textually predetermined.

Nevertheless, we should acknowledge that an author's or stationer's pre-assumptions may have swayed some Renaissance readers; an audience member need not have been especially impressionable to want to identify with the "Christian" or "knowing" readers to whom a book was targeted. Positioning readers within a book's preliminary leaves served, moreover, as a compliment: readers were being told that they mattered. The chorus of people represented at the start of a book – the dedicatee, publisher, and reader – had to accompany the writer in making the text meaningful.

That more than one third of the 1,097 Renaissance works that I examined in the Carl H. Pforzheimer Collection include some kind of formal note "to readers" suggests such introductory appeals occur often in seventeenth-century literature.[79] This number would likely double if we were to take into account books with multiple prefaces and the many other less explicitly labeled advertisements, epistles, notes, and prologues that still direct some

---

[77] These specific introductory appeals appear, among other places, in the following works: "Christian" in William Prynne, *Histrio-mastix* (London, 1633; STC 20464), **6r–***3r; "courteous" in John Cotgrave, *The English Treasury of Wit and Language* (London, 1655; Wing C6368), π2r–π3v; "discrete" in W. H., *Englands Sorrow Or, A Farewell to Essex* (London, 1606; STC 12582), A3r; "impartial" in Thomas Durfey, *Butler's Ghost* (London, 1682; Wing D2703), π3r–π4r; "iudiciall" in Thomas Heywood, *An Apology for Actors* (London, 1614; STC 13309), A4r–v; and "knowing" in Robert Davenport, *King John and Matilda, A Tragedy* (London, 1655; Wing D370), π2r.

[78] Ullrich Langer, *Divine and Poetic Freedom in the Renaissance: Nominalist Theology and Literature in France and Italy* (Princeton, 1990), p. 32.

[79] I have excluded broadsides, proclamations, and ballads from my count (Pforz 86–114, 532, 533, 668, 669, 907, 911, and 996) but included the eleven items listed as "recent acquisitions" in the Pforzheimer Catalogue (Pforz app. 1–11).

remarks to readers. Dekker in *The Shomakers Holy-Day* (1610), for example, includes a preface "To all good Fellowes, Professors of *the Gentle Craft*," Robert Greene in *Greene's Arcadia* (1616) writes "To the Gentlemen Students of both Universities," and the anonymous author of *The Pourtraiture of Truths Most Sacred Majesty* (1649) prefers the politically charged title "To the Seduced People of England."[80] Some untitled notes and prefaces are also directed at readers, such as the pair of couplets printed above the errata in Robert Herrick's *Hesperides* (1648) (*"Condemne the Printer, Reader, and not me*," A4r) as well as, we will see in chapter 5, some of his collection's poems ("To the Soure Reader," B2r). Even some seventeenth-century dedicatory epistles represent a type of readerly address, as the publisher, author, or one of the author's acquaintances asks a specific reader to bestow favor upon the text.

And as with dedicatory epistles, notes to generic readers served as both a defense mechanism and a foregrounding of the audience's activity.[81] In the case of a formal dedication, however, the writer or stationer sought a distinguished patron's favor and protection; with a preface "to the reader," writers now appealed to an unseen, general audience to purchase and watch over their publications. Thus, John Guillim, in a fairly standard gesture, disavows future responsibility for his treatise on heraldry: *"Looke now who will heeron, / My* taske *is past, and all my* care *is gone.*"[82] Jonson also accepts that he must "*leave*" his play *Cataline* to his readers' "exercise" and "medling": he admits somewhat reluctantly, "*It is your owne. I departed with my right, when I let it first abroad*" (A3r). Other prefaces conventionally announce that readers are responsible for arriving at their own conclusions. Introducing George Herbert's *The Temple* (1633), for example, Thomas Buck and Roger Daniel decide to "leave it free and unforestalled to every mans judgement, and to the benefit he shall finde by perusall" (¶2r).[83] In like manner, the bookseller Thomas Walkley prefaces a 1622 quarto of

---

80 Dekker, *The Shomakers Holy-Day* (London, 1610; STC 6524), A3r; Robert Greene, *Greene's Arcadia* (London, 1616; STC 12275), A2r–B4r; and *The Pourtraiture of Truths Most Sacred Majesty* (London, 1649; Wing M267), A3r–A4v. Kevin Sharpe adduces a few seventeenth-century books with more than one dedication to argue that multiple dedications "represented a hierarchy of authority and obedience and positioned the text within that order. They also enabled the writer to identify and construct a community of readers." See Sharpe, *Reading Revolutions: The Politics of Reading in Early Modern England* (New Haven, 2000), pp. 53–54.

81 For a discussion of Renaissance prefaces as important sites for self-authorizing rhetoric, see Dunn, *Pretexts of Authority: The Rhetoric of Authorship in the Renaissance Preface*, especially pp. 7–16.

82 Guillim, *A Display of Heraldrie*, O01v.

83 As Randall Ingram has shown, the textual apparatus in Margaret Cavendish's *Poems, and Fancies* (1653) similarly "acknowledges and . . . promotes individuated readings." See Ingram, "First Words and Second Thoughts: Margaret Cavendish, Humphrey Moseley, and 'the Book,'" *Journal of Medieval and Early Modern Studies* 30.1 (2000): 101–24, this quotation, p. 114.

Othello by telling the reader that he will "*leave it to the generall censure*" (A2r).

Although these statements, in particular the use of "leave" in the above examples, imply that the books' creators were turning over their works to readers, we need to remember that both authors and stationers still wanted to avoid interpretations that they considered erroneous. As John Kerrigan notes, authors remained "wary of abandoning their works to misconstruction. That could lead to imprisonment, or worse."[84] The empowerment of Renaissance readers did not, in other words, require that early modern authors relinquish complete control of their writings. Authors and stationers instead devised strategies to encourage readers to arrive at what they deemed a text's correct meaning. The Renaissance protocol of attaching a preface addressed to readers represents, once again, both an affirmation of an audience's authority and an attempt by authors and stationers to direct that audience's interpretation.

READERS IN ACTION

This same tension expresses itself in emblem books, a genre that further suggests the kind of participation often expected of readers during the sixteenth and seventeenth centuries.[85] On the one hand, readers had to take an active role in constructing the meaning of the emblems they read; on the other hand, authors attempted to impose limitations on readers' participation. That John Wilkins catalogues "Emblems" among other forms of covert communication such as smoke signals, invisible ink, and shorthand reveals the demanding nature of these readers' activity.[86] Readers had to piece together an emblem's meaning from three parts: a symbolic picture, an ambiguous motto, and a verse commentary that hinted at the picture and motto's relationship. Thomas Blount in *The Art of Making*

---

[84] Kerrigan, "The Editor as Reader," p. 114. John M. Wallace similarly discusses the period's "wide latitude of response permitted within the pale of unrestrained interpretation." See Wallace, "'Examples Are Best Precepts': Readers and Meanings in Seventeenth-Century Poetry," *Critical Inquiry* 1 (1974): 273–90, this quotation, p. 275.

[85] As evidence of the popularity of emblem books, William Camden's *Remaines of a Greater Worke Concerning Britaine* reached eight editions between 1605 and 1674; and Francis Quarles's two collections, *Emblemes* and *Hieroglyphikes*, were published together and separately in a total of thirteen editions between 1635 and 1696. Emblem books became so popular in England by the end of the sixteenth century that Gabriel Harvey complained about Cambridge students who were devoting so much time to these works that they had begun to neglect Aristotle. Gabriel Harvey, *Letter-Book*, ed. Edward John Long Scott (London, 1884), pp. 78–79.

[86] John Wilkins, *Mercury: or the Secret and Swift Messenger* (1641; Wing W2202), in *The Mathematical and Philosophical Works of the Right Reverend John Wilkins* (London, 1708), p. 55.

Devises (1646) emphasizes the expressive potential of well-made "devises" – which he defines as everything from "Hieroglyphicks, Symboles" to "Armes, Blazons" and "Cyphres" – but he insists that the best decorations ought to require some effort to interpret them.[87] He claims "it is of absolute necessity" that sovereigns' devices use only Latin or Greek mottoes (F4v), for example, and asserts as a more general rule, "by how much this way of expression is lesse usuall with the common people, by so much is it the more excellent" (C3r).

Writing on royalist literature from the Civil War and Interregnum, Lois Potter has uncovered various methods of encryption that suggest readers by the middle of the seventeenth century had considerable experience interpreting secretive language, both visual and literary. As Potter observes, "the civil war was a period when encoding and decoding had more than a metaphorical meaning."[88] Both royalists and independents used secret communications in everything from poetry to paintings to political pamphlets. Leah Marcus specifically notes that "royalist and royalist sympathizers coped with the loss of public ritual and festivity by recasting old ceremonies in more private forms and surrounding them with cryptic language and hermetic symbolism – barriers against the intrusion of hostile outsiders."[89] Sometimes a book's codes were communicated through its physical design. Milton's *Pro populo Anglicano Defensio* (1651) contains a printer's ornament that furtively undermines his defense of republicanism, while William Walwyn's *A Helpe to the Right Understanding* (1645) imitates the design and typography of William Prynne's *Independency Examined* (1644) as part of a larger strategy to trick Prynne's supporters into thinking he endorsed Walwyn's argument.[90]

In all these cases of covert communication, the Renaissance reader's activity was still prescribed in advance: as with medieval allegory, readers were being asked to decode meanings that writers had deliberately planted in their texts. Yet, given the subtlety of these secret codes and the corresponding demands put on early modern readers – Blount, we recall, especially lauds a writer's obscurity and a reader's effort – we should not be surprised that some readers would begin to intervene in their texts more actively than authors had imagined. It is this phenomenon, as I show in the next chapter,

---

[87] Thomas Blount, *The Art of Making Devises* (London, 1646; Wing E3350), A1r.

[88] Lois Potter, *Secret Rites and Secret Writing: Royalist Literature, 1641–1660* (Cambridge, 1989), p. 38; and see Sharpe, *Reading Revolutions: The Politics of Reading in Early Modern England*, pp. 51–52.

[89] Leah S. Marcus, *The Politics of Mirth: Jonson, Herrick, Milton, Marvell, and the Defense of Old Holiday Pastimes* (Chicago, 1986), pp. 213–14.

[90] Dobranski, "Burghley's Emblem and the Heart of Milton's *Pro populo anglicano defensio*," *Milton Quarterly* 34 (2000): 33–48; and Achinstein, *Milton and the Revolutionary Reader*, pp. 143–44.

that occurred with Sidney's *Arcadia* during the seventeenth century: audiences sometimes approached "plain" texts as secretive ones. How could they not? If even Scripture, as Chillingworth argued, had become "a rule only" and "not a judge of controversies," readers might suppose that other texts were also open to various interpretations.

Such unscripted readerly activity is one of the distinguishing characteristics of the early modern period; seventeenth-century readers, we will see in this chapter's last section, often appropriated another writer's work with their own goals in mind. Here we may detect the influence of not only Protestant hermeneutics but also the polemical approach to learning that shaped early modern pedagogy. Disputation remained the primary means of learning in seventeenth-century universities, and students proved their competence by orally defending positions in a series of debates. This rhetorical method, casting learning as a dynamic, social process, surely influenced how students would also have experienced printed materials. Reading, like learning, need not be limited to a single person's ideas or arguments; instead, it required discussion, or, as Milton summarizes, "much arguing, much writing, many opinions" (*CP* 2: 554).

That all Renaissance authors began as readers also helps to explain the reader's increased activity: writers who borrowed from and appropriated other writers' works set a precedent for their own readers to become writers and, in turn, use the writers' works for their own purposes. As readers saw how older texts were translated, excerpted, and annotated, they naturally would feel less hesitant to interact with newly printed books.[91] Bacon's famous indictment of "schoolmen" as spiders, spinning ideas out of their heads, "admirable for the fineness of thread and work, but of no substance or profit," was an attack not on readers' active appropriation of other writers' works but on the readers' self-absorption and "small variety of reading."[92] Bacon specifically deprecates the humanists' habit, as he saw it, of "hunt[ing] more after words than matter" and quibbling over "all the smaller sort of objections" (pp. 139, 141). He instead wants readers who will weigh what they read with what they observe, and "hunt" in books "after the weight of matter, worth of subject, soundness of argument, life of invention, or depth of judgment" (p. 139). The solution for avoiding the humanist interpreters' fruitless activity, in other words, required a more dialectical encounter with other writers' works, not less activity, and certainly not, as

---

[91] See Cave, "The Mimesis of Reading in the Renaissance," p. 155.

[92] Francis Bacon, *The Advancement of Learning*, in *Francis Bacon*, ed. Brian Vickers (Oxford, 1996), pp. 120–299, this quotation, p. 140. All subsequent references to the text are taken from this edition and cited parenthetically by page number.

Bacon emphasizes, confining a reader's wit "in the cells of a few authors (chiefly Aristotle their dictator)," the way scholars had formerly been "shut up in the cells of monasteries and colleges" (p. 140).

Writing forty years later, Milton in *Areopagitica* prefers a metaphor of selection to describe the effort that effective reading entails, ultimately granting that it is readers who determine a book's merit. Reading, Milton argues, requires the same "incessant labour to cull out, and sort asunder" that Psyche undertook to separate Venus' "confused seeds" (*CP* 2: 514). While he insists on his own authority as a writer – describing a "good Booke" in the tract's most often quoted passage as "the pretious life-blood of a master spirit" (*CP* 2: 493) – Milton also emphasizes the reader's role in creating meaning. Books "contain a potencie of life in them to be as active as that soule was whose progeny they are" (*CP* 2: 492). The word "potencie" indicates a capacity or potential, and the infinitive "to be" casts the progeny's activity in the future. Only when "sown up and down" in readers' minds, can the "pretious" seed stored in books give birth – "chance to spring up" – people "armed" with the author's insights (*CP* 2: 492).

To illustrate the effort of active reading, Milton switches to metaphors of digesting food and compounding medicine. Whereas "Bad meats will scarce breed good nourishment in the healthiest concoction," a "discreet and judicious Reader" can digest even "bad books," making them useful "to discover, to confute, to forewarn, and to illustrate" (*CP* 2: 512).[93] That books also resemble "usefull drugs and materialls wherewith to temper and compose effective and strong med'cins" emphasizes once again the potential that books contain and the work that they require: readers must first actively transform a text into something useful, then actively apply it in their pursuit of knowledge (*CP* 2: 521). Thus Milton compares a good reader to "a good refiner" who "can gather gold out of the drossiest volume," even using "errors" – when they are "known, read, and collated" – for "the speedy attainment of what is truest" (*CP* 2: 513, 521). Here, too, the act of reading is a demanding process, whereby readers' efforts can compensate for a writer's mistakes. People must choose and read for themselves, according to Milton, because "faith and knowledge thrives by exercise" (*CP* 2: 543). He objects to Parliament's licensing policy in part because it restricted such "exercise" and

---

[93] In George Gascoigne's *A Hundreth Sundrie Flowres Bounde Up in One Small Poesie* (London, 1573; STC 11635), the printer Henrie Bynneman offers a similar argument: "the well minded man may reape somme commoditie out of the most frivolous works that are written. And as the venemous spider will sucke poison out of the most holesome herbe, and the industrious Bee can gather hony out of the most stinking weede: Even so the discrete reader may take a happie example by the most lascivious histories" (A2v).

impeded readers who wanted to continue seeking wisdom. Personifying Truth as a dismembered virgin, he would like readers to "imitat[e] the carefull search that *Isis* made for the mangl'd body of *Osiris*" by "gathering up limb by limb" the "dessever'd peeces" of Truth "scatter'd" through various pamphlets and books (*CP* 2: 549, 550–51).

Other contemporary texts similarly cast the pursuit of truth as a laborious searching and gathering. While a seventeenth-century edition of Plutarch's *Morals* (1603) primarily explains how to use poetry for "the framing or reforming of maners," it echoes both Bacon and Milton in emphasizing the effort involved in effective reading.[94] When readers discover "some wicked and ungodly speech," they "must confute it," either by locating "contrarie sentences of the same author in other places" or by tracking down "contrarie sentences of other famous authors" that can be "weighed and compared" (C1v, C2r). Sometimes a reader must extrapolate what a poet means, "whereby a sentence may be stretched farther than the bare words import" (D5r); at other times, readers must work to uncover the "many profitable and holsome lessons" that are "covertly couched" in a literary work (D1r). A preface in Virgilio Malvezzi's *Discourses upon Cornelius Tacitus* (1642) suggests that authors should deliberately encourage this type of readerly intervention. Malvezzi praises an author's "obscurity" because it forces the reader to discover "the true meaning" by "labouring about it" and, thereby, inspires the reader to new insights: "then he counts it an issue of his own braine, and taking occasion from those sentences, *to go further then the thing he reads*" (my emphasis). Malvezzi describes reading and writing as a reciprocal practice: an "understanding" reader will take greater delight in an author who has "cunning," according to Malvezzi, "because by it he discovers his owne."[95]

Presumably many of these recommendations for active reading owed something to the fragmentation and social upheaval brought about by and prompting the Civil War. Aside from the use of secret communication that flourished, as we have seen, during the war period, reading was linked physiologically with the country's political troubles. Seventeenth-century thinkers tended to attribute contemporary conflicts at least in part to the internal war waged between the understanding and imagination within each individual.[96] Because this ongoing "Intestine Strife," as the natural

[94] Plutarch, "How A Yoong Man Ought to Heare Poets," D1r, B3r.

[95] Virgilio Malvezzi, *Discourses upon Cornelius Tacitus*, trans. Richard Baker (London, 1642; Wing M359), A6r.

[96] Johns, *The Nature of the Book*, p. 403. Without attempting a full analysis of Renaissance physiology, we need to remember that human beings after the fall could no longer trust in their senses to

philosopher Thomas Willis punningly described it, afflicted all people, the larger body politic was also harmed. Writing toward the end of the seventeenth century, Willis emphasized the seriousness of each person's internal struggle, using language that again recalls England's recent history: he refers to the individual's "wicked Combinations, troublesom Contests, and more than Civil Wars."[97]

Reading during the seventeenth century could be part of the solution or part of the problem, able either to promote understanding or to provoke sometimes dangerous passions. Excessive or, more important, undisciplined reading was thought to stir up a person's imaginative faculties, causing errors in judgment, and in the worst cases, inciting rebellion, death, or madness. Writing about himself in the third person, Robert Boyle, for example, blamed his short attention span on poor reading habits: he complained that reading a romance as a boy had "accustomed his thoughts to such a habitude of roving, that he has scarce ever been their quiet master since, but they would take all occasions to steal away, and go a-gadding to objects then unseasonable and impertinent."[98] Robert Burton in like manner warned undisciplined readers that they could "prove in the end as mad as Don Quixote" if they "read nothing but Play-books, idle Poems, Jests, [or romances such as] Amadis de Gaul, the Knight of the Sun, the Seven Champions, Palmerin de Oliva, Huon of Bordeaux, &c."[99]

Such descriptions of the harmful effects of books recall the classical and medieval emphasis on a reader's relative passivity; most immediately, we may be reminded of Dante's Francesca and Paolo and the sinfulness that their reading prompted. The solution offered during the seventeenth century required that people not only choose good books but also develop

gain knowledge. In Paradise, understanding produced knowledge, but in the post-lapsarian world, each person was guided by passions. While the understanding continued to enable rational activity, passions played the equally important role of providing ideas for the mind to contemplate. Modern historians such as Johns accordingly refer to a "problem of knowledge" during the Renaissance, for the faculties of understanding and imagination frequently clashed. Because passions failed to distinguish between sensory and imaginary stimuli, the apprehensions they communicated to the brain might prove false. See also Johns' earlier essay, "The Physiology of Reading in Restoration England," in *The Practice and Representation of Reading in England*, ed. James Raven, Helen Small, and Naomi Tadmor (Cambridge, 1996), pp. 138–61.

97 Thomas Willis, *Two Discourses Concerning the Soul of Brutes*, trans. S. Pordage (London, 1683; Wing W2856), G2r, A2v.

98 Robert Boyle, "An Account of Philaretus [i.e. Mr. R. Boyle], during his Minority," in *The Works of the Honourable Robert Boyle*, ed. Thomas Birch, 5 vols. (London, 1744), 1: B1v–D2r, this quotation, C1r.

99 Robert Burton, *The Anatomy of Melancholy*, ed. Floyd Dell and Paul Jordan-Smith (New York, 1955), p. 459 (part 2, section 2, member 4).

active reading habits – what Erasmus earlier had called the judicious pursuit of "right reading."[100] Only when read constructively could books help readers to cure their melancholy or reach divine insights. As Adrian Johns notes, "Habits were held to be the best hope an individual had of countering immoral, unhealthy, excessive, or erroneous passions," and intellectual processes such as learning to read or speak depended precisely on this type of repeated conditioning.[101] Milton thus recommends books for the "constituting of human vertue" because reading allows a person to "scout into the regions of sin and falsity" without actually committing sins or speaking falsehoods (*CP* 2: 516–17); John Locke suggests "the arrangement and regular dispersal of our thoughts in a well ordered and copious common-place book" as the best way "to obviate the inconvenience and difficulties attending a vacant or wandering mind"; Bacon prescribes "fit studies" to cure any "stond or impediment in the wit"; and Burton, citing authorities from Seneca to St. Paul, extols the benefits of "study" for people "overrun with solitariness, or carried away with pleasing melancholy and vain conceits."[102]

Reading could specifically cure "solitariness" and melancholy in part because it represented a social activity.[103] Just as the translators of the King James Bible encourage readers "to seeke ayd of our brethren by conference" (B2r), Burton in the above passage suggests not only that people read books but also that they talk about them. Following the esteemed Muslim philosopher ar-Razi, he recommends "continual conference" and "perpetual discourse of some history, tale, poem, news, &c., which feeds the mind as meat and drink doth the body, and pleaseth as much."[104] Based on surviving anecdotal accounts, seventeenth-century reading often differed from the silent, solitary activity that we might undertake today when we describe ourselves as "studying." At the beginning of the century, as we have seen, Bacon opposed the isolated reading of "schoolmen . . . shut up

---

[100] While Erasmus' concept of "right" or "authentic" reading (*sensus germanus*) does not occur in *Ratio verae theologiae*, it is a central idea in, for example, his later *Ecclesiastes* (1535). See Cave, *The Cornucopian Text*, pp. 88–94.

[101] Johns, *The Nature of the Book*, p. 405.

[102] John Locke, *Essay Concerning Human Understanding* (1690; Wing L2738), as qtd. in Peter Beal, "Notions in Garrison: The Seventeenth-Century Commonplace Book," in *New Ways of Looking at Old Texts: Papers of the Renaissance English Text Society, 1985–1991*, ed. W. Speed Hill (Binghamton, NY, 1993), pp. 131–47, this quotation, p. 140; Bacon, "Of Studies," p. 439; and Burton, *Anatomy of Melancholy*, p. 458. Burton seems to envision "study" as a specifically masculine activity. For women, "instead of laborious studies," he prescribes "curious needlework, cut-works, spinning, bone-lace, and many pretty devices of their own making, to adorn their houses, Cushions, Carpets, Chairs, Stools . . . confections, conserves, distillations, &c. which they shew to strangers" (p. 463).

[103] Richardson, *Printing, Writers and Readers in Renaissance Italy*, p. 112.

[104] Burton, *Anatomy of Melancholy*, p. 459.

in the cells of monasteries and colleges," and as late as 1667 John Evelyn was still warning against the extreme dangers of private reading. Evelyn argues that a life spent in "*Chambers* and *Closets* crowded with shelves" ultimately "produces *ignorance*, renders us *barbarous*, feeds *revenge*, disposes to *envy*, creates *Witches*, dispeoples the *World*, renders it a *desart*, and would soon *dissolve* it." He instead urges his readers to use their book-learning: they must "*read men* . . . converse with *living Libraries*," and apply their knowledge to public action and "active *Conversations*."[105]

Renaissance readers frequently followed Evelyn's advice, supplementing the material they perused with lectures and discussions. As William Sherman observes, "throughout the early modern period reading and conference were set alongside each other as the twin means to fruitful instruction."[106] Employed as a professional reader/scholar, Gabriel Harvey, for example, was called upon to read and discuss the political implications of Livy's Roman history with visiting courtiers and his patron, the Earl of Leicester. In one typical marginal notation, Harvey records, "The courtier Philip Sidney and I privately discussed these three books of Livy, scrutinizing them so far as we could from all points of view, applying a political analysis . . ."[107]

But while the popularity of scholarly facilitators such as Harvey had begun to wane by the beginning of the seventeenth century, his "persistent challenging of and intervention into the text" remained in fashion.[108] Seventeenth-century readers certainly continued to talk about books. Ben Jonson's surviving conversations with William Drummond, for example, focus attention on the author's literary opinions: although the two men's temperaments may have clashed, both shared an abiding passion for contemporary and classical writers.[109] John Donne similarly believed that "much of the knowledge buried in Books perisheth, and becomes ineffectuall, if it be not applied, and refreshed by a companion, or friend."[110] And Henry Wotton also pronounced that "A friend to confer readings together [is] most necessary." Taking particular pleasure in his discussions with John Milton, Wotton wrote to the young poet in the hope that he might enjoy his friend's "conversation again . . . at a poor meal or two,

[105] John Evelyn, *Publick Employment and an Active Life Prefer'd to Solitude* (London, 1667; Wing E3510), F7r, I3v.
[106] Sherman, *John Dee*, p. 63.
[107] As translated from the Latin by Jardine and Grafton, "'Studied for Action,'" p. 36.
[108] Jardine and Grafton, "'Studied for Action,'" p. 66.
[109] See Jonson, *Conversations with William Drummond*, in Herford and Simpson, 1: 128–78.
[110] John Donne, *Selected Prose*, ed. Evelyn Simpson, Helen Gardner, and Timothy Healy (Oxford, 1967), p. 122.

that we might have banded together some good authors of the ancient time."[111]

Seventeenth-century reading was, like writing, associated with various social sites. In London coffee houses, even illiterate customers could hear the government *Gazette* read aloud, or listen to political tracts such as Harrington's *Oceana* (1656), which was reportedly read "dayly at Coffe-houses" and "made many Proselytes."[112] Several patrons read the news at drinking houses; some patrons brought their own books and kept a library; some were inspired by the convivial atmosphere to write and/or share verses with other customers.[113] Ian Green reminds us that Bible-reading could be similarly social: "heads of household might read the Bible or an improving work out loud to servants who were illiterate," and "children in elementary schools were urged to read the Bible to their parents, especially if the latter themselves could not read."[114] The design of collegiate libraries, beginning probably in the sixteenth century, also offered readers opportunity to exchange ideas and experiences. Instead of providing individual seating areas, as in private studies, institutional libraries contained benches, revolving desks, and long tables built into bookcases that may have brought readers together at least temporarily.[115]

All these practices and circumstances suggest the active labor that constituted reading during the seventeenth century. Readers were conditioned to participate in their books – whether through conventions of decoding, studying, lecturing, or socializing – so that interpretation required, above all, readers' active engagement in determining an unfixed meaning. Again and again, we find accounts of readers *using* their books – interacting with them, both to improve their own quality of life and to make the most of authors' ideas.

But, as we have seen in printed prefatory matter, these practices of active reading occurred at the same time that the Renaissance author's authority was also emerging. As a final extension of the reader's interpretive activity, some readers envisioned themselves conversing directly with the authors of their books. These readers imagined, to borrow Milton's metaphor from

[111] Logan Pearsall Smith, *The Life and Letters of Henry Wotton*, 2 vols. (Oxford, 1907), 2: 381. Wotton's letter to Milton is also printed in *Poems of Mr. John Milton, both English and Latin, Compos'd at Several Times* (London, 1645; Wing M2160), E4r–E5r.

[112] Aytoun Ellis, *The Penny Universities* (London, 1956), p. 46; Dobranski, "'Where Men of Differing Judgements Croud': Milton and the Culture of the Coffee Houses," *The Seventeenth Century* 9.1 (1994): 35–56; and John Aubrey, *Brief Lives*, ed. Oliver Lawson Dick (Ann Arbor, 1957), p. 124.

[113] See Peter Clark, *The English Alehouse* (New York, 1983), p. 13.

[114] Woolf, *Reading History in Early Modern England*, p. 101; and Ian Green, *Print and Protestantism in Early Modern England* (Oxford, 2000), p. 25.

[115] See John Willis Clark, *The Care of Books*, 2nd edn. (Cambridge, 1909).

Areopagitica, that books preserved an author's "pretious life-blood" and allowed even deceased writers to communicate with them personally. The conventional metonymy of *authors* for *books* hints at the elevated status granted some writers during the early modern period. William Harvey refers to those who "read authors," as opposed to those who read books; Donne describes his "poor Library, where to cast mine eye upon *good Authors* kindles or refreshes sometimes meditations not unfit to communicate to near friends"; and Burton imagines if he were held prisoner, "I would desire to have no other prison than that Library, and to be chained together with so many *good Authors* and *dead Masters*" (my emphasis).[116] Describing the possible benefits of reading, Bacon offers the similarly provocative distinction, "Histories make men wise; poets witty; the mathematics subtile; natural philosophy deep; moral [philosophy] grave; logic and rhetoric able to contend."[117] Instead of sustaining a parallel construction, Bacon disrupts the neat categories of "histories," "mathematics," and "natural philosophy" with the more personal term, "poets." His diction implies that readers of literature may approach verse as the expression of an individual identity. As Leah Marcus notes, "Our modern age of pervasive secondary orality has dulled us to some of the early shock value of print's ability to facilitate ready conversation with deceased authorities."[118] Marcus refers to Machiavelli's account of reading the ancients as the locus classicus of the personal connections readers sometimes felt with writers. In a letter to his friend Francesco Vettori, Machiavelli describes how each evening

I enter the courts of the ancients, where affectionately greeted by them, I partake of that food which is mine alone and for which I was born; where I am not ashamed to talk with them and inquire the reasons of their actions; and they out of their human kindness answer me, and for four hours at a stretch I feel no worry of any kind.[119]

Here Machiavelli casts reading as a social relationship – nourishing ("I partake of that food"), intimate ("which is mine alone"), and interactive

---

[116] Harvey, *Anatomical Exercitations, Concerning the Generation of Living Creatures* (London, 1653; Wing H1083), ¶5r; Donne, *Selected Prose*, p. 127; and Burton, *Anatomy of Melancholy*, p. 457. Burton's specific image recalls the Renaissance practice of chaining library books to their shelves.

[117] Bacon, "Of Studies," p. 439. Presumably, the single adjectival form in this list, "moral," refers elliptically to "moral philosophy," since it immediately follows "natural philosophy."

[118] Leah Marcus, *Unediting the Renaissance: Shakespeare, Marlowe, Milton* (London, 1996), p. 200. Lisa Jardine similarly uses Erasmus's *Epistolae* to address "the ability of the familiar letter to capture and communicate highly wrought emotion from absent friend to reader" during the second half of the sixteenth century. See Jardine, "Reading and the Technology of Textual Affect: Erasmus's Familiar Letters and Shakespeare's *King Lear*," in *Reading Shakespeare Historically* (London, 1996), pp. 78–97.

[119] Roberto Ridolfi, *The Life of Niccolò Machiavelli*, trans. Cecil Grayson (Chicago, 1963), p. 152.

("and they . . . answer me"). This sentiment continues to find expression in some seventeenth-century books, such as Edward Blount's introduction to John Lyly's comedies.[120] Having jokingly *"dig'd up the Grave of a Rare and Excellent Poet"* (A5r), the bookseller offers now to bring *"him to thy Acquaintance"* (A6r). Blount describes reading Lyly's book as a personal visit with its writer: *"when Old* Iohn Lilly, *is merry with thee in thy Chamber, Thou shalt say, Few (or None) of our Poets now are such witty Companions"* (A6r).

Such a close, interactive relationship further illustrates that the demands placed on Renaissance readers did not eliminate the author from the calculus of a work's meaning. On the contrary, although some authors were concerned about readers having too much authority, an audience's participation could help to elevate, not erase, the author. When booksellers appealed directly to readers in prefaces and notes, they were not merely introducing those individual texts but attempting to advance the authors' – and their own – authority. The immediate goal may have been profit-driven, but over time such rhetoric generated the name recognition that is at the core of the author's emerging status. Thus the bookseller Francis Kirkman tells readers of *A Cure for a Cuckold* (1661) that he *"need not speak any thing in its Commendation, the Authors names,* Webster *and* Rowley, *are (to knowing men) sufficient to declare its worth."* Kirkman wants readers to approach the text as the function of the writers' identities but he also understands that authors need astute readers ("knowing men") to maintain their reputations.[121] In like manner, the bookseller Moseley assures readers of *The Last Remains of Sir John Suckling* (1659) that the book contains Suckling's "real and genuine Works." Anyone doubting the authenticity of these poems need only peruse the collection and "seriously consider the Freedom of the Fancie, the Richness of the Conceipt [*sic*], proper Expression, with that air and spirit diffus'd through every part, and he will find such a perfect resemblance with what hath been formerly known, that he cannot with modestie doubt them to be his."[122] Moseley is acknowledging the value of a reader's efforts and the interconnection between readers, authors, and stationers. A bookseller can praise an author, but must still call on a

---

[120] John Lyly, *Six Court Comedies* (London, 1632; STC 17088).

[121] John Webster and William Rowley, *A Cure for a Cuckold* (London, 1661; Wing W1220), A2r. Compare the printer Richard Ihones who tells readers in Marlowe's *Tamburlaine the Great* (London, 1590; STC 17425) that he realizes the "Great folly" of trying "to commend unto your wisedomes, either the eloquence of the Authour that writ them, or the worthinesse of the matter it selfe." He consequently decides to "leave unto your learned censures, both the one and the other, and my selfe the poore printer of them unto your most curteous and favourable protection" (A2v). Ihones implies that readers are responsible not only for evaluating the play's worth but also for establishing the author's and stationer's reputations.

[122] *The Last Remains of Sir John Suckling* (London, 1659; Wing S6130), A2v–A3r.

discerning audience to "seriously consider" both the book's meaning and the author's unique merits.

A 1653 edition of William Harvey's *Anatomical Exercitations* provides a last example of this collaborative relationship between authors and readers.[123] From the start, Harvey's book emphasizes his authority, containing both a frontispiece portrait of the author's bust (A1v; see figure 1a) and highlighting his name and credentials on the opposing title page, "By *WILLIAM HARVEY*, Doctor | of *Physick*, and Professor of *Anatomy*, | and *Chirurgery*, in the COLLEDGE | of Physitians of *LONDON*" (A2r; see figure 1b). The book then opens with an anecdotal account of Harvey alone, hard at work in the *"tranquillity"* of his laboratory, *"deeply searching into the Causes of natural things"* (A6r, A3r–v). Both this dedicatory epistle and the following commendatory poem lavishly establish Harvey's ethos: he is *"that Eminent Person, the chiefest Glory and Ornament of our Colledge"* (A3r), "the Incomparable Dr. HARVEY" (a1v), and a person whose *"Virtue, Candor, and Ingenie, are long since very well known"* (A8v).

But while celebrating Harvey's reputation and achievements, the text simultaneously foregrounds his position within a larger community that shares responsibility for his finished work. Harvey himself repeatedly calls attention to writers who came before him, most notably Galen and "Natures most diligent searcher," Aristotle (a5r), and the text's physical design hints at other, more immediate contributors, such as the frontispiece's engraver, probably Richard Gaywood; the physician Martin Lluelyn, who has written a poem about Harvey's accomplishments (a1v–a4v); the physician George Ent, who claims to have proofed advanced sheets (A8v–a1r); and the printer James Young and the bookseller Octavian Pulleyn, both of whose names appear on the title page.

In addition to these various types of collaborators, Harvey enlarges his circle of participants by directly addressing his audience. He acknowledges that he especially needs a "friendly Reader" (¶5r) to make his ideas meaningful and influential. Instead of accepting the book's arguments passively, readers should test what Harvey has written "in the steady scale of experiment; and give no longer credit to it, then thou perceivest it to be securely bottomed, by the faithful testimony of thy own eyes" (¶5r–v). For Harvey, those who "read authors, and do not, by the aid of their own Senses, abstract true representations of the things themselves" will fail to learn anything. Inactive readers are left with "deceitful *Idols*, & *Phantasms*; by which means they frame to themselves certaine *shadows* and *Chimaera's*" (¶5r).

---

[123] William Harvey, *Anatomical Exercitations, Concerning the Generation of Living Creatures* (London, 1653; Wing H1083). All quotations of Harvey's treatise are taken from this edition and cited parenthetically.

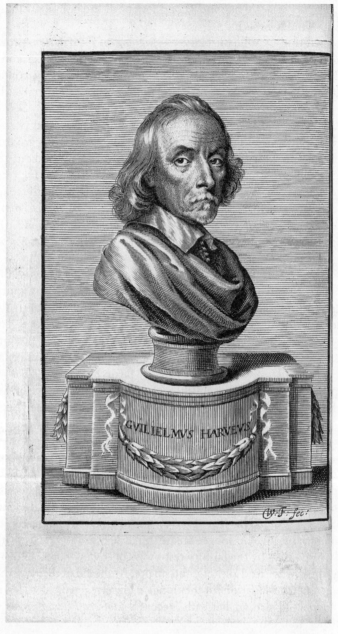

Figure 1a. Portrait frontispiece from William Harvey's *Anatomical Exercitations* (1653).

ANATOMICAL EXERCITATIONS,

Concerning the

GENERATION

Of Living Creatures:

To which are added Particular Difcourfes, of *Births*, and of *Conceptions*, &c.

By *WILLIAM HARVEY*, Doctor of *Phyfick*, and Profeffor of *Anatomy*, and *Chirurgery*, in the COLLEDGE of Phyfitians of *LONDON*.

LONDON,

Printed by *James Young*, for *Octavian Pulleyn*, and are to be fold at his Shop at the Sign of the Rofe in St. *Pauls* Church-yard. 1653.

Figure 1b. Title page from William Harvey's *Anatomical Exercitations* (1653).

FILLING IN THE BLANKS

Within this collaborative context, Renaissance omissions represent another way that readers could shape the meaning of what they read while simultaneously helping to advance an author's authority. Thoughtfully perusing a text with actual missing pieces, Renaissance readers were then invited to think, infer, and write in, if only imaginatively, what an author withheld. The omissions that I examine in this book formally encode what readers were already being asked to do in thousands of readers' prefaces in thousands of Renaissance books.

In *Arte of English Poesie* Puttenham explicitly recommends that poets should sometimes withhold information so that readers become more actively involved in a text. He objects, for example, to two lines of poetry, "*The tenth of March when Aries received, / Dan Phoebus raies into his horned hed*," because the author – in this case George Gascoigne – has "blabbed out" the season which, through the figure of Aries, "should have bene covertly disclosed."[124] Puttenham re-writes the lines to make them more inductive: "*The month and daie when Aries receivd / Dan Phoebus raies into his horned head*." In this revised version, as Puttenham explains, "there remaineth for the Reader somewhat to studie and gesse upon, and yet the spring time to the learned iudgement sufficiently expressed."

Puttenham's recommendation for such an elliptical expression not only suggests the demanding subtlety of seventeenth-century literature – authors regularly expected readers "to studie and gesse upon" the meaning of their works – but it also reveals the degree of intervention that was accepted during this period. Early modern readers did not just read attentively; many, like Puttenham, went beyond an author's apparent intentions and re-wrote parts of another writer's works. Although not all Renaissance readers were able to write, those who could were then able to use that skill to personalize and/or appropriate some of the books they read.[125] During the seventeenth century "peruse," as we have seen, meant "to read thoroughly." That it also could mean to "reconsider" or "revise" suggests the overlap between carefully reading and partly re-writing a text.[126]

---

[124] Puttenham, *The Arte of English Poesie*, p. 194.

[125] For literacy during the Renaissance, see Margaret Spufford, *Small Books and Pleasant Histories: Popular Fiction and Its Readership in Seventeenth-Century England* (Athens, GA, 1981), p. 27; David Cressy, *Literacy and the Social Order: Reading and Writing in Tudor and Stuart England* (Cambridge, 1980); and Keith Thomas, "The Meaning of Literacy in Early Modern England," in *The Written Word: Literacy in Transition*, ed. Gerd Baumann (Oxford, 1986), pp. 97–131.

[126] *OED* II.4.a.

Thus Suckling, coming across what he called "an imperfect Copy" of *Lucrece*, decided to compose his own "Supplement."[127] He started with two stanzas of Shakespeare's poem, recast them according to the stanzaic structure of *Venus and Adonis*, and added fifteen lines of his own. A note in the margin after the ninth line reads "Thus far *Shakespear*," but Suckling has in fact provided more than a missing piece. Even the opening of Suckling's poem incorporates some changes, omitting, for example, all of Shakespeare's allusions to death (such as "entombed" and "monument," lines 390, 391) as well as Tarquin's imminent crime ("lewd unhallowed rape," line 392). Our evaluation of these changes and Suckling as a writer depends on how we rate him as a reader. While critics have traditionally assumed that Suckling would have passively accepted Shakespeare's language – Brisley Nicholson, for example, has accounted for some alterations by supposing that Suckling was working from an unpolished, earlier draft of *Lucrece*[128] – Suckling may deserve more credit as an astute reader of Shakespeare. Rather than simply transcribing *Lucrece*, he was playing a witty game of poetic one-up-man-ship and attempting to make the text his own. In stanza four of the "Supplement" (based on *Lucrece*, lines 400–406), for example, Suckling not only tries to improve Shakespeare's description of her "hair like gold threads play'd by her breath"; he attempts to dismiss his poetic predecessor. Only "dull men," Suckling claims, would describe Lucrece's hair as literally "hair" instead of his own preferred "beams" (line 19).[129]

But if by modern standards Suckling's "Supplement" seems merely an audacious plagiarism, we should not assume that contemporary readers would have thought such extensive revision a crime. Recent work on scribal publication and the evolution of Renaissance manuscript collections has shown that the boundary between reading and writing during the seventeenth century was often ill-defined. Translators regularly re-interpreted ancient texts, and readers relied on commonplace books to copy phrases and ideas that appealed to them – and that then found their way into the copiers' writings. Just the act of commonplacing transformed readers into

---

[127] Sir John Suckling, "A Supplement of an Imperfect Copy of Verses of Mr. Will. Shakespears, By the Author," in *The Works of Sir John Suckling: The Non-Dramatic Works*, ed. Thomas Clayton (Oxford, 1971), p. 16. Quotations of *Lucrece* are taken from Shakespeare, *The Poems*, ed. F. T. Prince (London, 1985), pp. 63–149.

[128] Nicholson in *The Shakspere* [*sic*] *Allusion-Book*, ed. John Munro, 2 vols. (1909; London, 1932), 1: 406. Clayton, ed., *The Works of Sir John Suckling*, has alternatively suggested that the minor discrepancies between the two works reflect Suckling's mnemonic corruptions (p. 227).

[129] Did Suckling intentionally leave lines 21–22 wildly imperfect in rhyme and meter so as to invite future readers' emendations of his own "Supplement"? The two lines read, "But these, as rude, her breath put by still; some / Wiselyer downwards sought, but falling short." See Clayton, ed., *The Works of Sir John Suckling*, p. 228.

authors, for it required a process of selecting, transcribing, and organizing that resulted in a "personal construction of meaning."[130] Keeping a commonplace book would have also conditioned readers to approach each new text with their own individual motives: what should they jot down? What might they later use? As Max Thomas observes, "writing teaches one what to read for, whether that writing is as brief as the demarcation of *sententiae* worth committing to memory, or as lengthy as a response to, alteration of, or translation of a poem encountered and re-produced."[131] Thomas suggests that "it might even be possible to see the compiler of a commonplace book as the paradigm for reading/writing practices in the Renaissance, insofar as the two practices cannot be separated and operate in tandem."[132]

The conflation of reading and writing also manifested itself in the ways that writers freely drew on their prior reading when composing their own works. Throughout the Renaissance, as Walter Ong has observed, "no one hesitated to use lines of thought or even quite specific wordings from another person without crediting the other person, for these were all taken to be – and most often were – part of the common tradition."[133] Ong explains that "even later, it was thought honorable and indeed commendably enterprising to avail oneself of preprocessed material and modes of expression."[134] Montaigne, for example, openly announces that his *Essays* contain various appropriations, which he invites readers to evaluate: readers should "see in what I borrow whether I have known how to choose what would enhance my theme." He modestly justifies that he has taken ideas from other authors because they "say what I cannot say so well, now through the weakness of my language, now through the weakness of my understanding."[135]

[130] Sharpe, *Reading Revolutions: The Politics of Reading in Early Modern England*, p. 279. Peter Beal calls commonplace books "the primary intellectual tool for organizing knowledge and thought among the intelligentsia of the seventeenth and probably also the sixteenth centuries." See Beal, "Notions in Garrison: The Seventeenth-Century Commonplace Book," p. 134.
[131] Max W. Thomas, "Reading and Writing the Renaissance Commonplace Book: A Question of Authorship?," in *The Construction of Authorship: Textual Appropriation in Law and Literature*, ed. Martha Woodmansee and Peter Jaszi (Durham, NC, 1994), pp. 410–15, this quotation, p. 409.
[132] Thomas, "Reading and Writing the Renaissance Commonplace Book: A Question of Authorship?," p. 415.
[133] Walter J. Ong, Introduction, in John Milton, *The Art of Logic*, *CP* 8: 187.
[134] Ong, Preface, in Joan Marie Lechner, *Renaissance Concepts of the Commonplace* (New York, 1962), pp. vii–ix. See also Harold Ogden White, *Plagiarism and Imitation During the English Renaissance: A Study in Critical Distinctions* (Cambridge, MA, 1935).
[135] Michel de Montaigne, "Of Books," in *The Complete Essays of Montaigne*, trans. Donald M. Frame (Stanford, 1958), pp. 296–306, these quotations, p. 296.

But the key for Montaigne and other Renaissance writers was not just selecting appropriate *sententiae* but effectively assimilating borrowed phrases and words:

We take the opinions and the knowledge of others into our keeping, and that is all. We [instead] must make them our own. We are just like a man who, needing fire, should go and fetch some at his neighbor's house, and, having found a fine big fire there, should stop there and warm himself, forgetting to carry any back home. What good does it do us to have our belly full of meat if it is not digested, if it is not transformed into us, if it does not make us bigger and stronger?[136]

Montaigne's fire metaphor emphasizes the need for readers to carry away ideas that will illuminate and enliven their own writings. His second, digestive metaphor similarly suggests that reading is not just a taking in but also a transforming process. Readers must actively use – "digest" – what they encounter in someone else's works.

Ben Jonson also introduces a gustatory metaphor to distinguish between thoughtless appropriation and "imitation," one of the requisites, he claims, for being a good poet. While Jonson frequently attacked plagiarism (as in *Epigrammes* 58 "On Poet-Ape" and 81 "To Prowl the Plagiary"), he praised the true poet's ability

to convert the substance, or Riches of another *Poet*, to his owne use. To make choise of one excellent man above the rest, and so to follow him, till he grow very *Hee*: or, so like him, as the Copie may be mistaken for the Principall. Not, as a Creature, that swallowes, what it takes in, crude, raw, or indigested; but, that feedes with an Appetite, and hath a Stomacke to concoct, divide, and turne all into nourishment.[137]

According to Jonson's logic, early modern authors were to develop their authority, first, by actively reading and, second, by relying on their own active audience. Here again the digestion metaphor emphasizes and naturalizes an audience's activity; readers must not only "make choise" but also "concoct, divide, and turne."

Manuscript (as opposed to print) publication might seem to have restricted this type of appropriation and offered Renaissance writers greater control over their writings – that is, poets could attempt to limit the circulation of their verses and fine-tune specific poems for a hand-picked audience. But readers, like Suckling with Shakespeare's *Lucrece*, still modified or supplemented the manuscript copies that came into their hands. As

---

[136] Montaigne, "Of Pedantry," in *The Complete Essays of Montaigne*, trans. Frane, pp. 97–106, this quotation, p. 101.
[137] Jonson, *Discoveries*, lines 2468–75, in Herford and Simpson, 8: 638.

manuscripts passed from one group of readers to another, some compilers
undertook the relatively innocent task of augmenting manuscript collections by incorporating notes about the poems' original social contexts;
other readers intruded more actively, making slight corrections, adding
new poems, or revising the existing verses.[138] As Mary Hobbs has shown,
authors such as Robert Herrick, Andrew Marvell, and the Oxford poet
William Strode often echoed, borrowed from, and responded to poems by
other manuscript writers.[139]

Nor did printed books – my subject here – prohibit readers' participation. After purchasing a book in the sixteenth and seventeenth centuries,
readers had to help create the physical text, first cutting the outer sheets
of books printed in smaller formats, and, for some editions, paying to
have their copies bound. Some readers took this opportunity to create
virtually new texts, either by having a work's sections rearranged, or, in
a few cases, by having sections from two different works combined. The
Huntington Library's copy of John Bate's *Mysteryes of Nature, and Art*,
for example, contains only one section of that book bound with nine
pages of manuscript notes and large parts of Henry Peacham's *Gentleman's
Exercise*.[140] Similarly, John Warburton's collection of manuscript papers on
churches and antiquities in Cheshire incorporates pages and illustrations
that he cut from William Camden's *Britannia* and Michael Drayton's *Poly-
Olbion*.[141]

When starting a book, readers were then expected to turn to the back,
or front, and write in the sometimes extensive corrections listed under
"Errata." Even publications that did not name specific errata could ask
for the reader's help. Guillim concludes his book on heraldry with a conventional request that "Each gentle Reader" should "rub away" the text's
"verball Blots" and "staines."[142] Isaac Walton similarly appeals to his readers
to help him improve *The Compleat Angler* (1653): "if this Discourse which
follows shall come to a second impression . . . I shall then for thy sake be

138 For a discussion of these practices, see Arthur F. Marotti, *Manuscript, Print, and the English Renais-
sance Lyric* (Ithaca, NY, 1995), pp. 14–16.
139 Mary Hobbs, "Early Seventeenth-Century Verse Miscellanies and Their Value for Textual Editors,"
English Manuscript Studies 1100–1700 1 (1989): 182–210. See also David Norbrook, "'This Blushing
Tribute of a Borrowed Muse': Robert Overton and His Overturning of the Poetic Canon," *English
Manuscript Studies 1100–1700* 4 (1993): 220–66, and Hobbs' book, *Early Seventeenth-Century Verse
Miscellany Manuscripts* (Aldershot, Hants; Brookfield, VT, 1992).
140 William H. Sherman, "What Did Renaissance Readers Write in Their Books?," in *Books and
Readers in Early Modern England*, ed. Jennifer Andersen and Elizabeth Sauer (Philadelphia, 2002),
pp. 119–37.
141 Woolf, *Reading History in Early Modern England*, p. 94.
142 Guillim, *A Display of Heraldrie*, Oo2r.

glad to correct what is faulty, or by a conference with any to explain or enlarge what is defective."[143]

Some readers took such instructions literally, either devising and inserting their own emendations, or, in the case of errata, methodically paging through their books, counting down the appropriate number of lines, and writing in each correct form. Walton, for example, appears to have been a man of his word, for in the preface to the second edition of *The Compleat Angler* (1655) he notes that the book now contains "many inlargements, gathered both by my own observation, and the communication of friends."[144] But that Henry S. Bennett discovered no manuscript corrections in 75 percent of the Renaissance books he examined suggests that early modern readers may have fallen short of authors' great expectations. Many readers, if they followed an errata's instructions at all, only imaginatively repaired their books.[145] Or did the most heavily annotated copies get used up and thrown out during the intervening centuries? We should note that during the nineteenth and early twentieth centuries readers and booksellers regularly effaced readers' marginalia.[146] Also, some Renaissance books required important corrections that would not have been easy to insert by hand. In Milton's *Poems, &c. upon Several Occasions* (1673), for example, readers are asked to envision some of the verses in a different order, while in Meric Casaubon's *Of Credulity and Incredulity* (1668) readers are given two lists of errata, "whether of the *Press*, or *Copy*," and a set of long additions that the margins could never hold.[147]

The errata list in Thomas Carew's *Poems* (1640) helps to illustrate how much effort repairing a book might entail. Readers are asked to make such minor, though substantive changes as replace "your" for "their" in the line "Like swallowes when their summers done" (B3r); replace "Iris struts" for "frisketh" in the line "That frisketh in when her mantl's spred" (M4v); and replace "not" for "it" in the line "And if it love, allow it rest" (D6r). In each case, Carew's uncorrected poem makes sense; the reader is implicitly

---

143 Isaac Walton, *The Compleat Angler* (London, 1653; Wing W661), A7r.
144 Walton, *The Compleat Angler*, 2nd edn. (London, 1655; Wing W662), A8r.
145 Henry S. Bennett, *English Books & Readers, 1603 to 1640* (London, 1970), p. 208. Bennett claims, somewhat vaguely, to have looked at "some thousands of books from the beginning of printing until 1640." In those books with manuscript corrections, he notes that "few readers persevered beyond the first fifty or sixty pages," and a book in which the reader has corrected all the errors "is rare indeed."
146 Monique Hulvey, "Not So Marginal: Manuscript Annotations in the Folger Incunabula," *The Papers of the Bibliographical Society of America* 92 (1998): 159–76, especially p. 161.
147 Milton, *Poems, &c. upon Several Occasions* (London, 1673; Wing M2161), πA4v; Meric Casaubon, *Of Credulity and Incredulity, in Things Natural, Civil, and Divine* (London, 1668; Wing C807), A8r, X6v–X8v.

being asked not just to fix the author's works but to recognize how the errata's changes improve the poems. Sometimes this is difficult: in the last revision – "not" for "it" in "And if it love, allow it rest" (D6r) – the reader must decide which "it" to replace, the first, second, or both. Because two other corrections name the wrong page numbers, readers would have also had to discover on their own that the revision of "I straight might feele" belongs in line 15 of "A Hymeneall Dialogue" (H8r), not, as the errata propose, line 15 of "Murdring Beautie" (B6r). And while the request to replace "Lovers" for "Souldiers" does indeed belong in "A Rapture," the correction needs to be made in line 7 on page 83, not as the errata indicate, line 7 on page 85.

Most seventeenth-century errata do necessarily limit readers' contributions: readers are following specific directions in making such repairs, not willfully rewriting an author's works. But to begin a book by making corrections and sometimes changing its meaning contradicts our modern perception of the fixity of print. Even if Renaissance readers did not regularly bother to repair their books' errors, as Bennett's survey suggests, they could still approach both printed and manuscript works as something not entirely complete, something in which they could – and were encouraged to – collaborate. And with pen already in hand, early modern readers, like today's students and scholars, might then add their own marginal notations. As John Kerrigan observes, "one kind of emendation quickly ran into others."[148] Students in particular sometimes had their books interleaved so as to accommodate additional notes, and the "feast" of handwritten marginal commentary that survives in late seventeenth-century books indicates "a culture steadily alert to reflection and innuendo, readers who knew, delicately and dangerously, to draw parallels and seek applications."[149] If errata limited readers' choices for how to change a text, the blank spaces in margins and on extra leaves allowed for each individual reader's extensive comments.

Thus the surviving volumes owned by the seventeenth-century yeoman-farmer William Dowsing, to take but one example, reveal a scrupulously methodical reader.[150] Dowsing evidently began a book by jotting down

---

[148] Kerrigan, "The Editor as Reader," p. 118.

[149] Sherman, *John Dee*, p. 68; and Steven N. Zwicker, "Reading the Margins: Politics and the Habits of Appropriation," in *Refiguring Revolutions: Aesthetics and Politics from the English Revolution to the Romantic Revolution*, ed. Kevin Sharpe and Steven N. Zwicker (Berkeley, 1998), pp. 101–15, these quotations, pp. 103, 105.

[150] See John Morrill, "William Dowsing, the Bureaucratic Puritan," in *Public Duty and Private Conscience in Seventeenth-Century England*, ed. John Morrill, Paul Slack, and Daniel Woolf (Oxford, 1993), pp. 173–203.

and completing all of the biblical citations; then, with each subsequent annotation, he actively appropriated the author's material. As John Morrill summarizes, Dowsing "frequently . . . added to the title-pages [*sic*] of books and sermons an index of items that were of particular interest to him; frequently he scored the margin with varying degrees of emphasis; and less usually he summarized a passage in the margin or engaged in argument with the author."[151] That Dowsing, like many Renaissance readers, also wrote his name on his books' title pages – in Dowsing's case, along with the dates of purchase and reading – not only indicates the reader's sense of ownership but also suggests the collaborative relationship between Renaissance authors and audiences. The joining of their names at the start of a book symbolizes their shared textual authority.

Sometimes this shared authority manifested itself in the composition of more fully developed replies. As we saw with Chaucer's canon in the introduction and will see again in the next chapter with Sidney's *Arcadia*, readers commonly had their own responses and counterarguments published in a series of answer-poems and pamphlet wars. Topical dialogues both before and during the war generated thousands of verses, broadsides, and pamphlets – between prelates and Presbyterians; royalists and republicans; misogynists and proto-feminists; or, among the many, more mundane conflicts, coffee-vendors and ale-merchants. William Riley Parker aptly describes the middle of the seventeenth century as a "period of multitudinous debate" when "laymen refuted the sermons of famous divines; ordinary citizens replied to speeches made in Parliament; anonymous writers argued, and were answered by anonymous writers."[152] The resulting publications further suggest the intimate link between writing and reading during the Renaissance: again and again, as readers became writers, their works were defined relationally, and the original writers were cast as readers of the newly published replies. John Selden accordingly cautions readers that "In answering a Book, 'tis best to be short." He explains that long answers, "give my Adversary a huge advantage; somewhere or other he will pick a hole."[153]

The Renaissance omissions that I describe in this book represent a specific type of hole that readers and authors could use to enter into conversation with each other. Whereas Selden suggests that the inclusion of too much detail will encourage readers' hostile responses and could diminish

[151] Morrill, "William Dowsing," pp. 182–83.
[152] William Riley Parker, *Milton: A Biography*, 2nd edn., ed. Gordon Campbell, 2 vols. (1968; Oxford, 1996), p. 196.
[153] John Selden, *The Table-Talk of John Selden*, ed. S. W. Singer (1847; Freeport, NY, 1972), p. 23.

an author's ethos, I am looking at how the omission of some information correspondingly invited readers to interact with books and helped to establish the authors' authority. These blank spaces required the attentiveness that characterized effective reading in the Renaissance and provided another opportunity for readers to intervene in a text. As Robert Davenport asserts in the preface to *King John and Matilda* (1655), "*A good Reader, helps to make a Book; a bad injuries it.*"[154] While Davenport's distinction between "make" and "injuries" reveals the limits that authors attempted to impose on their audiences, the infinitive "to make" suggests the work that Renaissance readers were literally expected to undertake: readers during the early modern period could help to make the books they read – by cutting the outer sheets, correcting the errata, writing in notes, transcribing commonplaces, and borrowing select words and ideas. In the case of omissions, authors and stationers took this relationship a step further and encouraged readers to fill in a text's blanks.

In a preface to a quarto edition of Beaumont and Fletcher's *Philaster* (1628), the stationer Richard Hawkins compares books to gold in describing the importance of active readers: "*The best Poems of this kind, in the first presentation, resemble that all tempting Mineral newly digged up, the Actors being onely the labouring Miners, but you the skilfull Triers and Refiners.*"[155] Hawkins' metaphor once again implies the collaborative basis of reading and writing: only through the readers' efforts can the play become truly valuable. Beginning with the next chapter we will see how Renaissance omissions facilitated such readerly participation and, in the specific case of Sir Philip Sidney's *Arcadia*, enhanced the value of authors and their books.

[154] Davenport, *King John and Matilda*, A2r.
[155] Francis Beaumont and John Fletcher, *Philaster* (London, 1628; STC 1683), A2v.

CHAPTER 2

Re-writing Sidney's Arcadia

A jest's prosperity lies in the ear
Of him that hears it, never in the tongue
Of him that makes it.
                    – William Shakespeare[1]

When Sir Philip Sidney died near the end of the sixteenth century, he
left unfinished his prose masterpiece, *The Countess of Pembroke's Arcadia*,
a work that friends and family then attempted to supplement and have
printed. If, as we saw in the previous chapter, readers during the Renaissance were encouraged to intervene in printed books – some even taking
the liberty of partially revising another writer's work – it is hardly sur-
prising that Sidney's incomplete romance would become a popular site
of authorship in the ensuing decades. Unlike some seventeenth-century
poets who tried to bolster their authority by appealing to readers in prefaces, Sidney did not actively seek his audience's participation. His posthumous reputation was instead improved by readers who found meaning in
his text's omissions. In fact, so many Renaissance readers used the omissions in Sidney's romance to write their own supplements and sequels
that a new genre of literature emerged during the seventeenth century,
"Arcadiaes."

In this chapter, I examine the evidence of readerly activity preserved
in these Arcadian response poems, focusing particular attention on one
contemporary verse that attempted to create a new omission in Sidney's
romance. First printed at the end of the *Arcadia's* tenth edition (1655;
Wing S3768), "A Remedie for Love" was, according to the sub-heading,
"WRITTEN BY Sr PHILIP SIDNEY" and "Heretofore omitted in the
Printed ARCADIA" (Iii4v–Iii5v; see figure 2).[2] This burlesque verse has the

---

[1] William Shakespeare, *Love's Labor's Lost*, in *The Riverside Shakespeare*, ed. G. Blakemore Evans
(Boston, 1974), 5.2.861–63.
[2] For the reader's convenience, I cite passages from Sidney's work parenthetically according to the
pagination in *The Countess of Pembroke's Arcadia*, ed. Maurice Evans (London, 1977). In cases where

poet describing his love for Pamela and Philoclea. When "gazing on their excellence," he becomes so "reft of sens" (lines 31–32) that, like the heroes Pyrocles and Musidorus, he "might have sadly said, Good night / Discretion and good fortune quite" (lines 23–24). The poet prescribes for himself a form of aversion therapy: he need only glimpse Mopsa, Dametas' uncouth daughter, to feel "heal'd, and cur'd, and made as sound / As though I ne're had had a wound" (lines 35–36). The rest of "Remedie" jokingly catalogues Mopsa's repulsive features – her offensive voice, appearance, and smell.

Given Sidney's mastery of sophisticated verse forms elsewhere in the *Arcadia*, we might initially doubt that active, seventeenth-century readers could have mistaken Sidney as the author of the apparently crude "Remedie." Yet "Remedie" occurs in the *Arcadia*'s subsequent seventeenth-century editions (1662 and 1674), and it so effectively imitates Sidney's writing that modern editors reprinted the poem in all collections of Sidney's works through the first half of the twentieth century.[3] It was not until 1950 that anyone attempted to disprove that "Remedie" was a genuine omission. William Ringler first argued that the poem's "Hudibrastic meter and scatological humor" are not only uncharacteristic of Sidney's other works, but one word, "puddle dock" (line 56), first came into usage in the middle of the seventeenth century when Puddle Dock at Blackfriars became "a laystall for the soil of the streets."[4]

While the identity of "Remedie"'s author remains uncertain, I am more interested here in the effect that such "omissions" would have had on

---

punctuation or spelling might affect my interpretation, I have verified these quotations with the 1655 text, *The Countess of Pembroke's Arcadia* (Wing S3768), held at the British Library, London, shelfmark C39.h.10. All citations to other aspects of the *Arcadia* are taken from this edition and cited parenthetically by signatures. The 1655 edition collates 2°: A⁴b-d⁴B-Z⁶Aa-Zz⁶Aaa-Iii⁶Kkk [$3 signed (-A1, A2, A3, b3, c3, d3, Tt2, Tt3)]. The 1655 volume, though entitled *The Countess of Pembroke's Arcadia*, actually includes Sidney's collected works, a convention established with William Ponsonby's third edition of 1598. Following the *Arcadia* in 1655 are printed "Certain Sonnets" (Yy2v–Zz6r), *The Defense of Poesie* (Zz6v–Ccc1v), *Astrophel and Stella* (Ccc2r–Ggg3r), and "Her most Excellent Majestie walking in Wanstead Garden" (Ggg3v–Ggg6v).

[3] The following editions of Sidney's works also include "A Remedie of Love": *The Works of the Honourable Sr. Phillip [sic] Sidney*, 14th edn., 3 vols. (London, 1724–25), 3: 131–34; William Gray, ed., *The Miscellaneous Works of Sir Philip Sidney* (1860; New York, 1966), pp. 213–16; Alexander B. Grossart, ed., *The Complete Poems of Sir Philip Sidney*, 2 vols. (London, 1873), 2: 174–77; and Albert Feuillerat, ed., *The Complete Works of Sir Philip Sidney*, 4 vols. (Cambridge, 1912–26), 2: 344–47. The poem also occurs in Alexander B. Grossart, ed., *The Complete Poems of Sir Philip Sidney*, 3 vols. (1877), 3: 59–65, which was reprinted as late as 1970. Only Feuillerat places "Remedie" within an appendix of poems of doubtful authorship.

[4] William Ringler, "Poems Attributed to Sir Philip Sidney," *Studies in Philology* 47 (1950): 126–51, this quotation, p. 147. Ringler adduces some additional – though ultimately less compelling – "internal evidence" to prove that Sidney could not have written "Remedie."

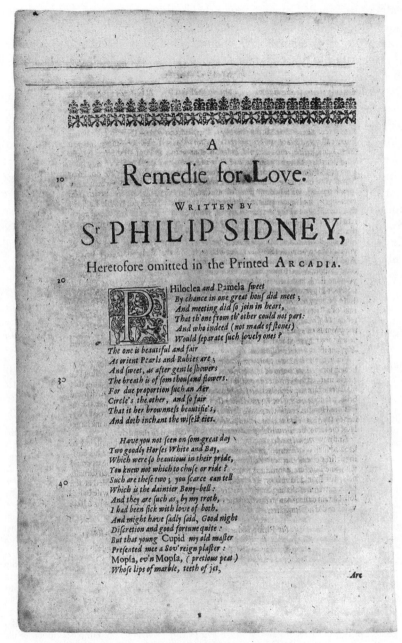

A

Remedie for Love.

WRITTEN BY

Sr PHILIP SIDNEY,

Heretofore omitted in the Printed ARCADIA.

Hiloclea *and* Pamela *sweet*
By chance in one great houf did meet ;
And meeting did fo join in heart,
That th'one from th'other could not part:
And who indeed (not made of ftones)
Would feparate fuch lovely ones ?
The one is beautiful and fair
As orient Pearls and Rubies are ;
And fweet, as after gentle fhowers
The breath is of fom thoufand flowers.
For due proportion fuch an Aër
Circle's the other, and fo fair
That it her brownneſs beautifie's,
And doth inchant the wifeſt eies.

Have you not feen on fom great day
Two goodly Horſes White and Bay,
Which were fo beautious in their pride,
You knew not which to chufe or ride ?
Such are thefe two ; you fcarce can tell
Which is the daintier Bony-bell :
And they are fuch as, by my troth,
I had been fick with love of both,
And might have fadly faid, Good night
Difcretion and good fortune quite :
But that young Cupid *my old maſter*
Prefented mee a Sov'reign plaſter :
Mopfa, *ev'n* Mopfa, *(pretious peat)*
Whofe lips of marble, teeth of jet,

Are

Figure 2. First page of "A Remedie for Love" in Sir Philip Sidney's *The Countess of Pembroke's Arcadia* (1655), sig. Iii4v.

Sidney's romance.[5] Once we accept that he did not compose "A Remedie for Love," the question becomes what a bawdy doggerel poem is doing in the courtly world of the *Arcadia*. Because some surviving manuscript copies also identify the poem as "An ould Ditty of Sr Phillip Sydneys omitted in the printed Arcadia," Ringler inferred that the publisher, deceived by the scribal attribution, inserted the poem into the 1655 text.[6] But why do these manuscripts also claim that the poem was written by Sidney? Why did the poem's author create a false omission? In this chapter I examine Sidney's incomplete *Arcadia* in relation to seventeenth-century conventions of reading and writing. Although the alleged omission of "A Remedie for Love" may seem less significant in the context of the many sequels Sidney's romance inspired, this one poem helps to expose the tension between the author's emerging status and the collaborative practices of early modern reading. Through the character of Mopsa, the poet of "Remedie" uses the lie of an omission specifically to adapt Sidney's romance to the political culture of seventeenth-century England.

RENAISSANCE ADDENDA

Few Renaissance books have a more complicated textual history than *The Countess of Pembroke's Arcadia*, and a brief overview of its collaborative genesis helps to explain how the text would come to accommodate so many contemporary supplements. Originally conceived as a five-book romantic

---

[5] Ringler claimed that "Remedie" was "probably" composed by either Sir John Mennes or James Smith, two seventeenth-century burlesque poets. But that "Remedie" also appeared in Mennes and Smith's humorous collection, *Musarum deliciae: or, The Muses Recreation* (1655; 1656), does not necessarily mean, as Ringler seems to assume, that either Mennes or Smith wrote it. This collection contains verses by various royalist authors who circulated their works in manuscript during the reign of Charles I. As Timothy Raylor has more cautiously conceded, the poem "may be" by Smith or Mennes – it shares, for example, the "playful, drolling style" of Mennes and Smith's verse epistles. But it could have just as well been written by poets such as William Davenant, William Bagnall, John Weeks, or even Robert Herrick, who all experimented with the same type of jocular verse during the seventeenth century. See Ringler, *The Poems of Sir Philip Sidney* (Oxford, 1962), p. 351; Ringler, "Poems Attributed to Sir Philip Sidney," p. 147; and Timothy Raylor, *Cavalier, Clubs, and Literary Culture* (Newark and London, 1994), pp. 239–40.

[6] I have examined the poem in Brit. Lib. MS Add. 25303, ff. 137r–138r ("An ould Ditty of Sr Phillip Sydneys omitted in the printed Arcadia") and Brit. Lib. MS Harl. 6057, ff. 10v–11v ("An old dittie of Sr: Phillipp Sidneyes omitted in the Printed Arcadia"). Ringler has also found the poem in Emmanuel College Cambridge MS I. 3. 16, ff. 4–5v under the title "An ould Ditty of Sr Phillip Sydneys" but without the explanation about its previous omission. And Raylor refers to another copy in The Folger Shakespeare Library MS V. a. 276 Part 2, fol. 10v. See Ringler, "Poems Attributed to Sir Philip Sidney," p. 147, and Raylor, *Cavalier, Clubs, and Literary Culture*, p. 239. For a description of the poem's manuscript and textual variants, see Feuillerat, ed., *The Complete Works of Sir Philip Sidney*, 2: 347.

adventure, Sidney's self-described "idle work" (A2r) was written for the "delight and entertainment onely" (Ff1v) of his sister, the Countess of Pembroke, who lent her title to its name. This first version, known today as the *Old Arcadia*, circulated in manuscript, "passed from hand to hand; and was never Printed" (Ff1v), as we read in a note in the 1655 edition, a process that resulted in emendations by various scribes. Although Sidney's death in 1586 cut short his plans to reshape the narrative, an unfinished expanded version, known as the *New Arcadia*, was printed four years later in 1590, prepared for the press by the poet Fulke Greville, the translator John Florio, and the physician-poet Matthew Gwinne. Whereas the *Old Arcadia* focused attention almost exclusively on Pyrocles and Musidorus' efforts to woo Philoclea and Pamela, for the revised text Sidney had begun to convert his romance into an epic, interpolating digressions about past and present wars and loves that complicate the primary plot-line.

In a folio edition published in 1593, Sidney's sister attempted to complete the revised text. The *New Arcadia* had ended abruptly, in mid-sentence, as Pyrocles (disguised as Zelmane) battled Anaxius, who was threatening to marry the captive Pamela:

But *Zelmane* strongly putting it by with her right hande sword, comming in with her left foote, and hande, woulde have given him a sharpe visitation to his right side, but that he was faine to leape away. Whereat ashamed, (as having never done so much before in his life)[7]

According to a note in 1655 by Hugh Sanford, a secretary to the Earl of Pembroke who assisted the countess in her editorial efforts, the text's "disfigured face . . . moved" Sidney's sister to fix her brother's work, "to take in hand the wiping away those spots wherewith the beauties therof were unworthily blemished" (A3r).

What began as a simple touch-up, however, escalated into a major repair. Working from Sidney's "several loos sheets (being never after reviewed, nor so much as seen altogether by himself)" (Ff1v), Sanford and the countess – "most by her doing, all by her directing" (A3r) – re-organized some of the Eclogues and concluded the narrative by adding material from books 3 through 5 of the *Old Arcadia*.[8] Although a full discussion of all the revisions

---

7 Sidney, *The Countesse of Pembroke's Arcadia* (London, 1590; STC 22539), Z28v. In this and the following paragraphs, I am indebted to Jean Robertson, ed., *The Countess of Pembroke's Arcadia (The Old Arcadia)* (Oxford, 1973), and Victor Skretkowicz, ed., *The Countess of Pembroke's Arcadia (The New Arcadia)* (Oxford, 1987).

8 A note in some copies of the 1590 edition explains that the Eclogues "*were of Sir* Phillip Sidneis *writing, yet were they not perused by him, but left till the worke had bene finished, that then choise should*

made in 1593 lies outside the scope of my present argument, we should note that Sanford claimed to have only included "as much as was intended, of Arcadia." He insisted that the new edition did not institute changes "further than the Author's own writings, or known determinations could direct" (A3r).[9]

But if Sanford here evokes a notion of autonomous authorship by trying to respect Sidney's final intentions, the *Arcadia* – in its old, new, and composite forms – never existed as the work of a single man. Through each stage of its composition, the book had been shaped, and re-shaped, by readers interacting with the text. Sidney even began the work socially: he wrote the *Arcadia* reluctantly, and only because, he claimed, his sister desired it. As he reminds her in the dedication, he composed most of the narrative in her presence, "the rest, by sheets sent unto you, as fast as they were don" (A2v). In entrusting the finished manuscript to her possession – its "chief protection, the bearing the livery of your name" (A2v) – he admits his lack of control and anticipates her sharing the work with friends who, he can only hope, "wil weigh errors in the balance of good wil" (A2r).

Scribes who circulated later copies of the manuscript participated more actively in the text, creating numerous variants and, in some cases, personalizing their copies by incorporating poems by other writers, or, as in John Harrington's copy, including passages that appear to be their own.[10] Perhaps most obviously the printed editions of 1590 and 1593 required the collaboration of outside agents, editors, and stationers who pieced together Sidney's foul papers and saw the work through the press. Among this group we should include Sanford and Sidney's sister, as well as Frances Sidney, the author's widow, whom Fulke Greville provided with a manuscript copy of the *New Arcadia* and who presumably then approved his editorial decisions.[11]

These early printed texts reflect the *Arcadia*'s social conditions of authorship by including various preliminary materials that Sidney did not

---

have bene made which should have bene taken and in what manner brought in. At this time they have bene chosen and disposed as the over-seer thought best." See the facsimile reproduction of the 1590 *Arcadia*, ed. Carl Dennis (Kent, OH, 1970), A4v.

[9] While the additions from books 3 through 5 required some minor revisions so as to preserve the text's consistent use of names, the reasons behind other, substantial changes in 1593 remain more difficult to explain. The editors have omitted Musidorus' attempted rape of Pamela, for example, and similarly bowdlerized the scene where Pyrocles and Philoclea consummate their relationship. See Robertson, ed., *The Countess of Pembroke's Arcadia (The Old Arcadia)*, pp. lx–lxii; and Ringler, *The Poems of Sir Philip Sidney*, pp. 375–78.

[10] See P. J. Croft's discussion of Harrington's manuscript in Stephen Parks and P. J. Croft, *Literary Autographs* (Los Angeles, 1983), pp. 39–75.

[11] Margaret P. Hannay, *Philip's Phoenix: Mary Sidney, Countess of Pembroke* (Oxford, 1990), p. 73.

compose. The 1655 edition, for example, begins with an engraving by Renold Elstracke (A1v), the preface by Sanford (A3), a new biography by "Philophilippos" (A4r–c1r), an extract from William Camden (c1v), commendatory poems by Sidney's acquaintances (c2r–d4r), and an extract from Peter Heylyn (d4v).[12] In a series of editorial asides, the *Arcadia* also contains the narrative of its own composition, from its conception through the revision and editing: here we are told about the crucial roles played by Sidney's family, friends, and admirers in preserving and publishing the text.

As opposed to the emerging concept of the autonomous author, each of the *Arcadia's* editions represents a collective enterprise dependent on community as well as individual effort. Nor should we exclude Sidney's own literary sources, most notably Sannazaro, Heliodorus, and Jorge Montemayor, as well as his allusions to writers such as Virgil, Ovid, and Lucian. In a sequel to the *Arcadia*, Gervase Markham defended himself against the charge that his story lacked originality by astutely suggesting that Sidney had done a great deal of his own borrowing and should "himselfe confesse the honie he drew" from other classical and Renaissance writers.[13]

The paradox of the *Arcadia's* authorship lies in the fact that all of these contributions and influences helped to advance Sidney's individual identity. Although the *Arcadia's* early editions consistently arose out of a collaborative context, all of the book's forms – the old, new, and composite texts – reinforced Sidney's authority as the author of *Arcadia*. Thus, just as Sanford foregrounded "the Author's own writings" (A3r), an unsigned note in the 1655 edition emphasizes that, while the present volume contains a complete story, the final version of Sidney's work must remain lost, "onely known to his own spirit, where onely those admirable Images were (and no where els) to bee cast" (Ff1v). The book's other addenda and preliminary materials similarly focus attention on Sidney: although written by other people, they would have been relevant for early modern readers in so far as they commemorated "Divine Philippe" (c2r). The group cooperates to create the individual whose larger-than-life persona obscures the social conditions in which it occurs.

---

[12] Surveying contemporary editions of the *Arcadia*, Peter Lindenbaum concludes that it is the 1655 edition "to whose condition all the earlier sixteenth- and seventeenth-century editions can be said to have aspired and subsequent seventeenth-century editions replicated." See Lindenbaum, "Sidney's *Arcadia* as Cultural Monument and Proto-Novel," in *Texts and Cultural Change in Early Modern England*, ed. Cedric C. Brown and Arthur F. Marotti (New York, 1997), pp. 80–94, this quotation, p. 82.

[13] Gervase Markham, *The English Arcadia, Alluding his Beginning from Sir P. Sydnes Ending* (London, 1607; STC 17351), A2v.

Part of what makes *Arcadia*'s authorship so unique is that this group continued to expand so dramatically after Sidney's death. Following the precedent of Sanford and Sidney's sister, who in 1593 intended to present "the conclusion, not the perfection of *Arcadia*" (A3r), other contemporary writers also tried to fill in the omissions in Sidney's work. Sometime in the early 1600s, for example, William Alexander wrote a supplement to book 3, bridging Sidney's revised version with the materials added by the Countess of Pembroke. This addendum, beginning with some copies of the *Arcadia*'s 1613 edition, was bound in the text, inserted directly into the gap between the revised and original halves of book 3.

Readers who disliked Alexander's account of Pamela and Philoclea's release from captivity could instead turn to James Johnstoun's alternative supplement, first included in the 1638 edition with directions for repairing book 3's same "unfortunate maim" (Ffiv). And if readers felt dissatisfied with the ending of the composite text, they could peruse Sir Richard Beling's new conclusion, *A Sixth Book to the Countess of Pembroke's Arcadia*, first included in the 1627 edition, which describes Musidorus and Pyrocles' double marriage to Pamela and Philoclea, and presents a happy, if convoluted, resolution for Helen and Amphialus.[14]

While the authors of these supplements may take some liberties with Sidney's narrative (Johnstoun, for example, contradicts Sidney by absenting Mopsa from Musidorus and Pamela's promise of marriage, Iii4r), the three writers adopt a subservient tone. Alexander hopes his "little Essay" may "serv for a shadow to give a lustre to the rest" (Gg5v); Johnstoun admits "that whatsoever is wanting" in Sidney's *Arcadia* "can no more bee fill'd up but by himself" (Hhh1r); and Beling, recognizing "the danger of the enterprize," describes his sequel as an act of "rashness" and a "fault" (Tt3r). Like Sidney's sister in the 1593 edition, Alexander tries to justify his intrusiveness by emphasizing that he has "conformed my self to that which preceded my beginning, and was known to bee that Author's own" (Gg5v). His specific diction, "conformed my self," implies that to remain faithful to Sidney's vision he has consciously forfeited his own identity for the sake of Sidney's, the true "Author's own."

Johnstoun, too, announces that he is "bound within the limits" of Sidney's "own conceits," which, he reminds readers, "I durst not exceed" (Hhh1v). According to Johnstoun, his supplement grew out of his affection

---

[14] For a fuller discussion of Beling's sequel – and three other contemporary continuations of *Arcadia* – see Jennifer Klein Morrison, "Readers Turned Writers: The Dynamics of the Sequels to Sir Philip Sidney's *Arcadia*," diss., Yale University, 1997.

for Sidney's romance. Having read the *Arcadia* over and over, he became inspired by the two pairs of lovers: "while at length my brain transported with the Idea's of his own conceit, brought forth a little complement, of what was rather desired than wanting in him: desired, I say, because there is nothing missing but himself" (Hhh1r). The idea is to enhance Sidney's book without suggesting that it needs enhancing. These writers accordingly present themselves first as readers; their complements must be compliments so as to avoid potential criticism and instead draw attention to Sidney himself, the only thing, as Johnstoun notes, "missing" from their works.

In a nod to Sidney's absence, both Alexander and Johnstoun deviate from their source-text long enough to depict the death of his surrogate, Philisides. While Alexander and Johnstoun could be staking a claim for their own sovereignty by killing off their esteemed predecessor, they primarily seem to use this opportunity to mourn such a tragedy. They come to praise Sidney, not bury him. Alexander describes Philisides' death as an "irreparable loss" that causes Musidorus and Pyrocles much anguish (Gg1v), and Johnstoun celebrates how Philisides, "dying in the bed of honor, was buried in the everlasting monuments of fame, desired of all, and hated by none" (Iii1r).

Other seventeenth-century writers paid tribute to Sidney by departing even more freely from his text. Victor Skretkowicz has catalogued numerous other Arcadian works in prose, drama, and verse – allusions, appropriations, imitations, parodies, and sequels – too many to list here.[15] As Mary Ellen Lamb has shown, Sidney's romance especially inspired his women relatives to write literary works, most notably the also unfinished romance, *The Countess of Montgomeries Urania* (1621) by Mary Wroth, Sidney's niece.[16] James Shirley based *A Pastoral Called the Arcadia* (1640) on Sidney's narrative; Francis Beaumont and John Fletcher borrowed from the *Arcadia* for *Cupid's Revenge* (1612); and Francis Quarles converted part of Sidney's text into *Argalus and Parthenia* (1628). Not surprisingly, then, when William Prynne attacked "popular Stage-playes" in *Histrio-mastix* (1633), he listed "Arcadiaes" as a discrete category of writing along with "Comedies, Tragedies," "fained Histories," and "other prophane Discourses."[17]

So many sequels, like the involvement of so many collaborators, suggests both a dispersal and intensification of Sidney's authorial authority. These texts, in advancing the identity of their individual authors, chipped away at any claim Sidney might have had to exclusive control over Arcadia's

---

[15] Skretkowicz, ed., *The Countess of Pembroke's Arcadia (The New Arcadia)*, pp. xlv–lii.
[16] See Mary Ellen Lamb, *Gender and Authorship in the Sidney Circle* (Madison, WI, 1990), pp. 22, 142–93.
[17] William Prynne, *Histrio-mastix* (London, 1633; STC 20464), 6A2r, 6B3r.

pastoral world. But at the same time, especially when surveyed collectively, the *Arcadia*'s sequels bolstered Sidney's reputation by keeping alive his name and looking back to his book as their starting point. Strictly speaking, Sidney represented the "author" of these addenda: the title "Arcadia" and the name "Sidney" became labels signifying a specific set of conventions – generic, aesthetic, and in some cases, as we will see, political – that provided a sense of unity for an otherwise diverse group of texts.

That some of these addenda were published with the *Arcadia* also suggests that members of the book trade recognized the supplements' economic value. Beginning with the second edition in 1593, all subsequent sixteenth- and seventeenth-century copies of Sidney's works claimed to contain some new, previously omitted material. The 1655 edition, for example, reprints the supplements by Alexander, Johnstoun, and Beling, and includes for the first time "A Remedie for Love," "The Life and Death of Sir Philip Sidney" (A4r–c1r), and a glossary or "Clavis, whereby the Reader is let in to view the principal Stories contein'd in the *Arcadia*, as they stand in their proper places" (Iii6r–Kkk1v). The inclusion of these addenda not only reinforced Sidney's prestige, setting off his writings more advantageously, but, as advertised on the title page, they helped to create a new market for an old book.

In a few cases, writers nevertheless thought it necessary to defend their use of Sidney's romance. Gervase Markham, for example, writing in response to critics of his first sequel, *The English Arcadia*, derided the logic behind attacks on his borrowed title: such criticisms implied, he said, that *"none should be cal'd* Alexander *that could not conquer the world, nor any* Iacob *that could not deceive his brother; nor this* Arcadia, *except by many degrees it could exceed the whole world both in words and invention."*[18] These detractors, according to Markham, were also forgetting *"how many God-brothers, and selfe-like Pamphlets had past through the world with the same title"* (A4r). In the preface to the earlier sequel, Markham had defended his practice of *"allusion and imitation"* by placing it within a larger literary tradition: he borrowed from *"the onely to be admired Sir* Philip Sidney" just as had "Virgill [*sic*] *from* Homer, Ariosto *from* Baiardo, *famous* Spencer *from renowned* Chaucer."[19]

Publishers and writers could also defend their Arcadian additions by pointing to the explicit invitation at the end of Sidney's book. Here, fol- lowing the princes' marriages and the reconciliation of Gynecia and Basilius, we encounter a catalogue of other possible plots:

[18] Gervase Markham, *The Second and Last Part of the First Booke of the English Arcadia* (London, 1613; STC 17352), A4r.
[19] Markham, *The English Arcadia*, A2r.

But the solemnities of these mariages with the *Arcadian* pastorals full of many comical adventurs hapning to those rural lovers; the strange stories of *Artaxia* and *Plexirtus, Erona* and *Plangus, Hellen* & *Amphialus*, with the wonderful chances that befell them: the shepheardish loves of *Menalcas* with *Kalodulus* daughter: the poor hopes of the poor *Philisides* in the pursuit of his affections; the strange continuance of *Klaius* and *Strephons* desire: Lastly the Son of *Pyrocles*, named *Pyrophilus* and *Melidora*, the fair daughter of *Pamela* by *Musidorus*, who even at their birth entred into admirable fortunes; may awake som other spirit to exercise his pen in that, wherewith mine is already dulled. (Ttiv)

Among the many "spirits" who "exercised" their pens during the seventeenth century, Richard Beling for one took this advice to heart: with the exception of Pyrophilus and Melidora, his *Sixth Book* does not just discuss all these characters, but details their exploits in the order that they are listed here.

More generally, though, the *Arcadia*'s concluding invitation and the subsequent popularity of related works reflect the early modern practices of communal reading and writing that I examined in the introduction and chapter 1. Jennifer Klein Morrison has noted that requests for readers to compose continuations became a convention in Renaissance prose fiction, while E. F. Hart has identified the "answer-poem" as "one of the most characteristic poetic productions of the first forty years of the seventeenth century," a category he then divides into antitheses, extensions, imitations, and mock-songs.[20] Although Sidney's unfinished *Arcadia* represents an extreme example because it inspired so many responses and appropriations, Renaissance authors often used each other's ideas and wordings. Manuscript transmission, as Arthur Marotti explains, had an "inherently malleable" quality that carried over into print.[21] Thus Sidney's disciple, Ben Jonson, could translate and borrow whole passages from classical authors – or, in the case of, say, "Still to be neat," he could appropriate whole poems. As we saw in the previous chapter, Jonson distinguished sharply between plagiarism, for which he had only contempt, and "imitation," one of the requisites, he believed, for becoming a true poet.[22]

While I am not suggesting that all writing during the seventeenth century benefited from such a collaborative process, this context helps to explain the proliferation of seventeenth-century supplements that Sidney's *Arcadia*

[20] See Morrison, *Readers Turned Writers*, p. 3; and E. F. Hart, "The Answer-Poem of the Early Seventeenth Century," *Review of English Studies*, new series 7 (1956): 19–29.

[21] Arthur F. Marotti, *Manuscript, Print, and the English Renaissance* (Ithaca, NY, 1995), pp. 135–47.

[22] Ben Jonson, *Discoveries*, in *Ben Jonson*, ed. Ian Donaldson (Oxford, 1985), p. 585. Interestingly, Jonson based his *Discoveries* in large part on John Hoskyns' *Directions for Speech and Style* (c. 1599). See Gary R. Grund, "Ben Jonson, John Hoskyns, and the Anti-Ciceronian Movement," *Studies in English Literature* (Tokyo) 54 (1977): 33–53.

inspired. That "A Remedie for Love" explicitly named Sidney as author has important interpretive implications, as I discuss in this chapter's final section, but it was not an entirely isolated instance of false attribution. This verse instead states openly what other seventeenth-century works implied: Sidney had "authored" "Remedie" even if he did not write the poem. On the one hand, Sidney resembles an autonomous author in that his prestige and popularity encouraged readers to encounter a body of work in conjunction with his individual identity; on the other hand, the *Arcadia* represents a site of collaborative authorship, for these same factors prompted readers to participate in and expand his writings. To put it another way: these writers were mining Sidney's romance for source material, but symbolically he validated their works, like a celebrity offering a commercial endorsement. The *Arcadia*'s enormous popularity during the seventeenth century – it reached thirteen editions by 1674 – would have guaranteed, moreover, that booksellers and writers could find an audience for their ancillary works, even if subsequent authors forged only tangential links to Sidney's book. The *Arcadia* and its supplements had a mutually beneficial relationship. Sidney's prestige and popularity inspired – and increased readers' interest in – supplements and sequels to his epic, which in turn seem to have reinforced readers and publishers' interest in the original *Arcadia* and Sir Philip Sidney himself.

EIKON ARCADIA

Within this climate of frequent appropriation and collaboration, John Milton's comments about Sidney's *Arcadia* in *Eikonoklastes* (1649; 1650) sound anachronistic, almost unfair. Milton objects to the *Eikon Basilike* (1649) for presenting Pamela's captivity prayer "word for word" as one of Charles I's personal meditations (*CP* 3: 362). The late king, according to Milton, was trespassing against "human right, which commands that every Author should have the property of his own work reserved to him after death as well as living" (*CP* 3: 365).[23] While this argument looks ahead, as Mark Rose has noted, to the first Copyright Act of 1709, we need to remind ourselves that for Milton the "human right" Charles had violated pertains to all "authors" – that is, all creators – which in the case of books could

---

[23] Among the various revisions that Milton made to *Eikonoklastes* between the first and second editions, he expanded this specific point "somwhat larger then before" in response, he claims, to a "crew of lurking raylers, who in thir Libels . . . as I hear from others, take it so currishly that I should dare to tell abroad the secrets of thir *Ægyptian Apis*" (*CP* 3: 363).

encompass writers as well as their collaborators.[24] Primarily, Milton was finding fault with the king for cribbing a prayer from a secular romance instead of addressing God sincerely, "of his own proper Zeal" (*CP* 3: 364). This type of religious appropriation, unlike the other supplements that Sidney's *Arcadia* inspired, only worked in one direction. Silently recasting Pamela's prayer as one of the king's private reflections, the author of *Eikon Basilike* did not allow for a collaborative relationship. Charles I had "sharkd" this passage and offered nothing in return (*CP* 3: 367).[25]

The vehemence of Milton's attack in *Eikonoklastes* may also have been a response to the *Eikon Basilike*'s subtle alliance of Charles I with Sir Philip Sidney. The *Arcadia*, I show in this section, spawned so many supplements in part because the text's egregious omissions allowed readers to adapt the romance to the charged political climate of mid-seventeenth-century England. The text – and Sidney's reputation – became one of the ideological battle grounds for both sides during the Civil War. Thus the "good caution" (*CP* 3: 362) that Milton advocates in *Eikonoklastes* may have been an exhortation for readers to approach the *Arcadia* objectively rather than accept its compatibility to the king's cause. Writing in response to Milton, Joseph Jane in *Eikon Aklastos* (1651) defended the king's book in precisely these terms. While Jane doubts that the late monarch ever used this meditation, he emphasizes that this choice of prayers does not identify the king with a fictional heathen, as Milton alleges, but instead joins Charles I with "the Author," Sidney himself.[26]

Even before *Eikon Basilike*, as Milton must have realized, disenfranchised royalists had appropriated *Arcadia* in an effort to ally themselves with a charismatic aristocratic hero and the world of chivalric romance that he had described. Although in some regards the 1655 "Life and Death of Sir Philip Sidney" depicts the author as "progressive" – Sidney, for example,

---

[24] See Mark Rose, *Authors and Owners: The Invention of Copyright* (Cambridge, MA, 1993).

[25] The *Eikon Basilike*'s appropriation of Pamela's prayer was not, as Milton argued, entirely surreptitious (*CP* 3: 364). Given the *Arcadia*'s popularity, many readers of *Eikon Basilike* could have recognized the source for this particular meditation of Charles I's. Milton himself obviously knew Sidney's epic, and with so many other writers borrowing from and alluding to Sidney's romance, his style must have been familiar to much of the *Eikon Basilike*'s audience. Seventeenth-century rhetoric handbooks, for example, frequently culled passages from Sidney's work. According to one contemporary anecdote, when a would-be lover borrowed from the *Arcadia* to woo a lady, she immediately saw through his deception: she "was so well verst in his author, as tacitely she traced him to the bottome of a leafe." The anecdote continues: when the gentleman's memory failed, "he brake off abruptly. 'Nay, I beseech you, Sir,' sayd she, 'proceede and turn over the leafe, for methinke the best part is still behinde'; which unexpected discovery silenc't him for ever after.'" See *Anecdotes and Traditions Illustrative of Early English History and Literature*, ed. William J. Thoms (London, 1839), p. 64.

[26] Joseph Jane, *Eikon Aklastos* (London, 1651; Wing J451), Ll1v.

disdained marrying for money (b1v) – the portrait of the artist that dominated contemporary accounts remained largely conservative.[27] As Kevin Pask observes, by paying so much attention to Sidney's military accomplishments and death on the battlefield, such works "retroactively cast aristocratic glory upon his life" and distinguished him among "an increasingly non-military and proto-commercial nobility."[28] The 1655 biographer tells us first that Sidney "was descended of an antient Familie" (A4r), and, in describing Sidney's fatal gun-shot wound, the biographer nostalgically recalls the traditional weaponry of a "sword and buckler," cursing "that Frier of *Mentz*, who, by intelligence from hell, first invented and hatcht that brood of Guns, the sworn enemies to personal Valor" (b4v).[29] Through both his life and writings, Sidney provided seventeenth-century readers a window to quasi-mythical "antient ages" (b4v) when aristocrats were military heroes and murdered monarchs could be miraculously resuscitated. In contrast to Sidney, who lived in a golden world of personal honor and knightly behavior – he was "exemplarie to all Gentlemen," he "was never observed to decline danger" but "never gave provocation to any" (b2r) – the 1655 biographer bemoans "the sacrilege of our age" (c1r), a sidelong glance, it seems, at England's Civil War and/or Charles I's execution.

We can explain some of Sidney's glamorous reputation during the middle of the seventeenth century within a broader attempt by the king's defenders to sustain traditional English customs. As the new government instituted political and cultural changes, Lois Potter notes, "the Stuarts naturally became identified with the same golden past that had previously been associated with Elizabeth I."[30] The author of *Eikon Basilike* briefly allies Charles I with both Elizabeth and James, and a letter from Charles I appended to the text more explicitly invites members of the Commons to "remember how happy they have been of late years under the reign of Queen Elizabeth, the King my father, and myself until the beginning of these unhappy troubles."[31] The Stuarts wanted to continue traditional English pastimes that Elizabeth had so effectively exploited. Leah Marcus

---

[27] Pask, *The Emergence of the English Author*, p. 79.

[28] Pask, *The Emergence of the English Author*, pp. 60, 53. The collection of Latin commendatory verses included in the 1655 *Arcadia* also casts Sidney as a military hero – we read about *Marte* as often as *Musæ* – and both Alexander and Johnstoun's supplements similarly idealize the author in terms of warfare (Gg1v, Iii1r).

[29] This particular criticism of firearms was common during the Renaissance. See J. R. Hale, *Renaissance War Studies* (London, 1983), pp. 394–96.

[30] Lois Potter, *Secret Rites and Secret Writing: Royalist Literature, 1641–1660* (Cambridge, 1989), p. 28.

[31] *Eikon Basilike, The Portraiture of His Sacred Majesty in His Solitudes and Sufferings*, ed. Philip A. Knachel (Ithaca, NY, 1966), pp. 58, 190.

specifically identifies a "wave of antiquarian nostalgia for a vanishing 'Merry England'" that manifested itself under Charles I in such public events as the *Book of Sports* being reissued.[32]

The Countess of Pembroke's Arcadia, the epitome of Elizabethan culture, accordingly became a seminal Caroline text, appropriated and celebrated in various sequels and supplements.[33] Amidst the swelling nostalgia for "Good Queen Elizabeth" special attention was focused on her reign's most celebrated figures, Sir Walter Ralegh, Sir Francis Drake, and Sir Philip Sidney.[34] We can also trace Sidney's popularity during Charles I's reign to what Annabel Patterson has identified as a cultural "shift in generic consciousness."[35] Henrietta Maria consistently commissioned and participated in Arcadian romances, and the king, too, purposefully identified himself with the romantic figure of St. George. As a result, readers and writers began to take Sidney's *Arcadia* and its genre even more seriously. Instead of fictive adventure stories cut off from real experience, the romance developed into a self-consciously political, though necessarily guarded, mode of expression. Royalists during the Civil War and Interregnum could use romances to depict and interpret current events without exposing their views to the glare of parliamentarian censors.

The trouble with Sidney's *Arcadia* as royalist propaganda was that it also contained some vaguely republican, or at least anti-absolutist, intonations. The narrative introduces many ineffective rulers, most notably Basilius, but also Antiphilus, Cecropia, Demagoras, Helen, Plexirtus, Tiridates, and the tyrant king of Phrygia. "Most princes," according to Musidorus, "make themselves, as it were, another thing from the people . . . by a fallacy of argument thinking themselves most kings when the subject is most basely subjected" (p. 256). When King Euarchus agrees to replace the murdered prince and rule Arcadia, he insists on the title "protector" over "king," an uncanny premonition of Cromwell's preference when appointed in 1653 as Lord Protector for life. Euarchus humbly tells the Arcadians "not to have an over-shooting expectation of me" and reminds them, though he is the King of Macedonia, "I am a man – that is to say, a creature whose reason is often

---

[32] Leah S. Marcus, *The Politics of Mirth: Jonson, Herrick, Milton, Marvell, and the Defense of Old Holiday Pastimes* (Chicago, 1986), p. 14; see also pp. 4–21.
[33] C. S. Lewis described the *Arcadia* as a "distillation" of Elizabethan culture because Sidney "gathers up what a whole generation wanted to say." See Lewis, *English Literature in the Sixteenth Century, Excluding Drama* (Oxford, 1954), p. 339.
[34] Kevin Sharpe, *Criticism and Compliment: The Politics of Literature in the England of Charles I* (Cambridge, 1987), pp. 16–17.
[35] Annabel Patterson, *Censorship and Interpretation: The Conditions of Writing and Reading in Early Modern England* (Madison, WI, 1984), p. 171.

over-darkened with error" (p. 797). Sentencing Pyrocles and Musidorus to death, he similarly argues that their status as princes does not mitigate their accountability: "If a prince do acts of hostility without denouncing war, if he break his oath of amity, or innumerable other such things contrary to the laws of arms, he must take heed how he fall into their hands whom he so wrongeth, for then is courtesy the best custom he can claim" (p. 835). Although Euarchus is specifically addressing the limited power of a *foreign* ruler, the same logic would later inform arguments that Charles I should be held responsible for "acts of hostility" against his own people.[36]

When read during James I's reign, Sidney's treatment of monarchy – in particular, his treatment of the irresponsible ruler Basilius – must have appeared, as various critics have observed, "supernaturally clairvoyant."[37] But we also ought not to underestimate the book's continued applicability under James's son. Mid-century readers attempting to treat the *Arcadia* as a political work would have found especially relevant that book 2 describes a failed rebellion and that book 4 depicts the disorder and lamentation that follows a monarch's (apparent) murder. In this latter episode, the Arcadians' "diversified thoughts" look ahead to Republican and Leveller reactions to Charles I's execution:

For some there were that cried to have the state altered and governed no more by a prince: marry, in the alteration, many would have the Lacedaemonian government of few chosen senators; others, the Athenian, where the people's voice held the chief authority. But these were rather the discoursing sort of men than the active, being a matter more in imagination than practice. (p. 767)

While Sidney does not endorse any of these political views, he also does not reject them out of hand; as David Norbrook has suggested, "republicanism emerges rather as an easy academic indulgence."[38] Of course, when such thoughts are acted upon by the multitude, as in the rebel attack at the end

---

[36] For the argument that the *Arcadia* reveals Sidney's support of tyrannicide, see William Dinsmore Briggs, "Political Ideas in Sidney's *Arcadia*," *Studies in Philology* 28 (1931): 137–61. Emphasizing the trial scene with Euarchus, Irving Ribner claims, on the contrary, that the *Arcadia* is an absolutist text: "Had Sidney wished to deny the tenets of passive obedience he had no better opportunity in all of the *Arcadia* to do so than in Euarchus' reply to the plea of the princes, for it was the very issue involved." Ribner presents this negative argument as the "primary evidence" that Sidney "was utterly hostile" to "the anti-absolutist thesis." See Ribner, "Sir Philip Sidney on Civil Insurrection," *Journal of the History of Ideas* 13.2 (1952): 257–65, these quotations, p. 264.

[37] William Hunt, "Civic Chivalry and the English Civil War," in *The Transmission of Culture in Early Modern Europe*, ed. Anthony Grafton and Ann Blair (Philadelphia, 1990), pp. 204–37, this quotation, p. 222; and David Norbrook, *Writing the English Republic: Poetry, Rhetoric and Politics, 1627–1660* (Cambridge, 1999), p. 72.

[38] Norbrook, *Writing the English Republic*, p. 12. Briggs makes this same point in "Political Ideas in Sidney's *Arcadia*," p. 160.

of book 2, Sidney clearly mocks the participants. The rebels are "barbarous" (p. 382) and "right villains" (p. 379), resembling "enraged beasts" (p. 379) and full of "direct contrarieties" (p. 383); they fight among themselves, cannot agree on their demands, cannot agree on a spokesman, and quickly suffer defeat by Zelmane and Dorus. Presumably Sidney wants us to laugh as Zelmane brutally "strake off the nose" of a rebellious tailor – "a dapper fellow," "a suitor to a seamstress daughter, and therefore not a little grieved at such a disgrace." When the tailor stoops "to bring his nose to his head, Zelmane with a blow sent his head to his nose" (p. 380). The tailor's airs, the understatement of "not a little grieved," the pun on nose/blow, and the irony of the victim's occupation (the tailor dies trying to mend his face; Zelmane next cleaves apart a butcher) – all these details indicate Sidney's lack of sympathy for anti-monarchists. The sudden reversal of nose-to-head *versus* head-to-nose conveys the alacrity with which Arcadia's head of state regains authority.

Still, if Sidney never actually questions the legitimacy of monarchical government in the *Arcadia*, seventeenth-century readers, paging through the text, had the opportunity to make up their own minds. So much happens in the *Arcadia* – some of the inconsistencies no doubt a product of the texts' various omissions, collaborations, and supplements – that readers could privilege some moments and selectively ignore or downplay other parts of the book. Annabel Patterson, for example, has offered a nuanced reading of Philisides' fable about the beasts' request for a ruler. She uncovers "conflicting theories and arguments about the nature of monarchy and the rights and duties of subjects," and she argues convincingly that Sidney presents "a more subtle analysis of political tyranny than that available in Aesop."[39] But Patterson ultimately must admit that this one poem, which directly addresses social hierarchy, can support conflicting political interpretations, everything from "an incitement to rebellion" to an endorsement of Tudor absolutism.[40] As William Dinsmore Briggs also astutely observes, Sidney never specifies what type of monarchy Basilius' own government constitutes, either a limited or absolute kingship.[41]

---

[39] Patterson, *Censorship and Interpretation*, pp. 40, 38. In keeping with her "hermeneutics of censorship," Patterson ultimately argues that this particular poem is "about itself, about fabling, and about equivocation in the interests of safety." She concludes that Sidney intentionally wrote ambiguously so as to suggest "the *need* for ambiguity" and express "in effect . . . his desire for reform" (p. 39).

[40] Patterson, *Censorship and Interpretation*, p. 38; Briggs, "Political Ideas in Sidney's *Arcadia*," pp. 151–53; and Ribner, "Sir Philip Sidney on Civil Insurrection," pp. 260–61.

[41] Briggs, "Political Ideas in Sidney's *Arcadia*," p. 155. Briggs notes that most of the evidence of Sidney's favoring a mixed monarchy occurs in the *Arcadia*'s final book.

We cannot know how many of the *Arcadia*'s politically-minded readers focused attention on the text's bad rulers, nor, comparatively, how many championed the few good ones. And how would seventeenth-century readers have reacted to the composite edition's various inconsistencies, such as the passage mistakenly retained intact from the *Old Arcadia* which has the two princes receiving different punishments for Basilius' murder? For a book with such egregious omissions, Musidorus' warning to Pyrocles must have resonated with some early readers: "Let me, therefore, receive a clear understanding, which many times we miss while those things we account small, as a speech or a look, are omitted, like as a whole sentence may fail of his congruity by wanting one particle" (p. 140). Based on these criteria, Renaissance readers could not "receive a clear understanding" of the *Arcadia*, for surely, as we learn from the preliminary materials and other editorial notes, the composite text omits much more than a single "speech or a look." As readers perused the seventeenth-century text and had to choose, for example, between Alexander's and Johnstoun's supplements to book 3, interpretive uncertainty became one of the *Arcadia*'s themes. Responding to Basilius' pivotal decision to consult the oracle, the normative character Kalendar – "grave in years, great in authority . . . known honest" (p. 772) – criticizes the king's "vanity" for wanting to know too much: "there is nothing so certain as our continual uncertainty" (p. 82). At book's end, Sidney's narrator echoes this sentiment, gently undermining the apparently happy resolution: "So uncertain are moral judgements, the same person most infamous, and most famous, and neither justly" (p. 847).

This emphasis on uncertainty may further explain why the *Arcadia* spawned so many sequels: the book required them. Unfinished, long, and in places inconsistent, the *Arcadia* had to be read actively. Recounting the narrative of its own complex genesis, the text encourages readers to become writers and, following the example of Sidney's sister, bring the work closer to its conclusion by filling in its blanks. Fulke Greville, attempting in part to defend the *Arcadia* from critics' "carping eyes," insisted that "the most refined spirits" could find in the book various moral lessons, especially regarding "the Monarch's part . . . the growth, state, and declination of Princes, change of Government, and lawes."[42] While he claims to know Sidney's ultimate "purpose," Greville also emphasizes the need for "active

[42] Fulke Greville, *The Life of the Renowned Sr Philip Sidney* (London, 1652; Wing B4899), C1v. Greville specifically suggests that Sidney intended the *Arcadia* to critique "Soveraign Princes" who "play with their own visions . . . unactively charge the managing of their greatest affairs upon the second-hand faith, and diligence of Deputies" (B7r–v). Greville's *Life*, although written in 1612, was first published in this edition forty years later.

able" readers, willing to "exercise their Spirits" and "conceive" the romance's unfinished parts (C1r).

The pseudonymous author of the 1655 edition's "Life and Death" similarly compared reading the *Arcadia* to deciphering an Egyptian hieroglyphic:

as the antient Egyptians presented secrets under their mystical hieroglyphicks, so that an easie figure was exhibited to the eye, and an higher notion tendred, under it, to the judgment: so all the *Arcadia* is a continual Grove of moralitie; shadowing moral and politick results under the plain and easie emblems of Lovers: So, that the Reader may bee deceived, but not hurt thereby, when surpriz'd on a sudden to more knowledg than hee expect. (b3r)

Readers finding the *Arcadia* immoral, the biographer claims, are "Children" who "may rest in the shell"; discerning readers are "men" who will discover "a rich bank and bed of the choicest learning concealed therein" (b3v). But because readers lacked, as the biographer teasingly refuses to offer, "a *Key*, to unfold what persons were intended" (b3v), the *Arcadia's* seventeenth-century audience began to provide its own contemporary solutions.

These solutions presumably reflect the values and concerns of the *Arcadia's* diverse audience. While the expensive folio format must have restricted the book's purchasers, Sidney's work still appealed to a range of readers. William Hunt, for example, has documented various ways that "city folk" appropriated "both the code of knightly honor and the literary genres in which that code was inscribed."[43] I would add that the idea of reading the *Arcadia* as a secret allegory further explains why Sidney's work appealed to royalists during the Civil War and Interregnum. Royalist writing in general, as Lois Potter has shown, was characterized by its "obscurity, mystery, and playfulness," all essential attributes for a disempowered faction struggling to survive and unable to express its ideas openly.[44] Treating Sidney's romance as a roman à clef enabled royalists to relate the book more directly to their experiences. Sidney's book might be popular, according to this way of thinking, but only fit readers could decode its real significance.

Thus, one sequel, *The History of the Arcadia* (c. 1650), perhaps written by a member of the Digby family, claimed Sidney's book for Charles I by developing its royalist intonations into an overt critique of recent English history. In this supplement, a new oracle foresees that rebels will "thiere native country soe annoye, / That they both King and kingdome will destroye." And at the conclusion, the prediction proves true: rebels behead

---

[43] Hunt, "Civic Chivalry and the English Civil War," pp. 213, 208.
[44] Potter, *Secret Rites and Secret Writing*, p. 209.

the king and pass an edict eliminating monarchy, thereby, according to the author, reducing the government "into a confused chaos of Democracie." That the sequel stops here, Potter argues, indicates the strong link between monarchy and romance: without a king both the kingdom and the genre come to an end.[45]

The anonymous author of the octosyllabic verse, "A Draught of Sir Phillip Sidney's Arcadia" (c. 1645), takes the more radical tack of suggesting that Sidney was "soe wise" that he presciently described the events leading to Charles I's execution, "The rise, growth, fall of *Monarchie*."[46] Although the poet acknowledges that in an inclusive work such as the *Arcadia* "men may find / Whatever they fancie in mind" (lines 369–70), he wishes readers had paid particular attention to the poem's implied politics:

> That if men seriously but looke
> Is the thinge hinted in this booke,
> By which this nation might have learned
> And at distance something discerned
> Threatening a change in church and state,
> Not forseene, but seene when too late.
>
> (lines 323–28)

Finding fault with both the king's indulgences and the country's lack of foresight, the poet reserves his harshest criticism for the rebels, a "Heterogeneous Body" (line 63) resembling the drunken clowns who attack Basilius: "Scarce two agreeing in one mind / Only to mischiefe all inclinde" (lines 75–76). These rebels, the poet laments with hindsight, not only deceived the English people, but in the process massacred religion, hospitality, virtue, and patience (lines 227–30). He shudders now to think "What dolefull Scratches thei will make / Upon the face of Government" (lines 82–83).

The word "Draught" in this poem's title may refer to a preliminary outline, for in addition to purportedly uncovering the *Arcadia*'s secret meaning, the poet outlines the broad range of topics that Sidney's book addresses, "from the peasant to the King" (line 334). But the word "draught," also meaning a gulp of liquid or an inhalation of smoke, simultaneously suggests the culture of seventeenth-century drinking houses. Here, as Henry Vaughan described these establishments, "rich tobacco and quick tapers shine, / And royal, witty sack, the poet's soul, / With brighter suns than he

[45] Potter, *Secret Rites and Secret Writing*, pp. 94–95.
[46] Bodleian, MS. Eng. e. 2016, lines 27–30. A copy of this poem occurs in John Buxton, "A Draught of Sir Phillip Sidney's *Arcadia*," in *Historical Essays, 1600–1750, Presented to David Ogg*, ed. H. E. Bell and R. L. Ollard (London, 1963), pp. 60–77.

doth gild the bowl."[47] The title "A Draught of Sir Phillip Sidney's Arcadia" would thus cast the speaker as a talkative tavern-dweller, hoisting a few pints and sociably offering us "A Draught" of Sidney's romance.

Although this poem specifically describes anti-monarchists who "amids't their cupps doe prate / against the officers of state" (lines 237–38), it was Charles I's supporters who most often celebrated drinking houses in their writings; the praise of "*royal,* witty sack" became a common mid-century association. Royalist poets, both exiled courtiers and would-be gentlemen, followed the tradition established by Jonson and members of other early clubs in idealizing the pleasures of drinking, wit, and socializing, what Earl Miner has called the cavalier's "ideal of the good life."[48] The authors of these verses were in part attempting to escape the harsh reality of their current circumstance; in part recollecting nostalgically Charles I's golden days; and in part, as Timothy Raylor has argued, expressing subversively "cavalier bravado, libertinism, and antipuritanism."[49]

The alleged omission of "A Remedie for Love," as I show in the next section, emerged from this atmosphere. "Remedie" lacks the obvious political significance of other Arcadian sequels such as the *History* and "A Draught," but this verse also reflects seventeenth-century attempts by the king's supporters to ally themselves with Sidney and his romance. To understand "Remedie" as a royalist poem, we must first analyze its relationship to the *Arcadia* and consider why by 1655 the minor character Mopsa, on whom "Remedie" focuses attention, would have become important for Sidney's audiences.

LOVE AND MOPSA

Within the *Arcadia*, Kalendar first introduces Mopsa by way of her parents: Dametas, the "most arrant, doltish clown that I think ever was" (p. 77), and Miso, "so handsome a bedlam that only her face and splay-foot have made her accused for a witch" (p. 77). Kalendar sarcastically concludes that Mopsa is "fit woman to participate of both their perfections" (p. 77), but because "she goes for a woman," he refuses to criticize her, or at least so he pretends. He will "only repeat" a verse by an anonymous "fellow of my acquaintance":

[47] Henry Vaughan, "A Rhapsody," in *Ben Jonson and the Cavalier Poets,* ed. Hugh Maclean (London, 1974), pp. 351–53, lines 4–6.
[48] Earl Miner, *The Cavalier Mode from Jonson to Cotton* (Princeton, 1971), pp. 44, 84.
[49] Raylor, *Cavalier, Clubs, and Literary Culture,* p. 205.

What length of vers can serv brave *Mopsa's* good to show?
When virtues strange, and beauties such as no man them may know:
Thus shrewdly burdned then, how can my Muse escape?
The gods must help, and precious things must serv to shew her shape.
    Like great god *Saturn* fair, and like fair *Venus* chaste:
As smooth as *Pan*, as *Juno* milde, like goddess *Iris* fac't,
With *Cupid* shee foresee's and goe's god *Vulcan's* pace.
    And for a taste of all these gifts, shee steal's god *Momus* grace.
Her forehead Jacinth-like, her cheeks of Opal hue,
Her twinckling eies bedect with pearl, her lips as Saphir blue:
Her hair like Crapal stone; her mouth, O heavenly wide!
Her skin like burnisht gold, her hands like silver ure untri'd.
    As for her parts unknown, which hidden sure are best:
Happie bee they which well believ, and never seek the rest.[50]

Here the use of poulter's measure (rhymed couplets of iambic hexameter and iambic heptameter) highlights Mopsa's lack of virtue: even when a poet goes to such great lengths, Sidney implies in answer to the poem's opening question, he cannot redeem Mopsa's character.[51] As opposed to Philoclea and Pamela, whom Kalendar describes as "beyond measure excellent" (p. 76), the extra syllables of poulter's measure only emphasize Mopsa's coarse manners. Nominally, this verse form allies Mopsa with a vendor of domestic fowl; rhythmically, the plodding meter suggests her graceless lumbering.

From the start Sidney is inviting readers to laugh at Mopsa. Written according to the convention of *contreblazon*, the poem presents a list of antonymic allusions: readers can tick off each comparison and take satisfaction in the required reasoning; if the poem were a stage-play we might laugh aloud to demonstrate that we are in on the humor. Mopsa is as fair as Saturn, Saturn was ugly, therefore Mopsa is not fair; she is as smooth as Pan, Pan was hairy, therefore Mopsa is not smooth; and so on. The logic takes mere moments but in the process Sidney enhances the reader's sense of superiority, not only through the cumulative details of Mopsa's unrefinement, but because Mopsa, vain and easily duped by Dorus, would presumably not notice that the poem criticizes her. You readers, Sidney's poem assures us, are smarter than she is.

[50] *Arcadia*, pp. 77–78. I have followed the 1655 edition in spelling, capitalization, and punctuation (B6r). In the *Old Arcadia*, the verse is specifically attributed to Alethes, "an honest man of that time." See Robertson, ed., *The Countess of Pembroke's Arcadia (The Old Arcadia)*, p. 30, line 20.
[51] "Poulter's measure" takes its name from the traditional practices of poulters, who gave fourteen eggs in the second dozen. The poem accordingly consists of alternating lines of twelve and fourteen syllables.

Simultaneously, the poem introduces Mopsa's role as foil for Philoclea and Pamela, specifically foreshadowing Dorus' strategy of courting Mopsa insincerely. Dorus will later pay the same type of empty compliments to Mopsa – "she was the lodestar of my life, she was the blessing of mine eyes, she the overthrow of my desires" (p. 223) – with the same intention of setting Pamela in higher esteem. As Dorus explains, "in her foulness I beheld Pamela's fairness" (p. 223). He is suggesting in practical terms that he is permitted to see Pamela only in the presence of Mopsa's foulness, but he also implies that Mopsa's foul appearance comparatively improves Pamela's beauty.

Even Mopsa's name contributes to this sense of opposition: "Mopsa," as William Ringler has observed, ironically evokes the singing shepherd Mopsus from Virgil's Fifth Eclogue.[52] But, according to the *OED*, the name may also suggest a grimace or cleaning implement, while David McPherson detects a pun on the Dutch word *mops*, meaning "pug dog" and "country lout."[53] With the Latinized version *Mopsa*, Sidney can allude to all these possible origins, jokingly contrasting Virgil's pastoral ideal with Mopsa's frowning homeliness or doggy loutishness. Once again Sidney is appealing to readers' intelligence to discern, and distance themselves from, Mopsa's lack of sophistication.

The added layer of irony is that because Sidney so consistently and good-humoredly compliments Mopsa, readers may begin to feel – and suspect that he also feels – some affection for her. Perhaps, we think, the poet protests too much. Ugly, unintelligent, and ill-mannered, Mopsa snores, drools, and envies Pamela's beauty. When Dorus feigns "some supernatural contemplation," she experiences "such an itch of inquiry that she would have offered her maidenhead rather than be long kept from it" (p. 646). Yet, despite such egregious flaws, Mopsa is funny, lively, and, for the most part, harmless. When stuck listening to Dorus' self-serving tale, she sympathetically dozes; and when given the chance to ask Apollo for anything in the world, she shows herself a loyal monarchist and requests "a king to my husband" (p. 718). In keeping with the inverted logic of the *contreblazon*, Sidney characterizes Mopsa as one of those people who paradoxically "joys to see any hard hap happen to them they deem happy" (p. 645). That Mopsa takes pleasure from pain echoes our own experience as we enjoy reading about her painful mistakes and flawed character. The aphorism's

[52] Ringler, ed., *Poems*, p. 384.
[53] *OED* s.v. "mop," sb. 2 and sb. 3; and David C. McPherson, "A Possible Origin for Mopsa in Sidney's *Arcadia*," *Renaissance Quarterly* 21 (1968): 420–28.

stuttering alliterative wordplay ("hard hap happen . . . happy") again prevents us from judging her too harshly. We cannot thoroughly dislike Mopsa because Sidney makes it so much fun to read about her.

Even the usually reliable Kalendar enjoys the verses that he recites about Mopsa – which, he admits, "I have so often caused to be sung that I have them without book" (p. 77). Does Dorus' ruse to woo Pamela via Mopsa also reveal a perverse attraction to Mopsa's "sluttishness" (p. 223)? When Dorus asks "Which is my unworthiness, either of mind, estate, or both" (p. 226), Mopsa responds "In neither," unintentionally piercing his shepherd's disguise and ironically describing his true character. Such a generous reply, as Dorus himself acknowledges, suggests that beneath Mopsa's coarse exterior lies a "heart . . . tumbled with overmuch kindness" (p. 226). When Dorus insincerely compliments Mopsa's "greatness of . . . estate," and the "ornaments of that divine spark within you," she again cuts through the pretense of his courtly rhetoric. "Wagging her lips and grinning," she unknowingly lights on the truth, "In faith, you jest with me!" (p. 224).

In "A Remedie for Love," readers discover an amplified and ultimately more complex version of Mopsa's jocular, contrastive function, which demonstrates, above all, the care that the anonymous poet has taken in reading Sidney's romance. Modeled loosely on the poem that Kalendar recites, this added verse also works out of the *contreblazon* tradition. "Remedie" celebrates the paradoxically salubrious effect of Mopsa's offensive features, for as she again and again proves in the *Arcadia*, Mopsa is so bad that she is good. The octosyllabic meter of "Remedie," though much faster than the poulter's measure of Kalendar's recitation, has a similar effect: the poem's breezy, sometimes jagged rhythm implies Mopsa's lack of sophistication and hints at the poem's satiric intention. During the seventeenth century, as evident in "A Draught of Sir Phillip Sidney's Arcadia," such rough, octosyllabic verses developed out of a vernacular tradition. Although this unpolished style of writing appealed to some scholarly poets, it found most frequent use in broadsides, ballads, and parodies.

By choosing this form, the poet of "Remedie" also recalls Zelmane's more regular, octosyllabic *blazon* cataloguing Philoclea's physical attributes (pp. 190–95). Whereas Zelmane progresses methodically first down, then up Philoclea's perfect body ("pretty ears," "brave calves," "sugared flanks"), "Remedie" highlights Mopsa's repulsive features ("face of clout," "lips of marble, teeth of jet"). The coincidence of style and form allies the two portraits, sharpening the contrast between Mopsa and the princesses. Just as Kalendar's description of Mopsa in the *Arcadia* helps to set off

Pamela's beauty more advantageously, "Remedie" reinforces Mopsa's role as foil for Pamela and Philoclea. The irony of "Remedie" is that the poet openly acknowledges Mopsa's repulsiveness and praises her because of it.

This praise, as in the verse that Kalendar recites, incorporates allusions that appeal to educated seventeenth-century readers and comfortably distance them from Mopsa's coarseness. "Remedie" not only depends on an audience's familiarity with what must have been fairly obvious classical references – Apollo, Cupid, Medusa – but, more importantly, it assumes a knowledge of Sidney's romance. To appreciate fully the poem's humor requires that readers understand the references to Mopsa and the princesses, and recognize more subtle connections between this poem and the *Arcadia*'s similarly constructed verses. That Mopsa provides love's remedy in the alleged omission, for example, fits with her character as portrayed in the *Arcadia*. In a text fraught with tender emotions, Mopsa represents one of the few characters who appears immune to eros. Although Dorus claims that Mopsa felt a "certain smackering" towards him (p. 224), she mostly seems bemused by his feigned advances and never displays any reciprocal passion. In the episode of Apollo's ash tree, Mopsa gives little thought to obtaining Dorus as her husband and appears more interested in acquiring prestige and power (pp. 648, 717–18).

For the *Arcadia* to conclude with a love-cure also seems appropriate, since Sidney depicts erotic love as a potentially dangerous force. Love needs a remedy because it threatens, as Musidorus explains to Pyrocles, both a person's virtue and reason. Musidorus will recant his extended attack on love – "the basest and fruitlessest of all passions" (p. 133) – after he himself succumbs to Pamela: "all is but lip-wisdom which wants experience," he suddenly rationalizes (p. 170). But in Arcadia love remains a "deadly disease" (p. 427) that makes Philoclea "far more sick in mind than body" and Gynecia seem "likewise . . . somewhat diseased" (p. 675). Although not original to the *Arcadia*, the metaphor of love as sickness, so integral to "Remedie," grows out of Sidney's narrative and word choice.[54] Sidney describes lovers as "mind-infected people" (p. 114) and refers to love as a "fever," a "plague-sore" (p. 237), a "vile infection" (p. 138), a "sudden sickness" (p. 216), and a "languishing sickness" (p. 218).[55] When Pyrocles explains his passion for Philoclea to an unsympathetic Musidorus, he compares his

---

[54] On the origins of pathological love in ancient and medieval medicine, see Jacques Ferrand, *A Treatise on Lovesickness*, trans. and ed. Donald A. Beecher and Massimo Ciavolella (New York, 1990).

[55] For other examples of this metaphor, see *Arcadia*, p. 138 ("I am sick, sick to the death"), p. 140 ("mine eyes infected" and "know my disease"), and p. 377 ("saw sickness in her face").

friend to "a physician that, seeing his patient in a pestilent fever, should chide him instead of ministering help, and bid him be sick no more" (p. 138).

"A Remedie for Love" thus rewards readers familiar with Sidney's romance and lays claim to Sidney as author by responding so precisely to *Arcadia*'s characterizations, diction, and poetic forms. Seventeenth-century readers could have also recognized "Remedie" as a humorous adaptation of Ovid's *Remedia Amoris*.[56] While the Roman poet never prescribed looking at a physically repulsive woman as a cure for love, he does suggest that lovesick readers should distract themselves with other mistresses and focus their attention on lovers' least attractive features. As Ovid explains, "Revulsion" makes "you wish you'd never had a woman" (line 416), and he specifically recommends that the post-coital lover should "mark and remember every fault in [a woman's] body, / Turn a bright light on her defects" (lines 418–19). The poet of "Remedie" takes this idea a step further, inverting Ovid's later proposal to "compare *your* girl with famous beauties, / And who won't begin to find his mistress a bore" (lines 709–10). In "Remedie" a lover should instead compare his mistress with ugly Mopsa; one glimpse or whiff will not just deflect attention from a current mistress but should destroy all romantic desire.

Once again, the humor of "A Remedie for Love" depends in part on readers' ability to recognize how the poet wittily combines and builds on these sources. Like a tavern-dweller in a verse-competition, the poet of "Remedie" is vying with his poetic predecessors. He jokingly dismisses Ovid's "pretious shallow" as an ineffective love-cure (line 76), and in the same spirit mocks Sidney's idealized heroines as "Two goodly Horses" that look so attractive "You know not which to chuse or ride" (lines 16, 17).

Writing on seventeenth-century burlesque poetry, Timothy Raylor has identified this "competitive edge" as one of the general characteristics of an early modern comic style. Raylor notes that the scatological jokes and loose rhyme and meter in such poems similarly create "an impression of easy intimacy and mutual frankness."[57] He presents the now familiar dialectic that has come to characterize the New Historicism: working from Mikhail Bakhtin's theory of the carnival, Raylor argues that burlesque poetry "affords

56 All quotations from *Remedia Amoris* are taken from Ovid, *Cures for Love*, in *The Erotic Poems*, trans. Peter Green (London, 1982), pp. 239–63.
57 Raylor, *Cavalier, Clubs, and Literary Culture*, pp. 129, 133. Compare Raylor's analysis of James Smith's burlesque poem *The Loves of Hero and Leander*, which responds to the version of *Hero and Leander* written by Christopher Marlowe or George Chapman: "the earlier text is not mocked, it is exceeded. The burlesque aspects of the earlier poem are seized on and exaggerated beyond all proportion" (*Cavalier, Clubs, and Literary Culture*, p. 139).

an area of contained release from social and rational restraints, a fantasy world of pure play . . . but it does not transgress those limits." At heart, the burlesque remains "deeply conservative," because it consistently demon-strates "a commitment to traditional concepts of order and an espousal of classicism, good-fellowship, and wit."[58]

The ironic structure of "A Remedie for Love" neatly fits this dialectic. The poet's praise for Mopsa's repulsive features overturns traditional values, but only temporarily. While appearing to celebrate Mopsa's coarseness, the poem actually reinforces the finer qualities that the princesses embody and posits a highly literate reader, able to detect both classical and Arcadian allusions. By having readers laugh at Mopsa, "Remedie," like the *Arcadia*, puts her in her place – and elevates readers to theirs. Mopsa enacts the basic function of all seventeenth-century burlesque: just as cavalier poets some-times used a rough style of versifying to establish their status as gentlemen, Mopsa's rough features help to establish the princesses, the poet, and, by extension, the readers as people of good taste.

THE POLITICS OF LOVE

This type of social satire became political during the Civil War period, as we have seen with "A Draught of Sir Phillip Sidney's Arcadia," when supporters of Charles I attempted to re-assert traditional values in response to the defeat of monarchy. Jokes about social standing, Keith Thomas notes, "underlay the vast proliferation . . . of Royalist satire against enthusiasts and sectaries, tub-preachers and holy sisters," and Courtney Craig Smith describes how cavaliers compiled such verses into anthologies "as a weapon against their social and political foes." These so-called "drolleries" represent "the 'subversive propaganda' of an 'occupied' people who had lost out in the field, yet were unwilling to submit to the rule . . . of the 'Saints.'"[59]

We can begin to appreciate the political implications of "Remedie" by reading it within the context of the drollery *Musarum deliciae*, where the verse was printed under the title "Description of three Beauties" in 1655 and 1656. Few of the poems in this collection explicitly support monarchy, but when taken as a whole they insinuate loyalty to the king and evoke the cavalier's ideal of the good life; they address such comic subjects as "A Poet's farewell to his thred-bare Cloak," "Upon a Fart unluckily let,"

[58] Raylor, *Cavalier, Clubs, and Literary Culture*, pp. 132, 129.
[59] Keith Thomas, "The Place of Laughter in Tudor and Stuart England," *Times Literary Supplement* (21 January 1977): 77–81, this quotation, p. 78; Courtney Craig Smith, "The Seventeenth-Century Drolleries," *Harvard Library Bulletin* 6 (1952): 40–51, these quotations, p. 45.

and "Upon drinking in the Crown of a Hat."[60] The opening verse, "To Parson Weeks," establishes the volume's convivial tone, inviting the cleric of the title – as well as we readers – to London for camaraderie, wit, and "that old Sack / Young *Herric* took to entertaine / The Muses in a sprightly vein" (B1v). That the poet jokingly encourages us to "speak Treason there" (B2r) hints at the political affiliation of the friends that he wants to assemble. A later poem, "To a Friend upon his Marriage," similarly alludes to a political uprising and the unjust punishment of the cavalier William Davenant:

> You heard of late, what Chevaliers
> (Who durst not tarry for their eares)
> Proscribed were for laying a plot
> Which might have ruin'd God knows what:
> Suspected for the same's *Will D'avenant*,
> Whether he have been in't, or have not
> He is committed.   (B4v)

Perhaps most stridently, the final poem, "A Defiance to K. A.," describes a recalcitrant King Arthur who refuses, Samson-like, to abdicate his authority and shave his beard. If readers have overlooked the other poems' conservative allusions, "A Defiance" and the volume conclude with a more forceful image, an angry monarch threatening his opponent and shaking "his good Sword" (G4r).

Yet, even without the *Deliciae*'s royalist orientation, "A Remedie for Love" still succeeds as a political poem; setting the poem at the end of the *Arcadia* as an authorial omission enhances, not eliminates, the latent royalism in both works. The title "A Remedie for Love," for example, draws attention to one of the romance's central themes. The 1655 *Arcadia* begins with Strephon and Claius' unrequited love for Urania. In contrast to Sidney's metaphor elsewhere of love as sickness, the shepherds' love improves them. Claius claims that Urania's "sun-staining excellency" has inspired them to contemplate God, peruse "learned writings," and make themselves more worthy of her affection (p. 63). Instead of threatening Strephon and Claius' fellowship, Urania helps the shepherds maintain a friendly rivalry; instead of stirring up irrational passions, she has "thrown reason upon our desires . . . and taught the beholders chastity" (p. 64).

---

[60] Raylor similarly argues that this volume attempts to "memorialize a lost golden age of Stuart culture." See Raylor, *Cavalier, Clubs, and Literary Culture*, pp. 204–5; and Raylor, Introduction, *Musarum Deliciae (1655) and Wit Restor'd (1658): Facsimile Reproductions* (Delmar, NY, 1985), pp. 3–13.

In the book's second depiction of love, Parthenia and Argalus experience a "mutual affection" and "virtuous constancy" more spiritual than physical (pp. 89, 91). Their marriage also depends on both desire and reason: only after Parthenia "learned liking and misliking, loving and loathing" can she "out of passion . . . take the authority of judgement" and choose Argalus over Demagoras (p. 89). The "stories of Hercules" that the couple read suggest the heroic quality of their marriage:

> a happy couple: he joying in her, she joying in herself, but in herself, because she enjoyed him: both increasing their riches by giving to each other; each making one life double, because they made a double life one; where desire never wanted satisfaction, nor satisfaction never bred satiety: he ruling, because she would obey, or rather because she would obey, she therein ruling. (p. 501)

Like the epitaph that Basilius later has written for them, the balanced syntax of this passage conveys the balance of passion and reason that the couple achieves. The repeated phrases and parallel constructions also echo their fate: Parthenia and Argalus move through the *Arcadia* in perfect step with each other. He demonstrates his devotion to her by insisting on marriage after she is poisoned; she demonstrates her devotion to him by refusing to encumber him in such a match. He dies fighting Amphialus; she soon follows, fatally challenging Amphialus as the Knight of the Tomb. If Strephon and Claius' love for Urania represents a pastoral ideal, then Parthenia and Argalus' love for each other represents the ideal of matrimony. Instead of becoming paralyzed by their passion like the *Arcadia*'s lovesick protagonists, Parthenia and Argalus are suspended in a virtuous state of active loving, which inspires them to act honorably, both with each other and in their public lives.

That Amphialus, who also wants to act honorably, unintentionally kills both Parthenia and Argalus suggests, by comparison, the destructive force of passion unchecked by reason. Amphialus' immoderate feelings for Philoclea represent the third type of erotic attraction that Sidney examines in the *Arcadia*. For Amphialus, as for Sidney's main characters, love resembles a sickness that promotes idleness and overpowers virtue. "I cease to strive," a smitten Pyrocles pines (p. 131). Helen first describes the consequences of loving so excessively. The tears she sheds over Amphialus' picture, as if honoring an "idol" with "oblations" (p. 122), would have likely reminded Sidney's Protestant readers of Catholicism's specious rituals. Cruelly rejecting Philoxenus, she thinks of no one but herself: "in truth I cared not much how he took it," she admits, and "the forward pain of mine own heart made me so delight to punish him whom I esteemed the chiefest let in my way"

(p. 125). Helen's love for Amphialus not only destroys his friendship with Philoxenus, but because she deliberately allows Philoxenus to pursue his companion, she shares responsibility for his and his father's deaths.

Sidney seems to establish the three extremes of love early in the *Arcadia* – pastoral, ideal, and hurtful – so that we can then plot the romance's various attractions within these vertices. In the book's core debate about love, Musidorus warns Pyrocles, "the head gives you direction," and Pyrocles immediately counters, "And the heart gives me life" (p. 137). It is a conflict that Sidney in the *Arcadia* never entirely resolves. The argument reoccurs, for example, in an allegorical pastoral omitted from the *New Arcadia* but restored in the composite text: Reason says, "Who Passion doth ensue lives in annoy," and Passion responds, "Who Passion doth forsake lives void of joy" (p. 407). Although the shepherds performing these roles ultimately agree to "let us both to heavenly rules give place," Sidney undermines this apparent solution by having the shepherds then turn to the lovesick Basilius,

who framed his praises of them according to Zelmane's liking; whose unrestrained parts, the mind and eye, had their free course to the delicate Philoclea, whose look was not short in well requiting it although she knew it was a hateful sight to her jealous mother. (p. 408)

As opposed to the neat, parallel phrases that characterize Parthenia and Argalus' balanced affection, Sidney here strings together a series of dependent clauses so as to suggest these characters' tangle of emotions. The joke is that no one learns about the shepherds' "heavenly rules" because no one has been watching the pastoral. Art may quell a "skirmish betwixt Reason and Passion" (p. 407), Sidney suggests in this scene, but as we look at the love-struck members of Basilius' household, the war rages on.

Basilius and Zelmane's distraction hints, moreover, at the larger repercussions of having "unrestrained parts." Love without moderation in the *Arcadia* not only causes personal agony, but more importantly, as Blair Worden has observed, it disturbs public order.[61] Thus we are not surprised that the banished lover Demagoras would lead the rebellious helots. Amphialus takes up arms against the Basilians because of his infatuation for Philoclea; Queen Helen abandons the people of Corinth so that she can chase Amphialus; and Basilius ignores his duties as ruler because of his "doting love" for Zelmane (p. 149).

[61] Blair Worden, *The Sound of Virtue: Philip Sidney's* Arcadia *and Elizabethan Politics* (New Haven, 1996), p. 303. Compare Spenser's *The Faerie Queene*, in which the city-dwellers describe Cupid as "the disturber of all civill life, / The enimy of peace, and author of all strife." *The Faerie Queene*, ed. Thomas P. Roche, Jr. (New York, 1978), book III, canto 6, stanza 14.

The notion that love can lead to public disorder must have seemed significant in a work treated as an allegory during the middle of the seventeenth century. Adapting Aristotle's concept of the rational and irrational parts of a soul, Musidorus specifically uses a metaphor of monarchy and rebellion to describe the consequences of excessive passion:

the reasonable part of our soul is to have absolute commandment, against which, if any sensual weakness arise, we are to yield all our sound forces to the overthrowing of so natural a rebellion; wherein how can we want courage, since we are to deal against so weak an adversary that in itself is nothing but weakness? (pp. 132–33)

Although Pyrocles objects to Musidorus' attack on love and criticism of women, he still accepts this basic metaphor.[62] Pyrocles similarly casts his feelings for Philoclea as an "inward treason" accomplished by her "outward force." Having "lost the field," his "thoughts did faintly yield" and allow "poor reason's overthrow" (p. 131).

Seventeenth-century readers, already inclined to emphasize the book's political implications, could have heard in such language a premonition of contemporary attacks on Charles I. The king's critics commonly blamed his disloyalty and ineptitude on excessive devotion to Henrietta Maria. The author of *The Life and Death of King Charles* (1649), for example, criticized the deceased monarch for being "overpowred with the Inchantments of a Woman," and the first three annotations at the end of Charles' private correspondence in *The King's Cabinet Opened* (1645) focus attention on the "very pernicious consequences" of the queen's influence.[63] The anonymous commentator alleges that "the Kings Counsels are wholly managed by the Queen; though she be of the weaker sexe, borne an Alien, bred up in a contrary Religion, yet nothing great or small is transacted without her privity & consent."[64]

Surely the idea of curing unbridled passion, even when presented jokingly as in "A Remedie for Love," would have appealed to a seventeenth-century audience. Although cavaliers would presumably have disagreed with attacks by the king's critics on Henrietta Maria, Sidney's more basic depiction of passion as rebellion could have invited royalist readers to apply the poem to their contemporary predicament. In the context of the 1655 *Arcadia*, a "Remedie" for such destructive feelings would represent a way of resolving

---

[62] For other instances of this metaphor in *Arcadia*, see pp. 407, 632.
[63] *The Life and Death of King Charles* (London, 1649; Wing L2001), p. 214; *The King's Cabinet Opened* (London, 1645; Wing C2358), G2r.
[64] *The King's Cabinet Opened*, G2v.

England's recent turmoil, while the particular, wrong-headed solution of substituting Mopsa for the princesses might reflect the country's debasement since the monarchy had been overthrown. Whereas Sidney includes in the characters of Parthenia and Argalus a possible model for curing undisciplined passion, and he uses Strephon and Claius to suggest that even unrequited love need not be destructive, the poet of "Remedie" never looks beyond the self-consuming passion that Helen in the *Arcadia* embodies. Love in "Remedie" needs a cure because it leaves the poet "reft of sens" (line 31) and will, he predicts, ruin "good fortune quite" (line 24) – not unlike the fortunes of the king's defenders in the middle of the seventeenth century.

In 1655, as well as the successive editions of 1662 and 1674, "A Remedie for Love" enacts a process of restoration. It restores a poem that was allegedly missing from Sidney's text and, through the satire of Mopsa, restores a conservative social hierarchy. That the poet praises Mopsa as a "Sov'reign plaster" (line 26) indicates that she is, ironically, a potent curative and glances once again at the cavaliers' current crisis: the country's rebellion had been quelled, but only by turning to a fabricated ruler – a "Sov'reign plaster" – instead of a semi-divine king. In a world turned upside down after the revolution, the poem's ironic treatment of Mopsa, attributed to Sidney, offers royalist readers/writers a way of imagining things set right. But whereas Sidney's shepherds prescribe turning to "heavenly rules" (p. 408), the poet of "Remedie" instead responds to immoderate desire with cavalier bravado. He hides behind a sense of humor and the guise of an Elizabethan hero, out of fear, it seems, of losing control permanently. Through the lie of an omission he holds out hope that his heart, like Sidney's text – and perhaps even the country – can be remedied, "heal'd, and cur'd, and made as sound / As though I ne're had had a wound" (lines 35–36).

Another, more personal seventeenth-century verse, "An Imitation of Sir Philip Sidney's Encomium of Mopsa" (c. 1638), also focuses attention on Mopsa's character and, like "Remedie," borrows the *contreblazon* structure of the poem that Kalendar recites.[65] The "Imitation" tells the same joke about Mopsa (that is, "In Lowliness shee excells"), but the poet of this verse trusts his audience less than Sidney and the author of "Remedie." Comparing his lover's chastity to Venus' and her temperament to Medea's, he feels compelled to explain that Venus was not chaste, nor Medea mild. In the final couplet he also makes sure we understand that he has been

---

[65] Bodleian, MS. Eng. Poet. f. 27, pp. 99–101.

comparing Mopsa to "my Mrs Character, and if in / These lines her name you misse, 'tis faire Besse Griffin."

The effect of this verse, like "A Remedie for Love," resembles Mopsa's function in the *Arcadia*. The coarseness of both poems comparatively enhances Sidney's poetic accomplishments. Again and again in the romance Sidney himself had juxtaposed pairs of scenes and characters. Just as Dametas and Clinias' comic fight complements Argalus and Amphialus' heroic battle, or as Mopsa's unrefinement improves Pamela and Philoclea's grace and virtue, both "Imitation" and "Remedie" serve as comical contrasts. Preserved as an alleged omission by Sidney, however, "Remedie" alone lays further claim to Sidney as its actual author by mimicking his use of comic contrasts from the *Arcadia*'s style.

This punch line, that Sidney wrote the previously omitted "Remedie," also helps to establish the *Arcadia* as a royalist work. No longer just the grandfather of cavalier poetry, Sidney as of 1655 has himself become a cavalier. Whether Sidney would have actually approved of Charles I's actions must remain uncertain, nor can we know how many readers in 1655 would have accepted "A Remedie for Love" as a joke or real addendum. But the text is insistent, reprinting Sidney's name at the conclusion of "Remedie" (Iii5v), and the initial explanation, "Heretofore omitted in the Printed ARCADIA" (Iii4v), implies that the poem previously circulated in the *Arcadia*'s manuscript copies, a likely story given the romance's complex provenance. The distinction of print *versus* manuscript might also evoke a privileged audience of courtly readers, and, like the poem's precise allusions to the *Arcadia* and Ovid's *Remedia*, would reinforce the social hierarchy that its ironic praise of Mopsa implies.

Interestingly, no more seventeenth-century editions of *Arcadia* were produced after 1674 even though the genre of romance experienced an upsurge in popularity.[66] Readers began to prefer less expensive, more chivalric romances such as Emanuel Forde's *Parismus* and Richard Johnson's *Seven Champions of Christendom*. Perhaps with the restoration of monarchy, Sidney had become less politically viable; at least monarchists would have found the adroit use of Mopsa in "Remedie" less relevant. The anonymous poet concludes "Remedie" in 1655 with an image of personal honor that recalls both England's recent conflict and Sidney's death on the battlefield:

---

[66] Charles Mish, "Best Sellers in Seventeenth-Century Fiction," *The Papers of the Bibliographical Society of America* 47 (1953): 356–73. Studying readers' marginal annotations in the *Arcadia*'s successive editions, Peter Lindenbaum has observed that "as the seventeenth century wears on there seems to be less and less direct and serious engagement with the text, or at least less evidence of it." See Lindenbaum, "Sidney's *Arcadia* as Cultural Monument and Proto-Novel," p. 87.

Bee but my Second, and stand by,
(Mopsa) and I'le them both defie,
And all els of those gallant races,
Who wear infection in their faces:
For thy face (that Medusa's *shield)*
Will bring mee safe out of the field.
(lines 81–86)

In this final joke, the poet associates escaping love with escaping death. If Sidney had actually written these lines, he would be suggesting both that Mopsa could save his life and, as we will see with Ben Jonson in the next chapter, that he could achieve immortality through his poetic writings. The humor would stem from Sidney's aspiration to earn glory through lowly Mopsa instead of the *Arcadia's* more noble or at least more richly conceived characters.

Knowing that Sidney did not write "Remedie," however, we see that his immortality here depends on an unnamed "Second" who has written this fantasy of the author's survival and could stand for the many seventeenth-century readers who became writers to help preserve Sidney's work. These readers/writers resemble Mopsa-figures, improving not only the *Arcadia*, but also Sir Philip Sidney. Through the final artful allusion to Medusa, the anonymous poet pledges that Mopsa – and by extension such supplements – will protect Sidney's romance. Most obviously, Mopsa merits comparison to Medusa because both are hideous. But just as Medusa can turn onlookers to stone, both "Remedie" and Mopsa permanently memorialize Sidney and solidify his reputation for a contemporary audience. After Jason slew Medusa, he used her destructive countenance, according to some versions of the myth, to create or at least adorn Athena's aegis. Mopsa and this rough verse similarly help to protect and decorate Sidney as author. In a final ironic outcome worthy of the real Sidney, we can see that readers, such as the anonymous writer of "Remedie," did in fact help to bring Sidney "safe out of the field," re-calibrating the romance for seventeenth-century audiences, and, in the process, helping to preserve his body of work.

CHAPTER 3

Jonson's labors lost

For small erections may be finished by their first architect; grand ones,
true ones, ever leave the copestone to posterity. God keep me from
ever completing anything.
                                                    – Herman Melville[1]

In the preceding chapter we saw how a Renaissance reader could become
a respondent and use the pretense of omission to revise another writer's
work. In the case of "A Remedie for Love," the breadth of Sidney's *Arcadia*
made the anonymous poet's feigned omission more plausible: contemporary readers might believe that for such a long, unfinished work – one that
existed in so many manuscript and print versions – a new fragment actually
could have been discovered since the author's death almost a century earlier.

In this chapter, I examine an omission in one of Ben Jonson's poems
that also looks authorial. But whereas the anonymous poet of "A Remedie"
fabricated an Arcadian omission in an attempt to appropriate Sidney's
authority, Jonson, we will see, omitted part of his own "Epistle to Elizabeth
Countesse of Rutland" to establish himself as Sidney's poetic heir. Jonson's
incomplete verse epistle, addressed to Sidney's daughter, not only recalls
the unfinished form of *Arcadia*, but also, like that romance's seventeenth-
century editions, encourages readers to help commemorate the author.
Jonson may not explicitly invite "som other spirit to exercise his pen," as
does the note at the end of *Arcadia*, but the layout of the poem in Jonson's
1616 Folio invites active readers' participation by emphasizing that the poet
has removed some of the text.[2]

Jonson's specific omission comprises the epistle's final eight lines (see
figure 3). Recalling a time when verse "was once of more esteeme" (line 21),
the speaker initially bemoans the iniquity of his present age and looks
toward the day when those who have "done my *Muse* least grace, / Shall

---

[1] Herman Melville, *Moby-Dick, or The Whale* (New York, 1994), p. 142 (chap. 32).
[2] Sidney, *The Countess of Pembroke's Arcadia* (London, 1655; Wing S3768), Ttiv.

97

The Forreſt.   835

My gratefull ſoule, the ſubiect of her powers,
   I haue already vs'd ſome happy houres,
To her remembrance; which when time ſhall bring
   To curious light, to notes, I then ſhall ſing,
Will proue old ORPHEVS act no tale to be':
   For I ſhall moue ſtocks, ſtones, no leſſe then he.
Then all, that haue but done my *Muſe* leaſt grace,
   Shall thronging come, and boaſt the happy place
They hold in my ſtrange *poems,* which, as yet,
   Had not their forme touch'd by an Engliſh wit.
There like a rich, and golden *pyramede,*
   Borne vp by ſtatues, ſhall I reare your head,
Aboue your vnder carued ornaments,
   And ſhow, how, to the life, my ſoule preſents
Your forme impreſt there : not with tickling rimes,
   Or common places, filch'd, that take theſe times,
But high, and noble matter, ſuch as flies
   From braines entranc'd, and fill'd with extaſies;
Moodes, which the god-like SYDNEY oft did proue,
   And your braue friend, and mine ſo well did loue.
Who whereſoere he be . . . .
                 The reſt is loſt.

XIII.

Epiſtle.

To KATHERINE, LADY AVBIGNY:

'TIs growne almoſt a danger to ſpeake true
   Of any good minde, now : There are ſo few.
The bad, by number, are ſo fortified,
   As what th'haue loſt t'expect, they dare deride.
So both the prais'd, and praiſers ſuffer : Yet,
   For others ill, ought none their good forget.
I, therefore, who profeſſe my ſelfe in loue
   With euery vertue, whereſoere it moue,
And howſoeuer; as I am at fewd
   With ſinne and vice, though with a throne endew'd;
And, in this name, am giuen out dangerous
   By arts, and practiſe of the vicious,
Such as ſuſpect them ſelues, and thinke it fit
   For their owne cap'tall crimes, t'indite my wit;
I, that haue ſuffer'd this ; and, though forſooke
   Of *Fortune,* haue not alter'd yet my looke,

                           Or

Figure 3. End of Ben Jonson's "Epistle to Elizabeth Countesse of Rutland" in *The Workes of Benjamin Jonson* (1616), sig. Aaaa4r.

thronging come, and boast the happy place / They hold in my strange *poems*" (lines 79–81).[3] Helen of Troy was not uncommonly beautiful, the speaker explains, and "ACHILLES was not first, that valiant was" (line 51). They just had the best press agents. Their peers "lack'd the sacred pen" that "could give / Like life unto 'hem" (lines 56–57).

Jonson concludes the epistle by promising the Countess of Rutland the same abiding glory as these mythological figures:

> There like a rich, and golden *pyramede*,
>   Borne up by statues, shall I reare your head,
> Above your under carved ornaments,
>   And show, how, to the life, my soule presents
> Your forme imprest there: not with tickling rimes,
>   Or common places, filch'd, that take these times,
> But high, and noble matter, such as flies
>   From braines entranc'd, and fill'd with extasies;
> Moodes, which the god-like SYDNEY oft did prove,
>   And your brave friend, and mine so well did love.
> Who wheresoere he be . . . .
>
> *The rest is lost.*
> (lines 83–93)

Contrary to this sudden, editorial insertion, the "rest" of the epistle was not in fact "lost" but survives in two manuscript copies, Harley MS 4064 and Rawlinson poetry MS 31.[4] Here readers discover that the "brave friend" identified in line 92 represents the Countess's husband:

> Who, wheresoere he be, on what dear coast,
> Now thincking on you, though to England lost,
> For that firme grace he holdes in your regard,
> I, that am gratefull for him, have prepar'd
> This hasty sacrifice, wherein I reare
> A vow as new, and ominous as the yeare,
> Before his swift and circled race be run,
> My best of wishes, may you beare a sonne.[5]

---

[3] This and all subsequent references to *The Workes of Benjamin Jonson* (London, 1616; STC 14751) are taken from the copy held at the Harry Ransom Humanities Research Center at the University of Texas in Austin (Pforz 559). It collates 2°: ¶6A–Z⁶2A–2Z⁶3A–3Z⁶4A–4P⁶4Q⁴; 513 leaves. The "Epistle to Elizabeth Countesse of Rutland" is printed on sig. Aaaa3r–Aaaa4r; subsequent references to other poems by Jonson are also taken from this edition, unless otherwise indicated.

[4] It seems improbable that Jonson would have simply forgotten the poem's final lines in 1616. He admits in *Discoveries* that his memory "layes up more negligently" as he grows older "so that I receive mine owne (though frequently call'd for) as if it were new, and borrow'd." But Jonson also claims that he can still "repeate whole books that I have read, and *Poems*, of some selected friends, which I have lik'd to charge my memory with." See Herford and Simpson, 8: 578–79, lines 479–507.

[5] William Dinsmore Briggs, working from the Harley MS, first printed the missing text in "Recovered Lines of Ben Jonson," *Modern Language Note*s 29 (1914): 156–57. I am quoting the passage as it appears in Herford and Simpson, 8: 116. Anthony Miller, "Ben Jonson's 'Epistle to Elizabeth Countess of

Probably written in 1599, the first year of Elizabeth Sidney's marriage to Roger Manners, fifth Earl of Rutland, the poem in its restored form concludes with a traditional nuptial blessing.[6] Jonson's "best of wishes" is that the newlyweds will soon have a male heir, before "his" – perhaps the earl's; more likely, the year's – "swift and circled race be run."

Unfortunately, the Earl and Countess never had any children. In *Conversations with William Drummond*, Jonson was to observe, cryptically, that Elizabeth Sidney's husband "in effect . . . wanted the half of his. [*sic*] in his travells," and in a later epigram (*Underwood* 50) he praised the Countess for her discretion in living as "a widowed wife."[7] An elegy attributed to Francis Beaumont more candidly describes the couple's marriage as a "sacrament of misery," for the Countess had lived more "Like a betrothèd virgin than a wife" with a husband who "Could nothing change about thee but thy name."[8] Modern editors, beginning with C. H. Herford and Percy Simpson, have accordingly inferred that Jonson "tactfully cancelled" the last eight lines of his "Epistle to Elizabeth" because of the Earl's impotence: "the original conclusion would have excited derision in Court circles, apart from the pain it would have given the Countess."[9]

The omission of the poem's last lines hardly seems "tactful," however. The 1616 Folio does not just cancel the potentially offensive passage; it announces that part of the epistle is missing.[10] We know that for the publication of his *Workes* Jonson revised many of his plays and some of his

---

Rutland': A Recovered MS Reading and Its Critical Implications," *Philological Quarterly* 62 (1983): 525–30, discusses the differences between the two manuscript copies.

[6] For the possibility of a slightly later date of composition, see Joseph Loewenstein, "Printing and 'The Multitudinous Presse': The Contentious Texts of Jonson's Masques," *Ben Jonson's 1616 Folio*, ed. Jennifer Brady and W. H. Herendeen (Newark, 1991), p. 190, n. 17.

[7] Herford and Simpson, 1: 138, lines 220–22. In *Ben Jonson* (Oxford, 1985), p. 762, Ian Donaldson speculates that the full stop after "half of his" in *Conversations with William Drummond* probably indicates that a word or words had been suppressed in the manuscript. "A Epigram, To the honour'd – Countesse of –" is printed in the second folio edition of Jonson's works, sig. Gg3r–Gg3v. All citations of poems in this later book, *The Workes of Benjamin Jonson* (London, 1640; STC 14754), are taken from the copy held at the Harry Ransom Humanities Research Center at the University of Texas in Austin (Pforz 560).

[8] Francis Beaumont "An Elegy on the Death of the Virtuous Lady, Elizabeth Countess of Rutland," in *The Works of Beaumont and Fletcher*, ed. Alexander Dyce, 11 vols. (1843–46; New York, 1970), 11: 507–11.

[9] Herford and Simpson, 8: 10.

[10] Barbara L. DeStefano credits Jonson with taking seriously "his declared role as moral arbiter" because he refused to have printed in 1616 "the lines that are not true." DeStefano has overlooked, however, that Jonson could have fulfilled this role without claiming the epistle's final lines were "lost." In fact, the Folio's misleading declaration, "*The rest is lost*," suggests that Jonson was willing to have untrue statements printed when they suited his purposes. See DeStefano, "Ben Jonson's Folio Edition of His 'Epistle to Elizabeth Countess of Rutland' as Revealing Criteria of His Poetic Praise," *Concerning Poetry* 20 (1987): 11–17.

masques and poems – rewriting many of the dramatic texts substantially.[11]
Surely he could have amended his "Epistle to Elizabeth Countesse of
Rutland" so as to remove any hint of shame or scandal for the couple
or their families. At least he could have concluded the poem more neatly, if
somewhat abruptly, with the final couplet printed in the Folio, "Moodes,
which the god-like SYDNEY oft did prove, / And your brave friend, and
mine so well did love." Instead the poem is truncated in the middle of a
verse, the excision marked with eight full stops and a disingenuous explanation, *"The rest is lost."*

In this chapter I consider Jonson's motives for calling attention to the
poem's omitted passage and examine the implications of its shortened form
within the context of the 1616 Folio. As editor of his collected *Workes*, Jonson
anticipated the emergence of an autonomous author, arranging his volume's
individual texts as well as annotating, revising, and correcting early print
runs. The "Epistle to Elizabeth Countesse of Rutland" uniquely suggests
Jonson's ambivalence about such an enterprise. Building on the work of
Douglas Brooks, who has argued that the 1616 Folio reveals "a kind of
caesura in Jonson's authorship between theatre and court," I would suggest
that the book similarly preserves the shift in early modern England from a
courtly to a more professional mode of poetic writing.[12] As English literary
culture was changing from the older forms of manuscript and orality to print
transmission, Jonson's epistle looks forward and back, poised between the
court and printing house. By introducing the themes of error, omission, and
impotence, Jonson suggests his limitations as a poet but also, paradoxically,
asserts his authority, defending an author's primacy within the burgeoning
business of printed reproduction.

THE EPISTLE AND THE FOLIO

Probably the best known, incomplete Renaissance lyric remains John
Milton's "The Passion." First printed in his 1645 *Poems of Mr. John Milton,
both English and Latin,* "The Passion" concludes with a fuller, though similar
editorial insertion: *"This Subject the Author finding to be above the yeers he*

---

[11] See David L. Gants, "The Printing, Proofing and Press-Correction of Jonson's Folio *Workes*," in *Re-
Presenting Ben Jonson,* ed. Martin Butler (New York, 1999), pp. 39–58; Kevin J. Donovan, "Jonson's
Texts in the First Folio," *Ben Jonson's 1616 Folio,* pp. 23–37; and Herford and Simpson, 8: 7–10, 9:
13–84. Because no complete manuscript copy survives of *The Forest* as it was printed in 1616, we
cannot determine the extent that Jonson revised and/or oversaw the publication of these particular
poems.

[12] Douglas A. Brooks, *From Playhouse to Printing House: Drama and Authorship in Early Modern
England* (Cambridge, 2000), p. 111.

had, when he wrote it, and nothing satisfi'd with what was begun, left it unfinisht."[13] Milton or the book's publisher Humphrey Moseley may have included "The Passion" among the author's other minor poems so as to illustrate his poetic development and to help win over readers who only knew him from his controversial prose tracts. With "The Passion," Milton demonstrated his early intention to write an English vatic poem and, as one biographer has suggested, first let readers "see him . . . with his singing robes about him!"[14]

It is pleasing to speculate whether Moseley or Milton was specifically thinking of Jonson's "Epistle to Elizabeth" when they decided in 1645 to include an explanatory note with "The Passion," for both fragmented poems point to their respective authors' limitations: Milton found the subject of Christ's suffering to be beyond his years, and Jonson discovered over time the futility of his wish for the Countess and her husband. But that Milton's poem comes up short seems sincere and almost fits the tone set by the surviving stanzas. Early on we sense his lack of confidence as he stalls, trying to steel himself for such a daunting subject: "now to sorrow must I tune my song, / And set my Harpe to notes of saddest wo" (lines 8–9). He announces the subject of his poem (lines 10–25), describes the appropriate tone (lines 26–28), invokes Night as his Patroness (lines 29–33), and considers alternate expressions of sorrow (lines 34–56). The poem focuses on his trying to get started; the eight stanzas read like an extended drum roll. Jonson's epistle, in contrast, sounds confident, almost proud, as he addresses the Countess about the originality and potency of his writing. Comparing himself to Orpheus, the poet boasts, "I shall move stocks, stones, no lesse then he" (line 78), and, describing one of his contemporaries, he dismisses this mere "verser" as one who "doth me (though I not him) envy" (lines 68, 70). The inverted syntax, interrupted by a parenthetical aside, implies that the rival poet not only envies Jonson but also "doth" him – that is, tries to imitate Jonson's style.[15]

In this context, the omission of the final lines of Jonson's epistle seems to undercut his claims for poetic authority. Perhaps Jonson "allowed the

---

[13] *Poems of Mr. John Milton, both English and Latin, Compos'd at Several Times* (London, 1645; Wing M2160), sig. B2r. Subsequent quotations from "The Passion" are taken from this edition and cited by line number.

[14] William Riley Parker, *Milton: A Biography*, ed. Gordon Campbell, 2 vols. (1968; Oxford, 1996), p. 288. Moseley, a shrewd and enterprising Stationer, did not set forth Milton's 1645 *Poems* without taking some precautions. In addition to the volume's various commendatory notices celebrating the poet's abilities, he frames seventeen of the texts with terse, biographical tags stating Milton's age when he wrote a particular poem or – like the note at the end of "The Passion" – the circumstance surrounding the composition.

[15] See *OED* s.v. "do" B.I.4.

vatic role to carry him away," as Richard Newton suggests, and thus was admitting in retrospect that the subject of the Countess's offspring was beyond his powers.[16] The most Jonson could realistically offer Elizabeth Sidney was an opportunity to live forever in his writings. Whereas Milton in "The Passion" writes about the redemption purchased through Christ's suffering, Jonson's epistle presents a secular vision of the afterlife.[17] He claims that "the *Muse*, alone, can raise to heaven, / And, at her strong armes end, hold up, and even, / The soules, shee loves" (lines 41–43). He posits a kind of aesthetic Calvinist elect, for poetry, he emphasizes, will not save everyone: those "noble ignorants" who have "scorned verse" will not "find grace" (lines 28–30); "when they were borne, they di'd, / That had no *Muse* to make their fame abide" (lines 47–48).

We can trace Jonson's theme of "immortality through verse" – common among Renaissance poets – at least as far back as Ovid and Horace, the latter of whom Jonson specifically evokes in his simile comparing the Countess's image to a "rich, and golden *pyramede*" (line 83).[18] But given the epistle's bibliographic context in 1616, readers might have expected the poet to develop his poetic authority by alluding to the Folio. What better way for the Countess to outlast her peers than in such a handsome and imposing volume? Beginning with its engraved title page, *The Workes of Benjamin Jonson* announces itself as a lasting monument: it comprises 1,015 pages, including nine prefatory poems (¶3v–¶6v) and nine of Jonson's plays (A1r–Sss4v), each with a separate title page, dedication, and history of its publication and performance. The volume's 133 epigrams, published for the first time as a collection (Ttt1r–Zzz1v), also merit a separate title page and dedication (Sss5r, Sss6r–v), and some of the volume's masques have separate title pages along with the author's marginal notations (Bbbb1r–Qqqq4r).

---

[16] Richard C. Newton, "Jonson and the (Re-)Invention of the Book," in *Classic and Cavalier: Essays on Jonson and the Sons of Ben*, ed. Claude J. Summers and Ted-Larry Pebworth (Pittsburgh, 1982), pp. 31–55, this quotation, p. 54, n. 26.

[17] Both Milton and Jonson attribute their poetic accomplishments to divine inspiration. In "The Passion" Milton refers to Jerusalem, the seat of sacred poetry, as the place where "doth my soul . . . sit / In pensive trance, and anguish, and ecstatick fit" (lines 41–42), and Jonson, too, claims that "onely *Poets*, rapt with rage divine" can produce "high, and noble matter" (lines 63, 89).

[18] *Cf.* Horace, III.xxx: "*Exegi monumentum aere perennius / regalique situ pyramidum altius*" ("I have finished a monument more lasting than bronze and loftier than the Pyramids' royal pile"), in *The Odes and Epodes*, trans. C. E. Bennett (Cambridge, MA, 1968), pp. 278–79. See also Earl Miner, *The Cavalier Mode from Jonson to Cotton* (Princeton, 1971), pp. 143–44, and Ernst Robert Curtius, *European Literature and the Latin Middle Ages*, trans. Willard R. Trask (New York, 1953), pp. 476–77, which includes a summary list of classical allusions to "poetry as perpetuation."

While a few dramatists – including Jonson – had pursued the print publication of individual plays earlier in the century, Jonson's 1616 Folio helped to initiate a new way of looking at dramatic texts. His *Workes*, we need to remember, appeared sixteen years before Shakespeare's First Folio (1623; STC 22273), and more than thirty years before Francis Beaumont and John Fletcher's comparably sized collection, *Comedies and Tragedies* (1647; Wing B1581). The title's oft-noted seriousness – *The* Workes *of Benjamin Jonson* – sounds as far removed from the unruly crowds who enjoyed "plays" as it was from the spectacle that, Jonson believed, often marred "entertainments" at court.

The specific choice of printing Jonson's works in a folio format reflects, too, the growing authority granted authors during the seventeenth century. Because folios required both greater workmanship and more paper than was needed for books printed in smaller formats, they had traditionally been reserved for the period's most serious and important publications. Chapman's translations of the *Odyssey* and *Iliad*, for example, were published in folios (1609?, STC 13633; 1612?, STC 13634; 1615?, STC 13637), as were the King James Bible (1611; STC 2217) and the king's own collection, *The Workes of James, King of Great Britaine, France, and Ireland* (1616; STC 14344).[19] A brief survey of William Stansby's folio catalogue reveals mostly historical and philosophical texts. Before printing and publishing Jonson's volume, Stansby had worked on Richard Hooker's *Of the Lawes of Ecclesiasticall Politie* (1611; STC 13714), Walter Ralegh's *The History of the World* (1614; STC 20637), William Camden's first volume of his *Annales* (1615; STC 4496), and William Martyn's *The Historie, and Lives, or Twentie Kings of England* (1615; STC 17526).[20] These books, with their ample margins and generous layout, were both erudite and dignified – just what a poet/ dramatist like Jonson would have wanted to evoke in trying to establish his laureate status.

Nor could Jonson have ignored that England's most distinguished poets, Chaucer, Sidney, and Spenser, all had their works published in folios during the late sixteenth and early seventeenth centuries.[21] Some of these books' titles may have even helped Jonson to articulate his poetic

[19] Although King James' *Workes* was published the same year as Jonson's Folio, we do not know who influenced whom, nor which volume first went into production. See Brooks, *From Playhouse to Printing House*, p. 134.

[20] For a discussion of Stansby's reputation and output, see James K. Bracken, "Books from William Stansby's Printing House, and Jonson's Folio of 1616," *The Library*, 6th series 10 (1988): 19–29.

[21] Prior to 1616, folio editions of Chaucer's works were published in 1561, 1598, and 1602; of Sidney's works in 1605; and of Spenser's works in 1609 and 1611.

aspirations – the "Works of England's Arch-Poët, Edm. Spenser," for exam- ple, or "The Works of Our Ancient and learned English Poet, Geffrey Chaucer."[22] But, as evidence of the Renaissance author's increasing author- ity, these commemorative editions had been published posthumously, whereas Jonson in 1616 commissioned and directly participated in the pub- lication of his *Workes*. If we borrow his distinction from "To Penshurst," the folios of these other poets had been "built to envious show," but the author himself "dwells" in *The Workes of Benjamin Jonson* (lines 1, 102).

We may be surprised to discover, then, that Jonson does not address the Countess of Rutland's promised fame in terms of his Folio's esteem or permanence. Although the volume's first collection of verse, *The Epi- grammes*, begins with three poems that alternately address the reader, book, and bookseller, Jonson in his "Epistle to Elizabeth" seems disinterested in the material circumstances of his writing.[23] Readers could instead infer that he originally composed the epistle for scribal publication – perhaps a wedding present for the Countess, as he implies in the poem, or a gift given at the start of a new year.[24] Just as the textual apparatus included with Jonson's plays presents these works in the past tense, as if chronicling the author's past accomplishments, so the "Epistle to Elizabeth" repre- sents a cultural artifact, a glimpse into the world of the court that has been preserved in a snapshot. Jonson chose to have his manuscript poems printed, readers could infer, instead of producing new poems for the printed collection.

The editorial insertion at the end of the epistle enhances the sense of the Folio as historical record. By announcing that part of the poem has

---

[22] Spenser, *The Faerie Qveen* (London, 1611; STC 23084), π1r; and Chaucer, *Workes* (London, 1602; STC 5080), π1r.

[23] In "The Passion," by comparison, Milton dwells on the physical means of transmitting his words: he thinks "The leaves should all be black whereon I write, / And letters where my tears have washt a wannish white" (lines 34–35). Coming upon "that sad Sepulchral rock / That was the Casket of Heav'ns richest store" (lines 43–44), he appraises it as a potential writing surface: "on the softned Quarry would I score / My plaining vers as lively as before" (lines 46–47). In Jonson's first four epigrams, he seems to be addressing the particular collection entitled *The Epigrammes* rather than the Folio as a whole. Although *The Epigrammes* was licensed separately four years earlier and entered in the Stationers' *Register* by Jonson's bookseller, John Stepneth, on 15 May 1612, there are no surviving copies of a separate edition. These four poems are not, moreover, unique to the print culture of early modern England. Kathryn Anderson McEuen, *Classical Influence Upon the Tribe of Ben* (Cedar Rapids, IA, 1939), pp. 17, 65–66, describes the classical tradition that informs Jonson's opening epigrams.

[24] Sometimes authors put up the capital themselves to have their works printed; then they either personally circulated the edition or paid a bookseller to distribute it. Jonson could thus have distributed a separate printed edition of the epistle before its appearance in the 1616 Folio, but because no such copy survives, this possibility is less likely.

been lost, Jonson seems to privilege the original manuscript over the folio edition: he would rather have an incomplete poem printed than repair or restore the missing text. This staged gesture – like the epistle's opening attack on the "sway" (line 18) of "almightie gold" (line 2) – helps to identify Jonson as a court poet circulating his works in manuscript rather than a "verser" (line 68) writing for money. Indeed, throughout the 1616 *Workes*, as Joseph Loewenstein has observed, Jonson "presents himself as a man ambiguously engaged with the literary marketplace."[25] Although he collaborated in the Folio's production and was claiming through the book's format, layout, and dedications that his plays deserve serious attention, he did not entirely abandon the standard topos of the gentleman poet who disdains print. He asserts his seriousness and respectability as a poet in *The Epigrammes*, for example, by insisting that his bookseller not advertise the collection. Following Catullus, Horace, and Martial's classical precedent, Jonson would rather have his book's pages used as wrapping paper than appear to be a commercial writer who panders to his audience.[26] Even the epigraph on the Folio's title page reads "*neque, me vt miretur turba laboro: Contentus paucis lectoribus*" ("I do not labor so that the crowd might admire me, being content with few readers"). From the outset, Jonson establishes that he does not want to be popular and can be satisfied with a small, select audience.

This tension between patronage and the marketplace manifests itself most dramatically in the final lines of the "Epistle to Elizabeth Countesse of Rutland." On the one hand, Jonson wants to distance himself from the commercial implications of the printing trade and preserve the epistle as a personal document; on the other hand, he is producing a polished, updated edition of his works and cannot ignore the epistle's changing historical and material circumstances. The tension between these two forces ruptures the epistle's final lines, breaking off his now invalid wish for the Countess and her husband. If the complete poem had been printed in 1616, it would then have stood as a memorial to the Countess's fame and the poet's former optimism. Instead, the final lines are torn away in mid-verse, marring the epistle's 100-line perfection and symbolically suggesting Jonson's outrage over the Countess and Earl's plight.

---

[25] Joseph Loewenstein, "The Script in the Marketplace," *Representations* 12 (1985): 101–14, this quotation, p. 109. For more on Jonson's "deeply ambivalent attitude" toward the printing trade, see also Ian Donaldson, *Jonson's Magic Houses* (Oxford, 1997), pp. 198–215.

[26] Jonson wrote this particular epigram "To my Booke-Seller" in 1612, four years before the Folio's publication. For the sources of this classical gesture, see Donaldson, ed., *Ben Jonson*, pp. 647–48.

MERIT *VERSUS* BIRTHRIGHT

Before considering the implications of the poem's missing envoi, we need to remember that the Earl of Rutland had died in 1612, followed by his wife the Countess a few weeks later.[27] Contrary to the claims of editors such as Herford and Simpson, Jonson must have been more concerned in 1616 with preserving the couple's memory than hurting their feelings. Presumably, as Jonson implies in his later epigram to the Countess (*Underwood* 50), members of the court had heard rumors of the Earl's impotence.[28] Many of Jonson's readers would at least have known that the couple never had any children; a few may have been familiar with Jonson's original poem if it had circulated in manuscript. Although only this last group could have fully appreciated Jonson's motive for omitting the final passage, the poem's missing lines evoke the couple's absent heir. The statement "*The rest is lost*" implies not only that the remainder of the poem has been misplaced, but, more subtly, that the couple's final repose has been ruined.

When read outside of Jonson's 1616 Folio, the poem in its original, unabbreviated form ends with the possibility that the Countess "beare a sonne" (line 100) as another way for her to achieve abiding glory. This idea that parents after dying would live in their offspring was a commonly held belief in early modern England.[29] Compare several of Shakespeare's sonnets as he warns, "Die single and thine image dies with thee" and urges that "nothing 'gainst Time's scythe can make defense, / Save breed, to brave him when he takes thee hence."[30] Although Jonson initially claims that "It is the Muse, *alone*" that can make the Countess's "fame abide" (lines 41, 48; my emphasis), the epistle's original ending implies that her physical body could supplant, or at least supplement, the poet's literary corpus. According to Jonson's "best of wishes," if she "beare a sonne," part of her would survive into future generations. Similarly, in the next poem in the Folio, "Epistle. To Katherine, Lady Aubigny" (Aaaa4r–Aaaa5v), he suggests that Lady Aubigny's "blest wombe, made fruitfull from above" will "raise a noble stemme, to give the fame" to her family's "bloud" (lines 95, 97–98).

[27] According to *The Manuscripts of His Grace The Duke of Rutland*, 4 vols. (London, 1905), news of the Countess's death was reported on 12 August 1612 (4: 492).

[28] See "A Epigram, To the honour'd – Countesse of –" in the 1640 Folio, sig. Gg3r–Gg3v, especially lines 1–8.

[29] See Ralph A. Houlbrooke, *The English Family 1450–1700* (London, 1984), p. 127. Houlbrooke notes that aristocrats in particular might be pitied or, worse, criticized if they did not produce an heir.

[30] Shakespeare, *The Sonnets and Narrative Poems: The Complete Non-Dramatic Poetry*, ed. William Burto (New York, 1989). These quotations are taken from sonnets 3 and 12, respectively; see also sonnets 1, 2, 4, 6–11, 13, and 15–17.

Whether the Countess and her husband had a child must have especially concerned Jonson, not because of the Earl's lineage (his title passed on to his brother Francis, who became sixth earl of Rutland[31]), but because of the Countess's esteemed bloodline. As the only child of Sir Philip Sidney, she would determine if her father's genius continued into succeeding generations. In *Epigrammes* 79, "To Elizabeth Countesse of Rutland," Jonson had praised Elizabeth Sidney and her "noblest father" (line 2) while also quietly lamenting that

> the *destinies* decreed
>   . . .
> No male unto him: who could so exceed
> *Nature* they thought, in all, that he would faine.
>   (Uuu5v/lines 5–8)

In the subsequent "Epistle to Elizabeth," we sense Jonson's specific stake in the Countess's recent marriage as he compliments her poetic abilities. It would be a "sinne 'gainst your great fathers spirit," he tells her, if she did not inherit "His love unto the Muses," particularly because "his skill / Almost you have, or may have, when you will" (lines 31–34).[32] That he refers to her poetic "skill" as something to be achieved in the near future – when she "will" – suggests that she shows potential as a writer and that he is already thinking about future generations: if the Countess gives birth, she will soon have her father's talents embodied in a son. Throughout the poem Jonson uses words such as "birth" (line 26), "inherit" (line 32), "wombs" (line 46), "bred" (line 47), "borne" (line 47), and "borne up" (line 84); the words "beare" (line 97) and "reare" (line 100) from the excised final lines also occur earlier in the poem (lines 8, 18, 84). Moreover, by incorporating the Countess (along with "Lucy the bright") into "LUCINA's traine" (line 66), Jonson both allies the Countess with Queen Elizabeth as virgin goddess, and, through Lucina's specific role as the goddess of childbirth, hints at his forthcoming "best of wishes" for the newly married bride.

Jonson is conflating poetic and biological creation: he grants the Countess fame by promising to "reare" (line 84) her in his poems and use his "sacred pen" (line 56) to give birth – "give / Like life" (lines 56–57) – to her enduring image. Rather than resort to "tickling rimes, / Or common places" (lines 87–88), he will create her out of the more physiologically

---

[31] See *The Dictionary of National Biography*, ed. Leslie Stephen and Sidney Lee (1917; London, 1937–38), 12: 940–41.

[32] To Drummond, Jonson more emphatically pronounced that "The Countess of Rutland was nothing inferior to her Father S. P. Sidney in Poesie." See Herford and Simpson, 1: 138, lines 213–14.

suggestive "high, and noble matter, such as flies / From braines entranc'd, and fill'd with extasies" (lines 89–90). This latter image not only suggests the classical idea of divine poetic frenzy but also evokes contemporary theories of sexual generation.[33] Some early modern writers continued to attribute the production of male seed – "high, and noble matter" – to the brain.[34] In the conclusion of the *Timaeus*, Plato had described soul-bearing "seed" as a product of the "condensed marrow which comes from the head down by the neck and along the spine," and as late as the middle of the eighteenth century, S. A. D. Tissot, writing against onanism, endorses the findings of an anonymous "celebrated physician" who "pointed out the passages by which the brain is conveyed to the testicles."[35] When Jonson pledges to "show, how, to the life, my soule presents / Your forme imprest there" (lines 86–87), he specifically appropriates Aristotle's still current rhetoric from *De generatione animalium*: a child attains its form from the father's life-giving spirit. Whereas Aristotle in his treatise compares generation to artistry, Jonson is reversing the analogy's direction, describing his poetry in terms of sexual reproduction.[36]

The poet thus casts himself as the Countess's parent, offering her life through his verse.[37] He has already allied himself with Sir Philip Sidney by publishing his Folio *Workes* and, in the epistle, by comparing his own poetic inspiration to the "Moodes, which the god-like SYDNEY oft did prove" (line 91). Now, through this poem's imagery and diction, Jonson's poetic abilities allow him to take over Sidney's role as father. In appropriating

[33] For the theory of a poet's "divine frenzy," see Plato, *Phaedrus*, in vol. 1, *Plato*, trans. Harold North Fowler, 12 vols. (Cambridge, MA, 1982), 244a–245c. See also Curtius, *European Literature and the Latin Middle Ages*, pp. 474–75.

[34] For a discussion of the origin and development of this theory, see Anthony Preus, "Galen's Criticism of Aristotle's Conception Theory," *Journal of the History of Biology* 10.1 (1977): 65–85. Harold Love and Margreta de Grazia discuss sexualized metaphors of writing and printing. See Love, *Scribal Publication in Seventeenth-Century England* (Oxford, 1993), pp. 148–53; and de Grazia, "Imprints: Shakespeare, Gutenberg, Descartes," in *Alternative Shakespeares, Vol. 2*, ed. Terence Hawkes (London, 1996), pp. 63–94.

[35] Plato, *Timaeus*, in vol. 7, *Plato*, trans. R. G. Bury, 90e–91d; S. A. D. Tissot, *Onanism*, ed. Randolph Trumbach, in *Marriage, Sex, and the Family in England 1660–1800*, Series 13 (New York, 1985), pp. 50 ff.

[36] Aristotle, *De generatione animalium*, trans. A. L. Peck (Cambridge, MA, 1953), 730a25–730b30. Works by seventeenth-century physicians such as William Harvey and Nathaniel Highmore freely borrowed Aristotle's analogy comparing the processes of biological and artistic creation. Whereas Highmore, following Aristotle, compared the male seed to the artist, Harvey exalted the status of the woman's womb by comparing its power of conception to an artist's brain. See William Harvey, *Anatomical Exercitations Concerning the Generation of Living Creatures* (London, 1653; Wing H1085), and Nathaniel Highmore, *The History of Generation* (London, 1651; Wing H1969).

[37] As Raphael Falco observes, "Like few others in the Elizabethan period, the Sidney family lends itself to such a conflation of poetry and blood." See Falco, *Conceived Presences: Literary Genealogy in Renaissance England* (Amherst, 1994), p. 131.

"Sidney's poetic authority," as Don Wayne observes, Jonson creates a politics of intellectual merit that is, ironically, "antithetical to the court society Jonson had to serve."[38] But because Jonson simultaneously appropriates Sidney's parental authority, he also reinforces the values of court society where birthright matters more than merit. He concludes the original epistle by affirming the importance of heredity and predicting that the Countess will have a son.

Jonson is again relying on his power as a poet, however, to ensure the Countess's future, and thus even this, the poem's most traditional gesture, is qualified by his self-assertiveness. For Sidney's bloodline to endure requires the intervention of an author. "Onley *Poets*, rapt with rage divine," Jonson explains, can make the Countess "shine" brightly enough to fit into the starry train of the goddess of childbirth (lines 63–64). The epistle's envoi, missing from the 1616 Folio, accordingly sounds more incantatory than wishful: "Before his swift and circled race be run," Jonson begins prophetically, "may you beare a sonne" (lines 99–100). He raises this "ominous" "vow" through a "hasty sacrifice" (lines 97–98) – much like in the Folio's next poem, the "Epistle. To Katherine," where Jonson calls himself a "priest" of the Muses (line 101) and confidently foresees Lady Aubigny's "ripe and timely issue" (line 104). Jonson's "vow" at the end of his poem to the Countess of Rutland represents more than his earnest desire; according to another meaning of this word, he is making a solemn promise to perform an act in return for her favor.

Once we recognize that the Countess's promised fame is associated with the poem's allusions to birthing, Jonson's dilemma in the Folio becomes more understandable. How could he have revised the epistle to fit the new situational context of 1616 since, as James Garrison has observed, the concluding vow is "integral" to the "total meaning"?[39] Readers finish the poem, if not anticipating the poet's specific "best of wishes" for the Countess, at least expecting a gesture that unites the themes of birthing, merit, and immortality. Because the last lines printed in the Folio cryptically introduce the Countess's husband – her "brave friend" (line 92) – active, contemporary readers may have even suspected that the poet intended to address the couple's marriage in the passage that has allegedly been "lost."

[38] Don E. Wayne, "Jonson's Sidney: Legacy and Legitimation in *The Forest*," *Sir Philip Sidney's Achievements*, ed. M. J. B. Allen, Dominic Baker-Smith, Arthur F. Kinney, and Margaret M. Sullivan (New York, 1990), pp. 227–50, this quotation, p. 232.

[39] James D. Garrison, "Time and Value in Jonson's 'Epistle to Elizabeth Countesse of Rutland,'" *Concerning Poetry* 8.2 (1975): 53–58, this quotation, p. 57. While I agree with Professor Garrison's argument for the envoi's importance, I do not accept his conclusion that modern editions should, therefore, silently re-attach the final lines of the epistle.

The subsequent poems in *The Forest*, moreover, call attention to the theme of children and inheritance.[40] Whereas the two surviving manuscripts that contain the complete version of the "Epistle to Elizabeth" include four seemingly unrelated poems from *The Forest* – "To Sir Robert Wroth," "Song. To Celia," "To the Same," and "To Sicknesse" – the Folio has the "Epistle to Elizabeth" strategically grouped with verses that allude to its missing envoi.[41] Most notably, the next "Epistle. To Katherine," as we have seen, celebrates Lady Aubigny for her "blest wombe" and the "burthen which you goe withall" (lines 95, 103). The following "Ode to Sir William Sydney, on His Birthday" (Aaaa5v–Aaaa6r) also reminds readers of the Rutlands' absent son by honoring the heir of Sir Philip Sidney's brother. "Your blood / So good / And great" (lines 33–35), Jonson emphasizes, noting that great things are expected from William Sidney because of "your name, whose sonne, / Whose nephew, whose grand-child you are" (lines 41–42).[42] Even "To Penshurst" (Zzz2r–Zzz3r), written about the Sidney family's home, ironically calls to mind the Countess and Earl's missing heir. Complimenting the lord and lady's chaste love, Jonson concludes the poem by again looking toward the future: "His children thy great lord may call his owne: / A fortune, in this age, but rarely knowne" (lines 91–92).

While the ellipsis and editorial insertion printed in the 1616 Folio announce that something has been removed from the "Epistle to Elizabeth," the collection's intertextual design implies what the missing passage might have said. The uncertain tone of the truncated final line – "Who wheresoere he be. . . . . . ." (line 93) – suggests the truncated line of Sir Philip Sidney's family and hints at the uncertain future of Sidney's poetic inheritance. The omitted verse also illustrates Jonson's dependence on his patrons: the poet can distance himself from the marketplace, but only by reinforcing his subservience to his subjects. As the epistle's envoi suggests, Jonson wanted to think that he could control the Countess by granting her immortality

[40] We could also trace the more general theme of absence or "omission" in *The Forest*'s other poems, such as "Why I Write Not of Love" or "To the World. A Farewell for a Gentle-woman, Vertuous and Noble." For a discussion of how Jonson structures *The Forest*, see Alastair Fowler, "The Silva Tradition in Jonson's *The Forest*," in *Poetic Traditions of the English Renaissance*, ed. Maynard Mack and George de Forest Lord (New Haven, 1982), pp. 163–80, and Jonathan Z. Kamholtz, "Ben Jonson's Green World: Structure and Imaginative Unity in *The Forest*," *Studies in Philology* 78.2 (1981): 170–93.

[41] The two manuscripts, Harley MS 4064 and Rawlinson poetry MS 31, are held in the British Library and Bodleian Library, respectively. They are briefly described in Herford and Simpson, 9: 8.

[42] Don E. Wayne has described this ode to William Sidney as the "key to the design" of *The Forest* because it "carries resonances of the earlier poems and stands as something of a commentary on them." See Wayne, "Jonson's Sidney," p. 235.

in his verse and, more boldly, by granting her an heir. The absence of the epistle's final lines reminds us that the poet had to revise his works to suit his patrons' lives and characters. When his subjects failed to live up to his encomiums – as did, most famously, the "worthlesse lord" in *Epigrammes* 65 "To My Muse" (Vuu3v) – Jonson's poetry threatened to lose some of its value. We can only wonder what he would have done to the next poem in the Folio, his "Epistle. To Katherine," if after he promised Lady Aubigny a successful delivery, she had suffered complications or had a miscarriage.

Paradoxically, though, by calling attention to his poem's impermanence and incompletion, Jonson also reinforces his poetic authority. Omitting the possibility that the Countess "beare a sonne," he removes the temporal solution to her mortality and points up his role as provider of eternal glory: Elizabeth Sidney needed Ben Jonson's "sacred pen" (line 56) for her "forme" (line 87) to survive. The potent author has not just appropriated Sir Philip Sidney's authority; he has replaced the Countess's impotent husband. With the omission of the poem's final lines, "[i]t is the Muse, *alone*," as Jonson had predicted, that can make the Countess's "fame abide" (lines 41, 48; my emphasis). Aristocratic inheritance has failed, and she must now depend on the poet's ability – and, by extension, his 1616 Folio – rather than relying on her bloodline.

In "To Penshurst," poetic merit similarly supersedes birthright as Jonson usurps the lord's position: the poet first hopes that what "is his Lordships shall be also mine" (line 64) and later more audaciously imagines that Penshurst "wert mine, or I raign'd here" (line 74). By removing the final lines of the "Epistle to Elizabeth," Jonson again casts himself as Sidney's inheritor. Deleting the poem's envoi enacts the "hasty sacrifice" that Jonson had promised to perform for the Countess; in 1616 he forfeits the epistle's final lines so as to fulfill the omitted "vow" he made to her. Despite the ineffectiveness of the Countess's "brave friend," she has found an heir in Ben Jonson. He will not only give her life in his poems and his book; he will also carry on her father's poetic tradition.

THE REST IS LOST

Published with such a conspicuous omission in 1616, the "Epistle to Elizabeth" is unique among the poems included in Jonson's first Folio. It is not, however, the only incomplete poem of Jonson's that has been printed, nor the only work of his that has been "lost." In the 1640 Folio, for example, Jonson or his executor, Sir Kenelm Digby, left out parts of *Underwood* 20 "A Satirical Shrub" and *Underwood* 58 "Epigram, to my Book-seller." In the former poem, a missing couplet is marked with the editorial insertion "*Here something is wanting*," followed by two rows of 28 full stops each (Cc3v).[43] In the latter poem, brackets are used to indicate that a single, probably obscene word is missing: "Like a rung Beare, or Swine: grunting out wit / As if that part lay for a [ ] most fit!" (Hh1v/lines 11–12). Similarly, the title to *Underwood* 50 suppresses the name of the Countess of Rutland; instead, the title reads discretely, "A Epigram, To the honour'd – Countesse of –" (Gg3r).

The Underwood also contains *Eupheme*, Jonson's fragmentary, ten-poem eulogy to Digby's late wife, Venetia. Although the layout announces the titles of all ten pieces (Ll3r), poems 5–8 and 10 are absent. After the fourth piece, "The Mind," appears the explanation that

A whole quaternion in the middle of this Poem is lost, containing entirely the three next pieces of it, and all of the fourth (which in the order of the whole, is the eighth) excepting the very end: which at the top of the next quaternion goeth on thus. (Mm1v)

Then follows a prose paragraph signed "*B.I.*" in which the poet introduces his "last Legacie of Counsell" to Lady Digby's three sons and instructs the eldest to "read it to your Brethren" once he arrives "at yeares of mature Understanding." The subsequent poem "To Kenelme, John, George" advises the three boys not to rely on their titles, but to cultivate the virtue – which "alone, is true Nobilitie" (line 20) – that they inherited from their father.

The omission from *Eupheme*'s second poem, "The Song of Her Descent," most closely resembles the imperfect condition of the "Epistle to Elizabeth Countesse of Rutland":

> *And tell thou, ALDE-LEGH, None can tell more true*
> *Thy Neeces line, then thou that gav'st thy Name*
> *Into the Kindred, whence thy* Adam *drew*
> *Meschines honour with the* Cestrian *fame*
> *Of the first* Lupus, *to the Familie*
> *By* Ranulph ————

The rest of this Song is lost. (Ll4r/lines 13–18)

Although we ultimately do not know the provenance of all these omissions in the 1640 Folio, the smaller type face used for such annotations

---

[43] Herford and Simpson (11: 60) note that the last eight lines are a separate poem in MS Ashmole 38 and appear under the title "Lord Buckhursts Rodomandado upon his Mistris" in British Library, Add. MS 18220, f. 103.

suggests that we are encountering a different voice than the author's. Digby may have chosen to suppress parts of certain poems, or he may have been recording which poems Jonson himself had left unfinished. The incomplete tragedy, *Mortimer His Fall*, for example, was apparently interrupted by the author's death. Instead of announcing in the 1640 Folio that part of the play was "lost," Digby includes the fuller explanation, "Hee dy'd, and left it unfinished" (Qq4v).[44]

But while all the editorial asides included in the 1640 edition sound plausible – Jonson had died during its assembly, and Digby was piecing together *The Underwood* from the poet's manuscripts – the second Folio's various omissions also raise the question of Jonson's carelessness. If the poet believed that his subjects could live forever through his "strange *poems*" (line 81), would he not have taken better care of his writings? Based on Jonson's deception in his "Epistle to Elizabeth Countesse of Rutland," we at least ought to hesitate before accepting at face value similar claims about his other works. Had Digby in 1640 been genuinely unable to track down all of Jonson's complete texts? If so, had Jonson himself wanted to suppress some of them? Manifested in these omissions is perhaps the contradictory impulse that prompted Jonson to produce the physically imposing printed Folio in 1616 and yet identify himself as a court poet, sharing his verse in manuscript: Jonson's incomplete poems stake his claim for immortality through verse but imply through their omissions that his poetry is transitory and temporal. This near paradox, as Richard Helgerson has noted, consistently characterizes Jonson's literary ambitions.[45] Throughout Jonson's career, first as dramatist, then as court poet, he established his identity in opposition to the genres in which he worked, to the patronage system that he pursued, and, late in life as his health declined, to his own physicality. In 1616 and again in 1640, we glimpse the poet in opposition to the physical means of textual production. Although the printing trade guaranteed the accurate preservation of multiple copies of an author's work, Jonson ironically preserved fragments like the "Epistle to Elizabeth Countesse of Rutland." To understand fully Jonson's complete *Workes*, Renaissance readers had to proceed actively, logically filling in the poems' blanks and/or looking for the finished texts in manuscript.

[44] According to the catalogue of the Pforzheimer Collection, some copies of the 1640 Folio contain on this page the briefer editorial note, "Left unfinished." The other incomplete play included in 1640, *The Sad Shepherd*, concludes (after two and a half acts) with the potentially misleading statement, "*The End.*" (V4r). Herford and Simpson recommend that this latter note should be "taken to indicate that this was all [of the text] that, so far as any one knew, had ever existed" (2: 214).
[45] Richard Helgerson, *Self-Crowned Laureates* (Berkeley, 1983), pp. 101–84.

That three of Jonson's incomplete poems – the "Epistle to Elizabeth," "To Kenelme, John, George," and "The Song of Her Descent" – focus attention on the theme of inheritance raises the specific possibility that Jonson, consciously or unconsciously, was concerned about the prospect of not leaving behind a successor. Certainly when Jonson first wrote his "Epistle to Elizabeth" he could not have offered his final wish for the Countess without thinking about his own children. Jonson's second son, Joseph, was baptized in December 1599, around the time of the Countess's marriage. When Jonson's Folio was going to press, this association may have proven too painful. The Countess and her husband had died without issue during the interim, and Jonson had probably buried all of his legitimate children, Benjamin (age four and a half), Joseph (age three), and Mary (age six months).[46]

At least one of the poems in Jonson's 1640 Folio seems to contain a feigned omission like the one in his epistle to the Countess of Rutland. The title to *Underwood* 25 explains that "An Ode to James, Earle of Desmond" was "Writ in Queene Elizabeths time, since lost, and recovered" (Dd1r). While it is possible that Jonson, during the forty years between composition and publication, actually mislaid this poem, such a loss would not deserve notice in the poem's title, even if Digby or Jonson wanted to emphasize that the ode was one of the few poems in *The Underwood* written before 1616. More likely, "lost" here signifies that the author chose to suppress the ode because it subtly critiques Queen Elizabeth for the imprisonment of James Fitzgerald. If published when it was originally "Writ in Queene Elizabeths time," Jonson's "Ode to James" would have also been an unwelcome reminder of Elizabeth's failed scheme to put down the rebellion in Ireland by having Fitzgerald restored as Earl of Desmond.

For Jonson, then, a loss could represent a way of gaining something – in the case of "An Ode to James," perhaps political security; with the "Epistle to Elizabeth," the goodwill of the Rutland family and a more nuanced meditation on his own poetic authority. Throughout his career, Jonson had a habit of losing some of his writings, sometimes fortuitously, such as *The Isle of Dogs*, a "very seditious and sclandrous" satire, according to the Queen's Privy Council, for which Jonson was briefly imprisoned.[47] The poet's claim to Drummond that "half of his comedies were not in Print" has prompted Ian Donaldson to wonder whether "it was entirely through

---

[46] As David Riggs observes, we have no evidence that Joseph Jonson survived past the year 1603. See Riggs, *Ben Jonson: A Life* (Cambridge, MA, 1989), pp. 96–97.

[47] Riggs, *Ben Jonson*, p. 76. On Jonson's various lost texts, see William Dinsmore Briggs, "Studies in Ben Jonson, IV: Notes on the Canon of Jonson's Minor Pieces," *Anglia* 39 (1916): 219–52.

authorial decision or partly through accident" that Jonson misplaced some of his dramatic works.[48]

In *Underwood* 43 "An Execration Upon Vulcan" (Ff1r–Ff3v), the poet catalogues and mourns his various writings lost in 1623 when his library caught fire. Jonson mockingly chastises Vulcan, "Thou Executioner" (line 47), for his "Greedie flame" that did "devoure / So many my Yeares-labours in an houre" (lines 3–4). He claims to have lost "parcels of a play" (line 43); his translation of Horace's *Ars poetica* (lines 89–91); a grammar (lines 91–93); a "journey into *Scotland* song" (line 94); part of a translation of the Latin romance *Argenis* (lines 95–97); a "storie there / Of our fift *Henry*, eight of his nine yeare" (lines 97–98); and "twice-twelve-yeares stor'd up humanitie, / With humble Gleanings in Divinitie" (lines 101–2).

The poet's former friend, George Chapman, first raised the intriguing possibility that Jonson might have been exaggerating or lying about the extent of his losses:

> Thow doest things backwards, are men thought to knowe
> Mastries in th'arts with saying thay doe soe,
> And criing fire out In a dreame to kings.
> Burne things unborne, and that way generate things?
>
> (lines 117–20)[49]

Chapman bore considerable ill will toward Jonson, and we know that Jonson had in fact written or would ultimately compose at least some of these works. His translation of *Argenis*, for example, was entered in the Stationers' *Register* on 2 October 1623, prior to the fire, and two versions of his translation of *Ars poetica* were published posthumously in 1640.[50] Nevertheless, in light of Jonson's surviving fragmentary publications, we can appreciate the spirit, if not the letter, of Chapman's "Invective": its final lines are shrewdly omitted, and in their place we find an ellipsis with the Jonson-like disclaimer, "More then this never came to my / hands, but lost in his sickenes" (lines 198–99).[51]

In the particular case of Jonson's "Epistle to Elizabeth Countesse of Rutland," the omission of the poem's final lines is at once deferential, self-assertive, and provocatively ambiguous. The poet teases readers with things

[48] Herford and Simpson, I: 143, line 393; Donaldson, *Jonson's Magic Houses*, p. 215, n.32.
[49] *The Poems of George Chapman*, ed. Phyllis Brooks Bartlett (New York, 1962), pp. 374–78.
[50] See Herford and Simpson, II: 406–12, and Riggs, *Ben Jonson*, pp. 288–89.
[51] Bartlett's edition implies that Chapman wrote this final disclaimer, but, according to Arthur F. Marotti, the final lines were added by the manuscript's compiler, Nicholas Burghe (Bodleian Library MS Ashmole 38, p. 18). See Marotti, *Manuscript, Print, and the English Renaissance Lyric* (Ithaca, NY, 1995), p. 14.

unsaid and demonstrates his ability to manipulate the process of textual production. Jonson seems to have heeded his own advice to the Countess: he knew "there were brave men" whose names had been forgotten because they "lack'd the sacred pen" (lines 53, 56), and he consciously was trying to guarantee his own lasting reputation.

But in describing an age when "gold beares all this sway" (line 18) and a common "verser" is held up as a "*Poet*, in the court account" (lines 68–69), Jonson also apparently had little confidence in contemporary readers' judgments. He attempted to safeguard his authority by allying himself with "the god-like S Y D N E Y" (line 91) and by collaborating with William Stansby on the 1616 Folio. Neither tactic was foolproof: Sidney's fame could eclipse his respondent's, as we saw in the previous chapter with "A Remedie for Love." And while the elaborate presentation of Jonson's Folio *Workes* enhanced the author's status, it also transferred new authority to Jonson's audience. Not only could unseen readers interpret and appropriate his writings; owners of such an imposing and expensive volume could also exhibit it as a symbol of their – not Jonson's – status and learning.

Announcing that "*The rest is lost*" at the end of the "Epistle to Elizabeth" represents another way that Jonson tried to assert his authority in 1616. He formally marks the end of Sidney's bloodline and gently undermines the material process of printed production. He kicks away two of the chairs he has been standing on to create himself. As the seventeenth-century book trade threatened to demote authors to publishers' employees; as his patrons threatened to subvert his poems by failing to live up to his encomiums – Jonson reminds readers that he still wielded the ultimate control: the choice to circulate or suppress his writings.

Interestingly, no contemporary readers, to my knowledge, jotted in the book's margin their own final verses for Jonson's "Epistle to Elizabeth," nor did his other "lost" or incomplete works benefit from the kind of collaborative interventions that buoyed Sidney's reputation through much of the seventeenth century. Still, we ought not to assume a straightforward progression, from a social model of authorship (as associated with Sidney's works) to a more autonomous model (as characterizing Jonson's). That new sequels to Sidney's *Arcadia* continued to appear decades after Jonson's 1616 *Workes* belies any such linear narrative, and Jonson's poetic authority, like Sidney's, was augmented by active, contemporary readers who emulated his style and/or wrote their own response poems. A comparison of the omissions in Sidney's and Jonson's respective publications reveals instead a gradual development within the seventeenth-century book trade. As authors gained new authority, they could exert more practical influence over the material process of production. Readers' interpretive activity may have accordingly changed but it did not diminish. Readers intervened in Sidney's *Arcadia* through the omissions that they discovered – and created – in his text; they could participate in Jonson's Folio because his authorial presence gave them license to find potential meaning in even his poems' silences.

CHAPTER 4

The incomplete Poems *of John Donne*

When thou hast done, thou hast not done.
– John Donne[1]

Unlike Jonson, John Donne did not create deliberate omissions in his publications, much less use them to perpetrate textual deceptions (so far as we know). Instead, Donne, like Sidney, benefited posthumously from the omissions readers found in some of his poems. In Donne's case, his printer and publisher used blank spaces in *Poems, By J. D.* (1633) as part of a larger strategy to create an intimate text, evoking a manuscript miscellany, while suggesting at the same time that they have produced a definitive, collected edition.[2] Whether a shrewd attempt to please all possible readers, or a compromise made at the printing house, the book's bifocal perspective allows readers to see the author as both aloof and personal, directly involved though already deceased.

As the first printed edition of Donne's collected verse, published two years after his death, *Poems, By J. D.* is discussed today mostly in relation to the second edition's apparently more intentional design.[3] In the later book, published in 1635, the editors separated Donne's amorous verse from his religious poetry, disingenuously imposing a narrative structure: the author improves from a youthful rake to Dr. Donne, Dean of St. Paul's. In this chapter, I contend that the first edition possesses an equally provocative organization.[4] While Ted-Larry Pebworth and Ernest Sullivan have demonstrated that the 1633 *Poems* does not deserve its "anointed status"

---

[1] John Donne, "A Hymn to God the Father," in *John Donne: The Complete English Poems*, ed. A. J. Smith (London, 1996), p. 349 (line 11).

[2] In this chapter and throughout the book I use the term "publisher" to designate the person who put up the capital for a text's printing and distribution.

[3] See, for example, Catherine J. Creswell, "Giving a Face to an Author: Reading Donne's Portraits and the 1635 Edition," *Texas Studies in Literature and Language* 37.1 (1995): 1–15.

[4] All references to the 1633 text are taken from the copy of *Poems, By J. D.* (London, 1633; STC 7045) held at the Harry Ransom Humanities Research Center at the University of Texas in Austin (Pforz 296). I have also consulted the copy held in the British Library, London, shelfmark Ashley

as the preferred copy-text of modern editors, I would suggest that the collection nevertheless provides new insight into its individual texts as well as Donne's contemporary authority.[5] As Leah Marcus has observed, "the printer and publisher play a striking part" in creating the volume's "strong aura of authorial presence."[6] I want to pursue how the book's various omissions invite readers to participate in that aura as well. The author's presence – the impression that Donne oversaw this collection and was communicating directly with readers – emerged from a collaborative process that ironically required his absence or "omission" from the material production. The volume's other omissions, in apparently unfinished and partially censored poems, paradoxically reinforce Donne's authorial presence while highlighting the demands put on early modern readers. By examining these incomplete works, we see how Donne's collection, like Sidney's *Arcadia* and Jonson's 1616 Folio, represents a transitional volume. It anticipates a notion of autonomous authorship while still embodying the interactive practices of Renaissance reading.

THE CASE OF THE MISSING POET

That the printer Miles Flesher addresses the 1633 *Poems* to "The Understanders" – rather than the "*Readers*" – signals a crucial distinction at the start of the book (πA1r).[7] "Understander" during Donne's time could describe not only "one who has knowledge or comprehension," but also a person who feels sympathy or is accepting.[8] As Thomas Dekker explains in *A Strange Horse-Race* (1613),

> *Readers . . . are not* Lectores, *but* Lictores, *they whip Bookes (as* Dionysius *did boyes) whereas to* Vnderstanders, *our* libri, *which we bring forth, are our* Liberi *(the children of our braine) and at such hands are as gently entreated, as at their parents.*[9]

3082(2). The book consists of 210 leaves and collates 4°: A⁴ πA²B–Fff⁴ [$3 signed (-A1, -A2)]. In the Ransom Center's copy, the inserted pages containing the printer's preface and John Marriot's poem (πA1r–πA2v) occur after Donne's epistle (A3r–A4r, verso blank). In other copies, such as the one I examined at the British Library, the insert follows immediately after the title page (A2r, verso blank). All quotations of Donne's poetry not included in the 1633 *Poems* are taken from *John Donne: The Complete English Poems*, ed. A. J. Smith.

5 Ted-Larry Pebworth, "Manuscript Poems and Print Assumptions: Donne and His Modern Editors," *John Donne Journal* 3 (1984): 1–21; and Ernest W. Sullivan, II, "1633 Vndone," *Text* 7 (1994): 297–306, this quotation, p. 301.

6 Leah S. Marcus, *Unediting the Renaissance: Shakespeare, Marlowe, Milton* (London, 1996), pp. 193, 198.

7 Although "The Printer to the Understanders" is not signed by Flesher, I describe him as its author because he printed the 1633 *Poems*. Other critics have attributed this preface to *Poems*' publisher, the bookseller John Marriot.

8 Only this first definition appears in the *OED*, along with "understander" meaning a theatre-goer who stands on the ground during a play.

9 Thomas Dekker, *A Strange Horse-Race* (London, 1613; STC 6528), A3r.

Here Dekker's distinction between "Readers" and "Understanders" hinges on an audience's disposition more than its intellectual ability; he is contrasting "whip" with "gently entreated," instead of, as we might expect, appealing to how much his readers know or comprehend. Other seventeenth-century books seem to combine the term's two meanings. George Chapman in *Achilles' Shield* (1598), for example, describes an "Understander" as having both a "good nature" and a "solid capacitie."[10] Frustrated with the critical response to his earlier translations, Chapman attempts in this later book to address an exclusive audience: "not every bodie, to you (as to one of my very few friends) I may be bold to utter my minde."[11]

The preface to "The Understanders" in *Poems, By J. D.* similarly appeals to a select group of readers ($^\pi$A1r–$^\pi$A2r). "For this time I must speake only to you," the printer Flesher tells the book's understanders, "in hope that very few will have a minde to confesse themselves ignorant." Such a prescriptive gesture, as we saw in chapter 1, represents both an attempt to define readers' reactions and an awareness of readers' interpretive free will. The printer tries to influence his audience first by insisting that Donne's poems "were the best in this kinde, that ever this Kingdome hath yet seene" and then by criticizing readers if they refuse to accept these works on their own terms: anyone "who so takes [the book] not as he findes it . . . is unworthy of it," the printer avers. The author's poetic merits are accordingly associated with "The Understanders," whereas his works' potential shortcomings are preemptively transferred to mere "*Readers*." The collection needs an extraordinary audience, Flesher argues, because Donne's poems themselves are not "ordinary," "common," or "usuall"; readers who fail to appreciate the volume, he implies, lack sufficient intelligence and caring.[12]

---

[10] George Chapman, trans., *The Iliad: Achilles' Shield* (London, 1598; STC 13635), B1v. Among the Renaissance authors whose works I have examined, Jonson returns most often to this distinction between reading and understanding. As he announces at the start of *The Alchemist* (London, 1610; STC 14755), "*If thou beest more, thou art an understander, and then I trust thee*" (A3r).

[11] Chapman, trans., *The Iliad: Achilles' Shield*, B3r.

[12] That the leaves of the epistle are signed separately and were inserted in only some surviving copies of *Poems* suggests that Flesher decided to add the preface at the last minute, after the print-run had begun. The erroneous running title – it wrongly refers "to the Reader" ($^\pi$A2r) and was corrected to "Understanders" in all subsequent editions – further implies that the preface, or at least this version of it, was added in haste. Why would a publisher have bothered to pay for these extra leaves? The book's creators seem to have been particularly concerned about readers' reactions and potential sales. We know that Flesher already had experienced difficulty with the book's licensers, who, according to an entry in the Stationers' *Register*, refused to approve five of Donne's elegies and, initially, all his satires. An entry in the Stationers' *Register* on 13 September 1632 records that the publisher "John Marriott Entred for his Copy under the handes of Sir Henry Herbert and both the Wardens *a booke of verses and Poems* (the five *satires*, the first, second, Tenth, Eleventh and Thirteenth *Elegies* being

Elsewhere in the preface the printer uses irony to help define the book's exclusive readership. Flesher holds out various reasons for understanders to value Donne's *Poems* – only to snatch away these possibilities. The printer writes an epistle like we find in front of other seventeenth-century publications, but insists it is not "an Epistle, as you have before ordinary publications." He then invites readers to "imagine" how "I could endeare it unto you," but refuses to endear the publication to us. Flesher says he could note, for example,

that importunity drew it on, that had it not beene presented here, it would have come to us beyond the Seas (which perhaps is true enough,) that my charge and paines in procurring of it hath beene such, and such. I could adde hereunto, a promise of more correctnesse, or enlargement in the next Edition, if you shall in the meane time content you with this. (πA1r–v)

He concludes this list with a swift retraction, "But these things are so common, as that I should profane this Peece by applying them to it."

While Flesher's introductory double-talk may not exceed the ironic style of other seventeenth-century prefaces – often stationers printed introductory epistles or commendatory verses while insisting that they did not need to do so[13] – the specific appeal to "Understanders" in *Poems, By J. D.* makes the printer's irony seem more purposeful. Flesher is inviting the book's audience to enact its own worthiness: those who read beyond his literal meaning can identify themselves as "understanders" and can now feel qualified to appreciate Donne's unique merits. Flesher thus also includes thirty-four pages of commendatory verses but places them at the end of the collection because, he feigns, he does not want them to "have serv'd for so many Encomiums." Here again the printer allows knowing readers to catch him winking: understanders can distinguish themselves from less competent "readers" by noticing that the placement of the encomiums makes them no less complimentary. Moreover, understanders can observe, Flesher gets things both ways, printing the encomiastic verses at the end of the book but still calling attention to them in the opening pages.

excepted) and these before excepted to be his, when he brings lawfull authority . . . written by Doctor John Dunn." See Edward Arber, *A Transcript of the Registers of the Company of Stationers of London, 1554–1640 A.D.*, 5 vols. (1887; rpt. Gloucester, MA, 1967), 4: 285.

[13] In John Milton's *Poems* (London, 1645; Wing M2160), for example, the bookseller Humphrey Moseley prefixes various "*encomions*" to the collection – although he explains to the reader that "*it's the worth of these both English and Latin Poems, not the flourish of any prefixed encomions that can invite thee to buy them*" (a3r–a4v). On the use of the modesty topos and the ancient tradition of distrusting prefatory rhetoric, see Kevin Dunn, *Pretexts of Authority: The Rhetoric of Authorship in the Renaissance Preface* (Stanford, 1994), pp. 1–7.

These encomiastic verses, like Flesher's rhetorically adept preface, compose part of the stationers' larger strategy to guide readers' reactions by emphasizing Donne's authorial presence – what Leah Marcus has called the poet's "reliquary embodiment" in the 1633 volume.[14] Not only do the encomiums and preface frame the collection in terms of the poet's abilities, but also the book's design and organization, we will see, focus readers' attention on the author's authority.

The stationers initiate this strategy at the start of the book, with the collection's deceptively simple title, *Poems, By J. D.* Few Renaissance readers, we first need to remember, would have known immediately who "J. D." was. While recent studies have shown that manuscript copies of Donne's works circulated widely during the second quarter of the seventeenth century, that does not mean the 1633 *Poems'* understanders would have identified the "J. D." of the title page with "Doctor Donne, Dean of St. Paul's."[15] Although some manuscript verses referred to Donne in their titles, other copies circulated anonymously, and many became popular only after *Poems'* publication.[16] Even if the title page looks easily decipherable to our modern eyes, more than eighty authors with the same initials were having their works published during the same period.[17] And, as Franklin Williams has shown, contemporary readers had to approach such monograms cautiously, for Renaissance writers and stationers often transposed their initials or chose misleading letters as pseudonyms.[18]

In the case of the 1633 *Poems*, the title page simultaneously undercuts and elevates Donne's authority: "POEMS, | *By* J. D. | WITH | ELEGIES |

[14] Marcus, *Unediting the Renaissance*, p. 194.
[15] On Donne's manuscript publications, see Alan MacColl, "The Circulation of Donne's Poems in Manuscript," in *John Donne: Essays in Celebration*, ed. A. J. Smith (London, 1972), pp. 28–46. Working primarily from verse miscellanies and commonplace books, Deborah Aldrich Larson has concluded that Donne "had become something of a legend by his death in 1631" and "was remembered primarily as the Dean of St. Paul's who had flouted society's strictures and gotten away with doing so." Arthur F. Marotti suggests more conservatively that Donne "was known primarily as the dean of St. Paul's and by reputation as an eloquent preacher." See Larson, "Donne's Contemporary Reputation: Evidence from Some Commonplace Books and Manuscript Miscellanies," *John Donne Journal* 12 (1993): 115–30, these quotations, pp. 116, 124; and Marotti, *Manuscript, Print, and the English Renaissance Lyric* (Ithaca, NY, 1995), p. 250.
[16] MacColl has inferred from manuscript collections of Donne's poetry and the appearance of single verses in miscellanies that the poet's work achieved its greatest popularity between 1625 and 1650, "and was not very widely known before this. The peak seems to have come in the ten years or so following the publication of the first edition." See MacColl, "The Circulation of Donne's Poems in Manuscript," p. 40.
[17] I have arrived at this number by counting the authors with the initials "J. D." and "I. D." who are listed in *A Short-Title Catalogue of Books Printed in England, Scotland, and Ireland* (STC), rev. W. A. Jackson, F. S. Ferguson, and Katharine F. Pantzer, 2nd edn., 3 vols. (London, 1976–91).
[18] Franklin B. Williams, Jr., "An Initiation into Initials," *Studies in Bibliography* 9 (1957): 163–78.

ON THE AUTHORS | DEATH. | [single rule] | [single rule]" (A2r; see figure 4a). On the one hand, the title withholds the author's full name and subordinates his initials to the words "POEMS" and "ELEGIES," both printed in all upper-case letters in a larger font. On the other hand, the page's diction and layout emphasize J. D.'s status as the creator of these verses and, through the generous use of white space, establish his identity as the book's focal point. The author at once appears essential and expendable; the book's primary selling point is the author, but, incongruously, his name remains unknown. These contradictory impulses suggest two competing models of Renaissance authorship: *Poems'* title page glances back to the medieval tradition of a writer's relative insignificance, while looking ahead to the more modern practice of using a writer's name as an organizing principle to classify and interpret a body of work. The 1633 title page demonstrates that an author wrote these poems; exactly which author was evidently not as relevant.

The book's publisher John Marriot, we should recall, had no legal reason to conceal Donne's specific identity. Marriot already had licensed his copy of *Poems* using Donne's full name, and even if he perceived some opposition to the book's publication, he could have devised a better disguise than "J. D." More likely, if Marriot had concerns about the book, he would have concealed his own name, not that of his by now esteemed author. The title page instead contains a conventional announcement, "Printed by *M. F.* for IOHN MARRIOT, | and are to be sold at his shop in St *Dunstans* | Church-yard in *Fleet-street*. 1633." (A2r). Presumably Marriot used only Donne's initials, not as part of some grand subterfuge, but because the publisher did not deem the poet's full identity – like the printer's full identity – important enough to have increased sales.

More difficult to gauge is the general effect that the title page may have had on contemporary audiences. Did the book's understanders think that here, too, they were being invited to participate in the text, in this case by deciphering the poet's full name? Certainly the book does not sustain for long the mystery of J. D.'s identity. Some version of "Donne," "Jo. Donne," or "Dr. Donne" occurs on fifteen different pages throughout *Poems*, the first time on page 63, in the last line of "To Sr Henry Wotton" ("Sir, more then kisses").[19] The repetition of Donne's name – often as a signature at the end of a poem – makes the book seem more personal, while the author's anonymity on the title page helps to make these later references seem almost

---

[19] A form of Donne's name appears on the following pages: I4r, T2r, Yy4r, Aaa4r, Bbb3r, Cccir, Ccciv, Ccc2r, Ccc3v, Dddir, Ddd3r, Eeeir, Eee3r, Eee4v, and Fff3r. His initials are printed on Y2v.

POEMS,

By J. D.

WITH

ELEGIES

ON THE AUTHORS

DEATH.

LONDON.

Printed by *M. F.* for IOHN MARRIOT,
and are to be fold at his fhop in St *Dunftans*
Church-yard in *Fleet-ftreet.* 1 6 3 3.

Figure 4a. Title page of John Donne's *Poems, By J. D.* (1633).

revelatory: Donne again and again stands at center stage as if asserting his defining role in the volume. Especially the first placement of Donne's name seems calculated to enhance his presence. Donne concludes the poem to Wotton with a pun, "But if my selfe, I'have wonne / To know my rules, I have, and you have / DONNE" (lines 69–71/I4r). That the compositor has set off this last word from the rest of the text heightens the drama of Donne's delayed entrance. The poet's name appears in the typographical equivalent of a spotlight: "DONNE" stands out in upper-case letters in a slightly larger font.

Other elements similarly imply Donne's presence in the 1633 collection, such as an unsigned epistle by Donne that the stationers use to suggest that the author speaks directly to readers at the start of the volume (A3r–A4r). Although dated "16. *Augusti* 1601" and written as a preface to "The Progresse of the Soule," the letter seems to introduce the collection as a whole rather than a single work: a blank page separates the epistle and poem in some copies (A4v); in other copies Flesher's preface along with a short verse by Marriot also intervenes between the letter and "Progresse" (πA1r–πA2v). Thus when Donne twice refers to "this booke" in his letter, readers could not be faulted for thinking he referred to the 1633 *Poems*.[20] And when he specifically mentions "hee, whose life you shall finde in the end of this booke," readers could think he meant himself, because, as the title page promises, a series of elegies at the end of *Poems* celebrates J. D.'s life and accomplishments. Marriot's boast that "these" pages preserve Donne "living to Eternity" (πA2v) also encourages readers to approach the author's opening letter as an autobiographical introduction. The epistle's double title, "*Infinitati sacrum*" (sacred to infinity) and "*Metempsycosis*" [sic] (transmigration of the soul), could be describing the author's own spirit in Marriot's terms.[21] Donne's soul has migrated from his grave, the book's creators imply, and he survives forever in "these sheetes" of this book.

Surely the poem itself, "The Progresse of the Soule" (B1r–H1r), sounds as if Donne intended it for the start of *Poems*. "I Sing the progresse of a deathlesse soule" (line 1/B1r), the first stanza begins, extending Marriot's

---

[20] In fact, we do not know what "booke" Donne meant here. Perhaps he was referring to a manuscript, or he may have been planning to have "The Progresse of the Soule" printed separately. He also cryptically mentions "my picture," presumably referring to a manuscript portrait or an engraving intended for a print text, neither of which has survived.

[21] Donne's epistle and Marriot's verse would have been even more misleading in the second edition of *Poems, By J. D.* (London, 1635; STC 7046), where William Marshall's added engraving could have been interpreted as the "picture" of the author to which both Donne and Marriot refer (πA2v, A3r). For a thoughtful analysis of Donne's image and motto in 1635, see Creswell, "Giving a Face to an Author."

argument for the author's "living to Eternity" (ᵖA2v), or perhaps, as the stanza concludes, suggesting this specific collection's lasting life: "A worke t'outweare *Seths* pillars, bricke and stone, / And (holy writs excepted) made to yeeld to none" (lines 9–10/B1r). Once again, the printer and publisher have created the impression that the poet J. D. communicates personally with the book's audience. With the placement of both Donne's epistle and "The Progresse of the Soule," he would not only speak to readers but preternaturally oversee and introduce "this booke" from 1601.

Only after readers progressed through all of *Poems* could they appreciate why the book's creators positioned this verse first in the 1633 volume. Although unique among Donne's works as a satiric, Old Testament narrative, "The Progresse of the Soule" forecasts most of the collection's overarching themes – God, love, mortality, and corruption – while the poem's meandering journey evokes the haphazard arrangement of the book's individual texts. Like the migrating soul of this poem, Donne inhabits various poetic personae in his works, adopting the guise of men and women, sinners and penitents, new and jaded lovers. Given the collection's amatory verses, this first poem aptly describes the soul that occupies "the first true lover" (line 460/D4v), and given that the collection repeatedly returns to the subjects of sin and salvation, the first verse fittingly introduces Eve, Cain, and Noah. "Progresse" also anticipates the collection's intermixing of secular and sacred poems. This soul's migration from body to body announces from the start the dialectical interplay between the corporeal and spiritual that shapes many of Donne's writings.

Perusing these introductory materials that suggest the author's participation, we may need to recall that the deceased poet could not have had a hand in *Poems*' production.[22] The impression of Donne's presence instead depended on a collaboration between various people – Flesher, Marriot, and unnamed members of the printing house.[23] The ultimate effect in

---

[22] Donne apparently had intended to publish privately a small edition of his poems. In a letter to Sir Henry Goodyere from 1614, Donne claimed he had been "brought to a necessity of Printing my Poems, and addressing them to my L. Chamberlain . . . not for much publique view, but at mine own cost, a few Copies." But because no such authorial collection survives, we can probably discount Donne's assertion, "This I mean to do forthwith." In the same letter he complains "I am loath to hear my self" speak about such an "unescapable necessity," which suggests, as Ernest Sullivan and other critics have noted, "that Donne's heart was not in the enterprise." Donne, *Letters to Severall Persons of Honour* (London, 1651; Wing D1864), Cc2v–Cc3r; and Sullivan, "1633 Vndone," p. 300.

[23] Herbert J. C. Grierson speculated that Donne's close friend and fellow poet, Henry King, may have edited the collection. Harris Nicholas alternately suggested Isaac Walton as the book's editor, a possibility that David Novarr largely disproved. Novarr preferred either Sir Henry Goodyere, or, like Grierson, Henry King. See Grierson, ed., *The Poems of John Donne*, 2 vols. (London, 1966), 2: 255; and Novarr, *The Making of Walton's Lives* (Ithaca, NY, 1958), pp. 32–33.

1633 is a book that Donne seems to have been preparing for the press when he suddenly died. Of course, if Donne had been alive in 1633 and had participated in *Poems'* publication, our sense of the author would still have practically required that the poet cooperate in the production process. With the exception of Ben Jonson, as we saw in the previous chapter, few seventeenth-century writers had the inclination, authority, or resources to oversee the printing of their own poetry.

In 1633, however, the book's creators explicitly undertook this task as a monument to Donne. In the book's central paradox, J. D. does not just remain alive though dead; he remains alive *because* he has died. Again and again, the book's creators remind readers that the poet is deceased. The title page highlights "the Authors Death" (A2r), Flesher speaks of the poet in the past tense (ᵖA2r), Donne's acquaintances have written commendatory "elegies" (Bbb3r–Fff3v), and Marriot in his own introductory verse writes about Donne's "body in the grave" (ᵖA2v). This emphasis on death justifies the publication of *Poems* as a tribute to its author and assures readers that this edition will remain definitive. In practical terms, the poet's absence probably gave the stationers some liberty to collect and publish his verses.[24] But Donne's death also specifically occasions this book and inaugurates him as an "author": only now can the stationers dramatize the poet's immortality through verse to help dignify their volume; now they have reason to supplant the poet's physical body with this, his poetic corpus.

Ironically, when Donne does speak for himself in *Poems, By J. D.*, he shifts attention from himself back to his audience. As in the printer's preface, where Flesher acknowledges his audience's authority and tries to guide their responses, Donne's opening letter and poem reveal his own concern about reaching understanders. In "The Progresse of the Soule," for example, Donne sounds less particular than Flesher about his intended readers, but, like the printer, he posits a cooperative role for them: "Who ere thou beest that read'st this sullen Writ / Which just so much courts thee, as thou dost it" (lines 511–12/E2r). Donne, in other words, accepts the diversity of his unknown audience but still he would prefer understanders, readers who will "court" his poems and evaluate them favorably.

---

[24] The poet's son four years later petitioned the Archbishop of Canterbury because, he claimed, both the 1633 and 1635 editions of *Poems* were published "without anie leave or Autoritie." On 16 December 1637, the Archbishop ordered all parties "not to meddle any farther with the printing or selling" of Donne's works without his son's approval, "as they will answer the contrary at their peril." See *The Carl H. Pforzheimer Library: English Literature 1475–1700*, 3 vols. (New Castle, DE, 1997), 1: 287; and *Calendar of State Papers, Domestic Series, of the Reign of Charles I, 1625–1649*, 23 vols. (London, 1858–97), 12: 25.

In Donne's preceding epistle, he also explains that readers should not rush to judgment. Encountering a writer for the first time, he himself remains cautious: "Naturally at a new Author, I doubt, and sticke, and doe not say quickly, good. I censure much and taxe." He concedes that his own audience should have "as good hold upon me" and accepts that some will "reprehend" his writing (A3r). Donne has only one stipulation for his audience: he objects to readers who oppose specific "Authors, damning what ever such a name hath or shall write." According to Donne, "None writes so ill, that he gives not some thing exemplary, to follow, or flie" (A3v).

Paradoxically, Donne at the start of the 1633 *Poems* is challenging the principle of "a name" on which Marriot and Flesher have organized this volume. He does not just emphasize the need for generous-minded readers; he is suggesting that readers should not prejudge a work by its author. In contrast, the stationers, as we have seen, encourage readers to approach the poems in this collection in terms of J. D.'s excellence. Thus Flesher and Marriot have also included eleven samples of Donne's personal correspondence in the collection (T2r, Y2v, Yy4r–Bbb2v), and similarly justify printing thirteen commendatory elegies by the author's acquaintances because such poems illustrate "how much honour was attributed to this worthy man" (πA2r).[25] If Donne's argument about "a name" understates the writer's importance, his own status as author defines the relationship between these additional texts and gives them meaning. In 1633 the book's creators can justify the inclusion of such works because they are by or about John Donne.

Once again the volume bears witness to the Renaissance author's increasing authority. Donne's epistolary claims in the context of *Poems, By J. D.* expose the tension between two competing theories of authorship: the writer's relative unimportance *versus* an author-centered model. But, as Flesher's prefatory observations about readers suggest, poets and stationers, regardless of a book's orientation, must still hope for an understanding audience. Complementing the book's two models of authorship are two competing approaches to reading: readers who understand *versus* those who misconstrue. Donne's own instructions to his audience in the preface to "Progresse" indicate his concern that readers will fall into the latter category and take too much liberty with "this booke" (A3v). He elsewhere

[25] On the possibility that the stationers carefully selected which of Donne's correspondence to print in *Poems* so as to create "a manual of letter writing," see Novarr, *The Making of Walton's Lives*, pp. 35–38.

would define a "Critick" as a reader *"ingeniosus in alienis*, over-witty in other mens Writings," who "had read an Author better, then that Author meant," and in a letter to Henry Goodyere about the possibility of printing his poems, he worries, "I know that I shall *suffer* from many interpretations" (my emphasis).[26] In other letters he expresses similar concerns, about being "easily misinterpreted," about tackling "a misinterpretable subject," or about offering "misinterpretable and dangerous" conjectures.[27]

Yet Donne in the 1633 collection simultaneously grants readers considerable authority, inviting them, as we have seen, to "censure much and taxe." When he imagines his ideal audience in "Obsequies to the Lord Harringtons Brother," printed later in the volume, he stresses the need for readers' participation and good will:

> . . . a perfect reader doth not dwell,
> On every syllable, nor stay to spell,
> Yet without doubt, hee doth distinctly see,
> And lay together every A, and B.
>   (lines 93–96/T4r)

Here Donne calls for active readers – those who "distinctly see" and "lay together" every detail – but, perhaps in response to critics who found fault with the rough magic of Donne's poetry, the author warns readers not to treat his verses too severely.[28]

The decision to address specific people in so many poems – thirty-six of which are included in the collection – also reveals Donne's desire for his readers' involvement. Throughout his career, he wrote to, for, and about his friends, acquaintances, and would-be patrons. This highly visible social dimension in *Poems* underscores the reader's role in making Donne's texts meaningful. If the repetition of the author's name within the volume emphasizes his presence, then the even more frequent references to his various relationships indicate that no author is an island. As Donne deferentially writes in "The Storme" to his friend Christopher Brooke, "My lines" become valuable only "When by thy judgment they are dignifi'd" (lines 6–7/H4v). With the mere touch of Magdalen Herbert's "warme redeeming

---

[26] Donne, *A Sermon Preached at White-hall, Novemb. 2. 1617*, in *The Sermons of John Donne*, ed. George R. Potter and Evelyn M. Simpson, 10 vols. (Berkeley, 1953–62), 1: 232; and *Letters to Severall Persons of Honour*, Cc3r. And see *OED* s.v. "suffer" I.3.a.

[27] Donne, *Letters to Severall Persons of Honour*, D3r, N1v, Cc4r. See also Annabel Patterson, "Misinterpretable Donne: The Testimony of the Letters," *John Donne Journal* 1 (1982): 39–53.

[28] Ben Jonson, for example, reportedly claimed "That Donne, for not keeping of accent, deserved hanging." See Jonson, *Conversations with William Drummond*, in Herford and Simpson, 1: 128–78, this quotation, p. 133.

hand," he writes in another verse epistle, his "saples[s] leafe" will be "glorify'd" (lines 17–20/PIV).

We know that at least some seventeenth-century readers responded to the book's emphasis on the author's presence: Donne's *Juvenilia* is often found with his *Poems* in surviving contemporary bindings, while in other copies readers attached the author's signature to the title page (see figure 4b), or had his portrait inserted as a frontispiece.[29] Following the thread laid down in Flesher and Marriot's volume, these readers were collecting other texts based on Donne's status as author.

The sympathetic readers whom Donne and the volume's creators invoke thus did not diminish the author's textual authority. Instead, in another of *Poems'* multiplying paradoxes, understanders collaborated to construct a perception of the poet that belied their own participation. Just as the book's stationers forged the appearance of Donne's authorial presence in 1633, Donne also needed, as both he and Flesher seemed to realize, the efforts of these understanding readers. Together, they "author" the author – that is, the stationers and readers enhance the poet's presence in the volume and establish his status as an author worthy of having his collected poems printed. Here we may recall that "understand" during the Renaissance could also mean "to support or assist; to prop up."[30] The understanders that the 1633 *Poems* invokes are repeatedly being invited to support this book as a monument of Donne's authorship.

The concluding series of elegies in *Poems, By J. D.* represents the efforts of a specific group of Donne's understanders. As we will see with the book's poetic omissions, these contemporary tributes to Donne both re-affirm and undermine his authority. On the one hand, as they praise Donne's virtue and eloquence, the elegists convert the poet's absence into another occasion for his renewed presence in the volume. On the other hand, the elegists' words necessarily supplant the poet's; poems written "By J. D." become poems written by J. D.'s admirers.

But in a final turn, when the elegists insist that they cannot replace Donne, they, like the book's stationers, retreat to the background. Writing elegies about their inability to write elegies, Donne's contemporaries repeatedly find silence the most appropriate expression for commemorating his

---

[29] On contemporary bindings of *Poems, By J. D.*, see Sir Geoffrey Keynes, *A Bibliography of Dr. John Donne*, 4th edn. (Oxford, 1973), p. 197. Leah Marcus reports that the copy of *Poems* in the Harvard Library also has Donne's signature glued to the title page – a personalizing gesture, she observes, which further serves to "intensify" Donne's authorial presence. See Marcus, *Unediting the Renaissance*, p. 194.

[30] *OED* s.v. "understand" 9.

POEMS,

By J. D.

WITH

ELEGIES

ON THE AUTHORS

DEATH.

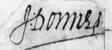

LONDON.

Printed by *M. F.* for IOHN MARRIOT,
and are to be fold at his fhop in St *Dunftans*
Church-yard in *Fleet-ftreet.* 1 6 3 3.

Figure 4b. Title page of John Donne's *Poems, By J. D.* (1633) with author's signature attached.

accomplishments. As Henry King tells the deceased author, "but thine owne, / No pen could doe Thee Justice, not Bayes Crowne / Thy vast desert" (lines 53–55/Bbb4r). A. E. B. Coldiron reads the elegists' exhortations to silence as a function of the genre's conventions, but I would note that a retreat to silence extends and develops the volume's paradoxical design.[31] As Robert Fallon observes, the elegies' theme "seems to surpass mere convention" in the "fervor with which it is pursued in poem after poem."[32] That half of the elegists also address Donne directly, as if he were still living, reinforces his presence at the end of the volume. And when the elegists then defer to the poet's silence as the best expression of grief and honor, they in effect efface themselves and allow the omitted poet once more to speak. Jasper Mayne wonders, "Who shall presume to mourn thee, *Donne*, unlesse / He could his teares in thy expressions dresse" (lines 1–2/Eee1r), and in reply the stationers provide the 1633 *Poems*, Donne's own eloquent expressions memorializing himself.

DONNE'S IMPERFECTIONS

Thus far we have seen how the first printed edition of Donne's poems establishes his poetic authority by positing an understanding audience. The accompanying tension, between the author's presence and absence, once again suggests the changing conditions of authorship in early modern England: that the poet is deceased should empower readers to interpret the collection freely, but the 1633 *Poems*, in emphasizing Donne's presence, instead prompts readers to help establish the author's ethos. In this section I show how the inclusion of Donne's incomplete verses in 1633 also invites readers to participate in authorizing the poet. These omissions represent another manifestation of his absence – parts of these poems are literally missing – but the book's layout encourages readers to peruse the remaining fragments as evidence that Donne deserves such a commemorative volume.

We assume that Donne did not finish "The Progresse of the Soule," for example, because the poem begins with the heading "*First Song*" (B1r), and none of the subsequent 52 stanzas contains a heading for a "Second," "Next," or "Final" song. In this verse, Jonson told Drummond, Donne's

---

[31] A. E. B. Coldiron, "'Poets Be Silent': Self-Silencing Conventions and Rhetorical Context in the 1633 Critical Elegies on Donne," *John Donne Journal* 12 (1993): 101–13.

[32] Robert Thomas Fallon, "Donne's 'Strange Fires' and the 'Elegies on the Authors Death,'" *John Donne Journal* 7 (1988): 197–212, this quotation, p. 198.

generall purpose was to have brought in all the bodies of the Hereticks from ye soule of Cain & at last left in ye body of Calvin. of this he never wrotte but one sheet, & now, since he was made Doctor repententh highlie and seeketh to destroy all his poems.[33]

Even if we doubt Jonson's specific account, as most critics have, the poem still feels unfinished.[34] Most notably, Donne suggests in stanza seven that Queen Elizabeth will become "the crowne, and last straine of my song" (line 65/B2v), a promise that he never fulfills.

While we do not know why Flesher and Marriot printed this unfinished verse first in their edition – was it the first poem in the copy from which the formes were set? – the stationers certainly did not attempt to disguise the poem's incompletion: the single division "*First Song*" is emphasized between a pair of horizontal rules. The overriding effect of the collection's design is a privileged glimpse into Donne's private cabinet, an effect intensified by beginning with the unfinished "Progresse."[35] In 1633 we encounter both poetry and prose; we find finished and unfinished works; we sift among the author's amatory, religious, and satirical poems.

Even earlier, in the preface, Flesher calls attention to Donne's incomplete poems as part of the argument for the author's excellence:

a scattered limbe of this Author, hath more amiablenesse in it, in the eye of a discerner, then a whole body of some other; Or, (to expresse him best by himselfe)

> *– A hand, or eye,*
> *By* Hilyard [*sic*] *drawne, is worth a history*
> *By a worse Painter made –.*   (πA1v)

That Flesher has chosen such an apt quotation from "The Storme" (lines 3–5/H4v), one among 149 verses by Donne printed in the volume, illustrates the care he has taken with Donne's writings.[36] But instead of demonstrating that the printer possesses "the eye of a discerner," Flesher's

---

[33] Jonson, *Conversations with William Drummond*, in Herford and Simpson, 1: 136.

[34] Grierson, for example, speculated that "Probably Donne mystified him [Jonson] on purpose." Grierson, ed., *The Poems of John Donne*, 2: 219.

[35] The stationers may have put "Progresse" first, we can also speculate, because it represented one of Donne's earliest efforts that they could confidently date – in which case the stationers were again using the author's identity, specifically his poetic development, as the book's organizing principle. On the manuscript tradition that informs the organization of the 1633 *Poems*, see John T. Shawcross, "The Arrangement and Order of John Donne's Poems," in *Poems in Their Place: The Intertextuality and Order of Poetic Collections*, ed. Neil Fraistat (Chapel Hill, 1986), pp. 119–63.

[36] Flesher and Marriot were not infallible, however. Two of the book's verses were not in fact composed by Donne, the translation of Psalm 137 (X3r–Y1r) and "An Epitaph upon Shakespeare" (Y3r).

discerning choice reinforces Donne's presence in the volume. The poet both authors and authorizes the collection: not only do we sense Donne's immediacy by peeking at his private papers, but Donne himself, Flesher implies, would have wanted it that way. To borrow one of the author's own puns, the 1633 *Poems*, by beginning with a text that is not done, evokes Donne all the more.

Flesher's argument of omission also exemplifies the reciprocal relation-ship between author and reader implied by the book's other appeals to "understanders." That "understand" during the 1600s could also mean "to supply mentally" or "to regard as present in thought, though not expressly stated or mentioned" suggests that the stationers were specifically seeking an active audience, one that would at least notice and perhaps fill in the text's various blanks.[37]

Interestingly, by quoting only part of "The Storme," the printer has in effect created another of the book's "scattered limbes." Following the passage that Flesher cites, Donne asserts that only readers can determine whether his poetry will achieve the status of Hillyard's paintings: as we saw in the preceding section, Donne tells his friend Christopher Brooke that "My lines" become valuable only "When by thy judgment they are dignifi'd" (lines 6–7/H4v). While Flesher's decision not to quote this concession from "The Storme" may at first seem to misrepresent Donne's claims for his power as a poet, the printer has actually fulfilled Donne's prediction. Excerpting part of a poem in the preface illustrates that a "discerner" – in this case, Flesher – does indeed have the authority to "dignify" Donne's verse on par with a painting by Hillyard.

In addition to "The Progresse of the Soule," the creators of the 1633 *Poems* have inserted two unfinished verses, "Resurrection, imperfect" (Y1r–Y1v) and "To the Countesse of Bedford" ("Though I be *dead*, and buried") (P4r). Although these poems raise various, ultimately unanswerable questions – why, for example, did Donne leave unfinished these particular works? – a brief examination of the poems' editorial apparatus reveals how the sta-tioners continue to encourage understanding readers to confirm Donne's authorial status, initiated in the collection's preliminary leaves.

Unlike "The Progresse of the Soule," both "Resurrection, imperfect" and "To the Countesse of Bedford" announce their incompletion at the end; both conclude with a Latin tag, "*Desunt caetera*" ("The rest is lacking"). Donne himself may or may not have added this tag: although two sur-viving manuscripts that contain "To the Countesse of Bedford" include

---

[37] *OED* s.v. "understand" 7.

this description, at least three manuscripts of "Resurrection, imperfect" do not.[38] A headnote with "To the Countesse of Bedford" explains further that the verse letter was "*Begun in France but never perfected*," but again we do not know whether Donne wrote this note or the terser explanation, "imperfect," included after the title "Resurrection." As Helen Gardner has cautioned, "it is so uncertain whether any of the titles of Donne's lyrics are his own that an attempt to use a title as a guide to interpreting a poem is unwarranted."[39] The one manuscript poem that survives in Donne's own hand does not have a title. The author has folded the paper into a small packet and addressed the verse letter on the outside, "To the Honourable lady / the lady Carew." The poem begins simply "Madame."[40]

If, however, Donne did write all or some of the titles and tags associated with "Resurrection, imperfect" and "To the Countesse of Bedford," he might not have intended them literally. George MacDonald was the first to suggest, in the nineteenth century, that "Resurrection, imperfect" seemed to him "complete," an idea that Ruth Falk and Raymond-Jean Frontain later developed.[41] According to this way of thinking, Donne chose "imperfect" and/or *Desunt caetera* to emphasize that the sunrise conveys Christ's resurrection imperfectly and that any attempt to describe Christ's resurrection must remain flawed.

[38] "To the Countesse of Bedford" ("Though I be *dead*, and buried") occurs in both the Dolau Cothi MS in the National Library of Wales (Group II) and the O'Flaherty MS Eng 966/5 at Harvard University (Group III); in the latter manuscript, the tag reads "The rest wants." For "Resurrection, imperfect," I have found the tag missing in the British Library, Add. MS 18647 (Group II), and, according to John T. Shawcross, it does not occur in the O'Flaherty, Harvard University, MS Eng 966/5 (Group III) and the Trinity College, Dublin, MS 877 (Group II). I have not been able to verify whether five other copies of "Resurrection, imperfect" contain the Latin tag: the Norton MS, Harvard University, MS Eng 966/3 (Group II); the National Library of Wales, Dolau Cothi MS (Group II); the Trinity College, Cambridge, MS R 3 12 (Group II); the Luttrell MS (Group III); and the Grey MS 2.a.II, South African Public Library, Capetown. See Shawcross, ed., *The Complete Poetry of John Donne* (New York, 1968), pp. 474, 486–87.

[39] Helen Gardner, "The Titles of Donne's Poems," in *Friendship's Garland: Essays Presented to Mario Praz on His Seventieth Birthday*, ed. Vittorio Gabrieli, 2 vols. (Rome, 1966), I: 189–207, this quotation, p. 207. The title for "A Hymne to Christ, at the Authors last going into Germany" (Qq4v), for example, appears to have been devised at the printing house. Even if we accept the unlikelihood that Donne would have referred to himself in the third person, the word "last" does not occur in any surviving manuscripts. As John T. Shawcross has also observed, Donne would probably not have known when he composed the poem that he had taken his "last" journey to Germany – although we should note that "last" here could simply mean "most recent." See Shawcross, "But Is It Donne's? The Problem of Titles on His Poems," *John Donne Journal* 7 (1988): 141–49.

[40] For a description of this manuscript, I am relying on Smith, ed., *John Donne: The Complete English Poems*, pp. 559–60.

[41] George MacDonald, *England's Antiphon* (1868), as quoted in *John Donne: The Critical Heritage*, ed. A. J. Smith (London, 1983, rpt. 1985), p. 462; Ruth E. Falk, "Donne's *Resurrection, Imperfect*," *The Explicator* 17.3 (1958): item 24; and Raymond-Jean Frontain, "Donne's Imperfect Resurrection," *Papers on Language and Literature* 26 (1990): 539–45.

No one to my knowledge has suggested, in contrast, that Donne had completed "To the Countesse of Bedford" ("Though I be *dead*, and buried"). Donne visited France with Sir Robert Drury between November 1611 and April 1612, and most likely this fragment, announcing itself "Begun in France," represents a failed attempt to appease his patroness, Lucy Harington, who was angry with Donne for over-praising Drury's daughter in the Anniversaries. This verse feels more unfinished than "Resurrection, imperfect." As printed in *Poems*, the letter ends abruptly, with a comma instead of a full stop: "May in lesse lessons finde enough to doe, / By studying copies, not Originals, / *Desunt caetera*." (lines 24–25).

That this poem seems so clearly incomplete challenges Falk and Frontain's arguments about Donne's strategy in "Resurrection, imperfect." Falk reasons that "it is in the examination of the tag phrase, *Desunt caetera*, together with the title, that we discern what Donne wanted to say," but the tag and headnote with "Bedford" appear more superficially descriptive. Did someone in the printing house borrow the Latin tag from "To the Countesse of Bedford" and mistakenly add it to "Resurrection, imperfect"? Did Donne himself defiantly insert the words "never perfected" beneath the Countess' name as a sly reminder that he had celebrated Elizabeth Drury's "perfection" in *The Second Anniversarie* (lines 312, 318/Mm3v)?[42]

Rather than trying to guess the tags' origins and meanings, I think it more important to note that readers of the 1633 volume are invited to treat both "Resurrection" and "Bedford" as incomplete poems. The repetition of *Desunt caetera* and "perfected" / "imperfect" – regardless of these terms' provenance – allies the works as equally unfinished in *Poems, By J. D.* Elsewhere in the collection, Donne uses "perfect" and its conjugates to mean both "complete," as in *Elegie II*: "The Anagram" (line 10/G3r), and "without flaws," as in "The Paradox" (line 2/Qq3v). The specific term "imperfect" occurs in only one other poem in the collection, a verse letter "To M. B. B." (O2r–O2v), where it describes the supposedly poor quality of Donne's writing. The poet complains that his muse has "Divorc'd her selfe" (line 20), leaving his rhymes "prophane, imperfect, oh, too bad / To be counted Children of Poetry" (lines 26–27).

---

[42] Almost any discussion of "To the Countesse of Bedford" and "Resurrection, imperfect" returns to such guesswork. Whenever I teach these poems, students want to speculate about the origin of the tags and titles, and the reasons Donne may not have finished these specific verses. Could he have been inviting the Countess of Bedford, also a poet, to collaborate with him by sending her an unfinished verse – something that *she* "never perfected"? Or perhaps he considered his "Resurrection" "imperfect" because, as he elsewhere tells the anonymous B. B., the poem had not been "confirm'd and Bishoped" by its original recipient (lines 26, 28/O2v).

As in this latter verse epistle, Donne often uses a form of "perfect" when addressing his friends and patrons about his writing. He implies that he needs these acquaintances to amend his poetry and/or bring it to completion. In a verse letter "To Mr E. G." not included in the 1633 edition, for example, Donne compares how "lame things seek their perfection" to his own "slimy rhymes" that require E. G.'s favor for their improvement (lines 1, 2). He similarly explains to "R. W." in another verse letter from the Westmoreland Manuscript that he finds inspiration and "new life" only through "thy song's perfection" (lines 1, 13). And if we return to the poem "To M. *B. B.*," Donne tells his friend that "these rhymes" will remain "prophane, imperfect" unless they are "confirm'd and Bishoped by thee" (lines 26, 28/O2v).

The layout of *Poems, By J. D.* does not, however, encourage readers in 1633 to devise their own endings to Donne's imperfect poems. On the contrary, the book's creators almost prohibit such participation by sealing off the poems, insisting through the tags and titles at the beginning and end of each that both verses remain fragments. Told at the start that each poem is unfinished, we reach the final line and read again that the two works are incomplete. The point of including such emphatically "imperfect" poems in 1633, it seems, is not to have readers finish Donne's work. Instead, as with Jonson's incomplete verse epistle, these fragments elevate Donne's status by, paradoxically, illustrating his limitations. Readers can infer not just that this deceased "worthy man" (πA2r) wrote some "imperfect" poems, but that this deceased man must be "worthy" because the book's creators consider even his admittedly "imperfect" poems worth reading. And if readers were to deem other poems in the volume less successful for any reason, the status that the volume confers on Donne remains intact because the stationers provide a ready-made category that forestalls future criticism: an unsuccessful poem can be bracketed off as merely another instance of what the creators have already acknowledged are the author's imperfect works. The stationers thus relieve Donne from having to live up to the volume's encomiums; not every poem in the collection has to be exceptional for John Donne to be an exceptional poet.

If we recall Flesher's preface, the collection's unfinished poems, like Hillyard's famous miniature paintings, encapsulate what Donne's readers had to accomplish throughout the volume. These unfinished parts are literally synecdochic; readers here confront a more extreme example of the effort that all his works require. "The Progresse of the Soule," "Resurrection, imperfect," and "To the Countesse of Bedford" spotlight how readers of such a collection proceed both inductively and deductively: working from the individual poems, we are to induce that the author merits this com-memorative volume; at the same time, beginning with the authority that the volume bestows on its author, we try to deduce why each of these poems deserves our attention. To borrow Flesher's terminology from the preface, the inclusion of the unfinished verses in the 1633 *Poems* exemplifies how all of the collection's works – none of them "ordinary," "common," or "usual" – demand both "understanders" and "discerners." We must understand Donne's worthiness and discern each poem's value.

DONNE OUT-DONE

The 1633 *Poems'* other type of omission entrusts readers with even more responsibility while alternately diminishing and building up the author's ethos. Whereas the collection's incomplete verses, as we have seen, enhance the poet's authority by empowering readers, the ultimate effect of these final omissions depends on how much understanding and discernment the book's other elements inspire. We have returned to the two modes of reading suggested in the preliminary matter: readers who understand *versus* those who misconstrue. If sympathetic contemporary readers used this opportunity to reconstruct the author's intentions, other readers may have taken more liberty and tried to compose their own replacement poems.

The final omissions occur in *Satyre II* and *Satyre IIII*, two partially cen-sored poems that together contain nine missing or incomplete lines. Because the licensers approved the satires almost a month after the book's original entry in the Stationers' *Register*, we may infer that these omissions repre-sent a compromise.[43] Perhaps the publisher Marriot received permission to print the satires only because he promised to excise the most objectionable lines and words. Whereas Donne could have written the tags and titles attached to his unfinished verses, the satires' omissions seem to announce the presence of someone else and indicate the poet's lack of authority over the publishing process. An unnamed censor, working either with the gov-ernment or as a member of the printing house, evidently had final say over how Donne's poems would appear.

---

[43] The relevant entry in the Stationers' *Register* reads as follows: on 31 October 1632, "John Marriott Entred for his Copy under the hands of Sir Henry Herbert and Master Aspley warden *The five Satires* written by Doctor J: Dun these being excepted in his last entrance." See Arber, *A Transcript of the Registers of the Company of Stationers of London, 1554–1640 A.D.*, 4: 287. For a useful introduction to the satires' textual history, see John T. Shawcross, "All Attest His Writs Canonical: The Texts, Meaning and Evaluation of Donne's Satires," in *Just So Much Honor: Essays Commemorating the Four-Hundredth Anniversary of the Birth of John Donne*, ed. Peter Amadeus Fiore (University Park, PA, 1972), pp. 245–72.

In *Satyre II*, for example, in the midst of Donne's portrait of the corrupt lawyer Cocus, readers encounter the following heavily censored verse:

> . . . now he must talke
> Idly, like prisoners, which whole months will sweare
> That onely suretiship hath brought them there,
>
> ___   ___   ___   ___
>
> ___   ___   ___
>
> Like a wedge in a blocke, wring to the barre,
> Bearing like Asses, and more shamelesse farre
> Then carted whores, lye, to the grave Judge; for
>
> ___   ___   ___
>
> ___   ___   ___
>
> As these things do in him; by these he thrives.
>
> (lines 66–76/Vv2r; see figure 4c)

I have quoted the passage at length to illustrate how disruptive these omissions are; the missing lines threaten to bring the poem to a halt as we puzzle out Donne's overlapping metaphors. Cocus "must talke / Idly, like prisoners" and must "wring" (meaning "writhe") his way "Like a wedge in a blocke" through the courtroom, already crowded with "Asses" like himself. Then, more shamelessly than a prostitute being carted to the whipping post, he must "lye, to the grave Judge." The broken lines within the text mark the removal of two additional comparisons. In the first place, as we learn from surviving manuscript copies, Cocus must "lie in everything / Like a king's favorite, yea like a king" (lines 69–70). In the second, Cocus' immorality exceeds even the king and clergy's: "Bastardy abounds not in kings' titles, nor / Simony and sodomy in churchmen's lives, / As these things do in him" (lines 74–76).

Although with hindsight we can easily understand the reason for removing these two irreverent passages, the text, as printed in 1633, renders the poem temporarily unintelligible and provides few clues about the satire's missing lines. Given the remaining references to "prisoners," "Asses," and "whores," contemporary readers could only presume that the omitted verses must have been more offensive. Surely the censor could have sharpened his shears and not gouged so deeply into the text, especially since elsewhere in the poem, as we will see, he trimmed two isolated words. This first omitted line in particular, "And to every suitor lie in everything" (line 69), describes Cocus and contains nothing overtly objectionable. It seems unlikely that the censor needed to cut this line to prevent readers from discovering the next rhyme, "king." By comparison, the decision *not* to omit "for" (line 73) and "As these things do in him" (line 76) as part of

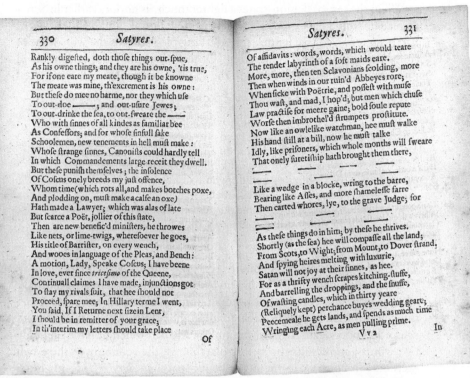

330   *Satyres.*

Rankly digefted, doth thofe things out-fpue,
As his owne things; and they are his owne, 'tis true,
For if one eate my meate, though it be knowne
The meate was mine, th'excrement is his owne :
But thefe do mee no harme, nor they which ufe
To out-doe ———; and *out-ufure* Jewes;
To out-drinke the fea, to out-fweare the ———
Who with finnes of all kindes as familiar bee
As Confeffors; and for whofe finfull fake
Schoolemen, new tenements in hell muft make :
Whofe ftrange finnes, Canonifts could hardly tell
In which Commandements large receit they dwell.
But thefe punifh themfelves ; the infolence
Of Cofcus onely breeds my juft offence,
(Whom time (which rots all, and makes botches poxe,
And plodding on, muft make a calfe an oxe)
Hath made a Lawyer; which was alas of late
But fcarce a Poët, jollier of this ftate,
Then are new benefic'd minifters, he throwes
Like nets, or lime-twigs, wherefoever he goes,
His title of Barrifter, on every wench,
And wooes in language of the Pleas, and Bench :
A motion, Lady, Speake Cofcus; I have beene
In love, ever fince *tricefimo* of the Queene,
Continuall claimes I have made, injunctions got
To ftay my rivals fuit, that hee fhould not
Proceed, fpare mee; In Hillary terme I went,
You faid, If I Returne next fize in Lent,
I fhould be in remitter of your grace;
In th'interim my letters fhould take place
                                              Of

Satyres.   331

Of affidavits : words, words, which would teare
The tender labyrinth of a foft maids eare.
More, more, then ten Sclavonians fcolding, more
Then when winds in our ruin'd Abbeyes rore;
When ficke with Poëtrie, and poffeft with mufe
Thou waft, and mad, I hop'd; but men which chufe
Law practife for meere gaine; bold foule repute
Worfe then imbrothel'd ftrumpets proftitute.
Now like an owlelike watchman, hee muft walke
His hand ftill at a bill, now he muft talke
Idly, like prifoners, which whole months will fweare
That onely furetifhip hath brought them there,
                                              ———
                                              ———
Like a wedge in a blocke, wring to the barre,
Bearing like Affes, and more fhamelesse farre
Then carted whores, lye, to the grave Judge; for
                                              ———
                                              ———
As thefe things do in him; by thefe he thrives,
Shortly (as the fea) hee will compaffe all the land;
From Scots, to Wight; from Mount, to Dover ftrand,
And fpying heires melting with luxurie,
Satan will not joy at their finnes, as hee.
For as a thrifty wench fcrapes kitching-ftuffe,
And barrelling the droppings, and the fnuffe,
Of wafting candles, which in thirty yeare
(Reliquely kept) perchance buyes wedding geare;
Peecemeale he gets lands, and fpends as much time
Wringing each Acre, as men pulling prime.
                              V v 2   In

Figure 4c. Omissions in John Donne's *Satyre II* from *Poems, By J. D.* (1633), sig. Vv1v–Vv2r.

the second excision only encourages readers to stop and ponder what "these things" signify. Like the broken horizontal rules that scar the text, these unfinished thoughts emphasize the poem's incompletion. They force readers to confront the book's material production and illustrate the author's limited authority over his poems' printing.

The satires' horizontal rules also allow readers to devise their own contributions to the text, thereby potentially diminishing Donne's presence further. Whereas the imperfect poems' tags and titles do not, as we have seen, promote this degree of audience participation, the satires' blank lines surely looked inviting to at least some contemporary audience members. And, aside from the verses' rhyme and meter, readers had virtually free rein: because the book's creators provide so few clues about what is missing, readers could invent various alternatives for the passages that were excised.

When the censor demonstrates a lighter touch, as he does earlier in *Satyre II*, readers would have even more likely paused, I think, and wondered what had been removed (see figure 4c). Attacking plagiarists as the worst type of sinful writer for "Rankly" digesting "Others wits fruits" and turning them into "excrement" (lines 26, 27, 30), the speaker claims to remain unaffected by such excess:

> But these do mee no harme, nor they which use
> To out-doe ———; and out-usure Jewes;
> To out-drinke the sea, to out-sweare the ———
> Who with sinnes of all kindes as familiar bee
> As Confessors; and for whose sinfull sake
> Schoolemen, new tenements in hell must make:
> Whose strange sinnes, Canonists could hardly tell
> In which Commandements large receit they dwell.
>
> (lines 31–38/Vv1r–v)

These two omissions momentarily turn the already waggish poem into a bawdy guessing game. The brevity of the missing passages would have allowed readers to count out the proper number of syllables and find something appropriately objectionable to fill in the blanks. Although the book's censor has once again silenced the author, the deft touch of removing only two words almost suits the satire's playfulness; the economy of these two excisions, in contrast to the other blank spaces in *Satyre II*, seems more careful, almost polite.

From surviving manuscripts, we know Donne's answers for these blank spaces: "Dildoes" and "Letanie" should be inserted, respectively, on the two lines. While readers could have inferred only that the first omission should be two syllables (stressed-unstressed), they should have had more success restoring "Letanie" in the second blank.[44] The eighteenth-century editor William Warburton specifically explained the latter "low allusion" as "a licentious quibble used at that time by the enemies of the English Liturgy"

---

[44] That the book's creators evidently deemed a reference to dildoes to be as objectionable as the collection's blasphemous and treasonous allusions points up the threat that women's sexuality posed for some early modern readers and/or the dangers associated with this so-called "fatal practice" during the Renaissance. Although ribald verses such as Thomas Nashe's "The Choice of Valentines" had a limited circulation in manuscript, the first popular pamphlet about masturbation did not appear until 1710. On contemporary references to masturbation, see Lawrence Stone, *The Family, Sex and Marriage in England, 1500–1800* (New York, 1977), pp. 512–16. The subject continues to bother some modern readers. R. B. McKerrow, for example, chose to exclude "The Choice of Valentines" from his edition of *The Works of Thomas Nashe*, 5 vols. (London, 1910) – even though, as he explains, "There can, I fear, be little doubt that this poem is the work of Nashe" (5: 141).

who objected to "the frequent invocations in the *Letanie*."[45] When Donne writes "out-sweare the Letanie," he thus equates the recital of such a repetitive prayer with taking the Lord's name in vain. If, as Warburton implies, the liturgy's critics used this expression commonly during the Renaissance, then some of the book's contemporary readers presumably could have filled in this blank according to the author's intentions. With the additional advantage of knowing that the missing word rhymed with "bee" in the next line, readers could have overcome the censor's intrusion and helped to restore Donne's presence in the 1633 *Poems*.[46]

All of the satires' blank spaces appear, on the one hand, to erode the poet's authorial status. The horizontal rules declare to even a casual reader that, according to someone else's standards, Donne's most brazen poems sometimes pushed too far. Or, in terms of the poet's own descriptions of excess in *Satyre II*, Donne in places had evidently been out-done by someone else.

On the other hand, we should not overlook that understanding readers might have been influenced by the book's overarching emphasis of Donne's identity and searched for the missing verses among the roughly 250 manuscript copies of his poems and prose then in circulation. More poems by Donne were transcribed during the sixteenth and seventeenth centuries than those of any other single author, and his satires were his most widely read early poems.[47] Readers would have accordingly found restoring these missing words less difficult than if, say, the book's censorial omissions occurred among Donne's *Songs and Sonnets*. Note, too, that the book's creators assist readers in repairing Donne's satires. Unlike the silent suppression of five elegies by Donne that the licensers rejected altogether, these poems call attention to their omissions.[48] If the stationers provide

---

[45] Alexander Pope, "The Satires of Dr. John Donne Versified," in *The Works of Alexander Pope, Esq. In Verse and Prose. Containing the Principal Notes of Drs. Warburton and Warton*, ed. William Lisle Bowles, 10 vols. (London, 1806), 4: 268. In this edition, which prints Donne's satire on the verso and Pope's versification on the recto, the original reference to the litany appears intact, but in place of "To out-doe Dildoes" occurs a series of eight full stops.

[46] Among all the book's censorial omissions, only "Letanie" was not replaced in *Poems*' second, third, and fourth editions, which may suggest that this liturgical controversy continued to 1669, or that so many early readers could guess "Letanie" that the omitted term was not actually missed until after the Civil War. It is also possible that the compositor of the second edition mistakenly omitted this word, and subsequent editions were set from the 1635 text. Instead of marking the omission of "Letanie" with a horizontal rule in *Poems*' second edition, the compositor has simply left off this word from the end of the line. I have consulted the copy of *Poems By J. D.*, 2nd edn. (London, 1635; STC 7046), held at the British Library, London, shelfmark 1076.a12.

[47] Peter Beal, *Index of English Literary Manuscripts*, 2 vols. (London, 1980–), 1: part 1, p. 245.

[48] Not printed in 1633 were Donne's most scandalous elegies – "Loves Progress" and "Going to Bed," presumably for their sexually explicit content; "The Bracelet," "Loves War," and "On His Mistress,"

few clues about exactly what is missing, they alert readers that *something* is. Rather than simply removing all the poems' objectionable passages, the stationers attempted to preserve at least the form of Donne's printable texts. They have left behind these dashes almost as a sign of respect, a textual I.O.U.

Even the book's less ambitious readers must have noticed how all these censorial omissions ironically verify the speaker's attack in *Satyre II* on contemporary abuses of language. Within the poem, Cocus "impaires / His writings" specifically by "leav[ing] out, *ses heires*" so that he can inherit his clients' land (lines 97–98). Cocus acts just as "slily" with his omissions, the speaker argues, as

> any Commenter goes by,
> Hard words, or sense; or in Divinity
> As controverters, in vouch'd Texts, leave out
> Shrewd words, which might against them cleare the doubt.
>
> (lines 99–102/Vv2v)

presumably for their political swipes at France, Spain, and Scotland. The book's designers also silently omit two other passages, lines 7–8 from *Elegie IV*: "The Perfume" (H1r–H2r) and lines 53–54 from *Elegie II*: "The Anagram" (G3r–G4r). In the first case, the omission from "The Perfume" likely originated with the copy from which the compositors worked, for these lines contain nothing obviously offensive ("Though he had wont to search with glazed eyes, / As though he came to kill a cockatrice") and all the surviving manuscripts in the collection known as Group I also omit these lines erroneously, as does the Dolau Cothi MS in Group II.

"The Anagram," however, is missing a reference to masturbation that appears to have been removed in 1633 at the printing house. Manuscript copies of the poem contain two additional lines (which I have underlined below):

> And though in childbirths labour she did lye
> Midwifes would sweare 'twere but a tympany
> Whom if shee accuse her selfe I credit lesse
> Then witches which impossibles confess
> Whom dildoes, bedstaves and her vellet glasse
> Would be as loath to touch as Joseph was.
> One like non, and liked of non fitter were
> For things in fashion every man will weare.
>
> (lines 49–56/G4r)

A full stop occurs after "impossibles confess" in the 1633 *Poems* (line 52), whereas the manuscripts that I examined necessarily use no punctuation so as to connect the dependent clause with the preceding sentence: the two parallel clauses – "Whom . . . I credit lesse / Then witches," and "Whom dildoes . . . / Would be as loath to touch" – must both modify "she" at the start of the passage (line 49). This change in punctuation suggests that a compositor deliberately cut the offensive passage, then altered the text to accommodate the couplet's omission. The inclusion of the omitted list in all but one primary manuscript collection (the single exception, the Dolau Cothi MS [Group II]) further supports that the book's creators purposely removed the couplet. Still, we do not know why Flesher and Marriot would have decided against a series of horizontal rules to mark this excision. Having examined over fifty partial and complete manuscript copies of "The Anagram," John T. Shawcross notes more generally, "Various lines are omitted in several texts." See Shawcross, ed., *The Complete Poetry of John Donne*, p. 438.

In all these instances, unscrupulous readers are using omission for their own benefit; they leave something out to make a text mean what they want – *contra* the authors' intentions. The book's censor could hardly have chosen a worse poem to meddle with, for Donne has here anticipated and outmaneuvered him: to remove any of Donne's own "shrewd words" allies the book's censor with corrupt lawyers, obtuse commentators, and dishonest controversialists. As M. Thomas Hester has argued, the speaker's final concession of his own ineffectiveness – "my words none drawes / Within the vast reach of th' huge statute lawes" (lines 111–12) – seems to reinforce the poem's thesis that "England suffers from the abuse and disregard of the truthful potential of language."[49] The omission of the speaker's most biting criticism would accordingly represent the ultimate proof that the power of truth has indeed been curtailed in Renaissance England: the poet's words are not just ignored; they have been excised by the same corrupt legal authority that he attacks for disrespecting truth and using language fraudulently.

The 1633 *Poems*' last cancelled passage, in *Satyre IIII*, similarly undoes itself, ironically complementing – rather than diminishing – the speaker's meaning. This omission also subverts Donne's authority, but, in another double move that characterizes so much in the volume, the poem's blank space may, with the reader's help, further augment the poet's presence. The omission occurs as the poet listens to a boorish courtier cataloguing lies and libels about other members of the court:

> Who wasts in meat, in clothes, in horse, he notes;
> Who loves Whores, who boyes, and who goats.
> I more amas'd then Circes prisoners, when
> They felt themselves turne beasts, felt my selfe then
> Becomming Traytor, and mee thought I saw
> One of our Giant Statutes ope his jaw
> To sucke me in, for hearing him. I found
>
> ⎯⎯   ⎯⎯   ⎯⎯   ⎯⎯   ⎯⎯
>
> ⎯⎯   Therefore I did shew
> All signes of loathing; But since I am in,
> I must pay mine, and my forefathers sinne
> To the last farthing.
>
> (lines 127–39/Xx3r)

These broken horizontal rules replace another omitted metaphor, "That as burnt venome Leachers doe grow sound / By giving others their soares,

[49] M. Thomas Hester, *Kinde Pitty and Brave Scorn: John Donne's Satyres* (Durham, NC, 1982), p. 52.

I might grow / Guilty, and he free" (lines 134–36). Here Donne seems to be mocking the idea of touching someone as a method of healing. He imagines the most repellent patients possible, "burnt venome Leachers," and suggests that they infect the healers who try to treat them.

Although we might initially infer that the censor objected to this missing passage for its potentially sexual content – specifically, the image of lecherous men with venereal sores – Donne's excised metaphor also seems to parody the "King's touch."[50] Up until the eighteenth century, doctors recommended that kings lay hands on their subjects to cure scrofula as well as various other sicknesses that caused blisters, ulcers, and sores. Patients would queue up at a special religious service and kneel one at a time before the king who gently pressed his hands against their faces while a member of the clergy read aloud from Scripture, "They shall lay hands on the sick, and they shall recover" (Mark 16: 18).[51] Charles I in particular considered rival healers or "strokers," as they were called, a threat to his exclusive right to cure sufferers by touch.[52] In 1632, the same year that Donne's *Poems* were licensed, the Privy Council ordered the Lord Chief Justice to examine a French prisoner who "takes upon him to cure the king's evil, and daily a great concourse of people flock to him." When the Chief Justice failed to prosecute Boisgaudre for "sorcery and incantation," the Council imprisoned him anyway, on the grounds he had committed "a contempt worth punishment."[53]

The censor's excision of Donne's allusion to this alternative medicine once again piques our curiosity: the removal of these lines from the middle of a sentence leaves us wondering what exactly the poet "found" upon "hearing" the boorish courtier. But this omission also unintentionally fits the meaning of Donne's poem. Worrying that he is "Becoming Traytor" by listening to the courtier's lies and libels, the poet imagines himself

---

[50] As further evidence that the omission was not made exclusively for the image's sexual content, the poem contains other, at least equally risqué passages, such as "Who loves Whores, who boyes, and who goats" (line 128), which the censor chose not to cut. Sullivan agrees that Donne is alluding to the king's healing ritual, whereas Wesley Milgate notes a seventeenth-century superstition of curing syphilis by infecting someone else. See Sullivan, "1633 Vndone," p. 303; and Milgate, ed., *John Donne: The Satires, Epigrams, and Verse Letters* (Oxford, 1967), p. 158.

[51] The practice became so popular during the Renaissance that kings began keeping "Registers of Healing," and the Book of Common Prayer started to include the ritual in 1634. Keith Thomas, *Religion and the Decline of Magic* (New York, 1971), p. 192.

[52] In *Biathanatos*, composed almost three decades earlier, Donne alludes to this same controversy. He accepts that healers can "cure diseases by touch, or by charme" but points out the inequity, that "vulgar owners of such a vertue" are "forbidden by divers Lawes" from doing so, "yet none mislikes that the Kings of *England* & *France*, should cure one sicknesse by such means." See Donne, *ΒΙΑΘΑΝΑΤΟΣ* (London, 1644; Wing D1858), Ee1v–Ee2r.

[53] *Calendar of State Papers, Domestic Series, 1631–33*, ed. John Bruce (London, 1862), pp. 252, 347–48.

prosecuted for treason according to the state's "Giant Statutes." He just begins to recognize his culpability – what Annabel Patterson has called the poet's "metamorphosis of complicity" – when the censor interrupts, silencing him.[54] The satire's omission either prevents the poet from erring or substantiates his fears; either he is cut off before he slips up, or he did become a traitor, and his words had to be excised. Both possible interpretations complement the poem, for cancelling these lines enacts the metamorphosis that Donne describes: the speaker and reader are momentarily "sucke[d]" into the blank space that the censor creates in the middle of the verse. The omission's interruption reminds us that we, too, have been listening to the courtier's accusations and we, too, may have been infected by his diseased words. When the satire resumes – "Therefore I did shew / All signes of loathing" (lines 136–37/Xx3r) – the poet suddenly sounds cured: he may have temporarily "flat-lined," but he now re-asserts control over himself and his verse.

Although few readers of the 1633 *Poems* could have arrived at such a detailed interpretation without additional hints about the omitted passage, they at least ought to have noticed the appropriateness of the censor intruding just as the poet senses himself "Becoming Traytor." Only those readers who knew the metaphor that the censor suppressed could then have appreciated how the omission allows a state-sanctioned remedy to replace the treasonous type of healing to which the poet – though only metaphorically – had almost turned. As soon as the poet felt himself falling ill, the king's agents laid hands on Donne's poem and wiped away anything they deemed infectious.

Clearly this omission, like the four censored passages in *Satyre II*, diminishes the author's presence in the 1633 volume. The dashes again signify that an outside agent oversaw the publication and had the authority to edit Donne's works, and these same dashes again allow readers to devise their own alternatives to fill in the book's blanks. But because this omission once again fits the meaning of Donne's poem, we can also see that the censor's cuts do not damage irreparably Donne's defining role in *Poems, By J. D.*

Nor should we, once again, underestimate the emphasis on Donne's identity elsewhere in the volume, which may have influenced readers' responses to the satires' blank lines. Because *Poems* contains so few of these censorial omissions, readers could have ignored their implications for the author's

---

[54] Annabel Patterson, *Censorship and Interpretation: The Conditions of Writing and Reading in Early Modern England* (Madison, WI, 1984), p. 93. Writing about censorship and Donne's satires, Patterson neglects to note that these poems were in fact censored in the 1633 volume.

authority; or, as we saw earlier, because Donne's satires enjoyed such a wide circulation, readers may have been able to locate manuscript copies containing the author's original words. If some readers, as we have seen, filled in *Poems'* title page by attaching Donne's signature below his monogram, they could have similarly tried to restore Donne's words on the satires' blank lines. Certainly some readers would have been motivated in part by a prurient curiosity: what could have been deemed unprintable, they might wonder, in poems that openly satirize bestiality and catamites? In the context of the other types of participation that were commonly expected of Renaissance readers – for example, correcting passages on the basis of sometimes extensive errata lists – the book's understanders may not have found the work required to complete Donne's satires all that strenuous. Early modern readers may have even been accustomed to filling in such blanks, for, as H. R. Woudhuysen reminds us, "documents – forms, broadsides, notices – were printed with spaces to be filled. Plague bills, leases, indentures, and trading documents had to be completed by hand; Church of England or heralds' visitation articles were left conveniently blank; almanacs were designed to leave space for notes and occasional memoranda . . ."[55]

Donne's *Satyre IIII* concludes, moreover, with the speaker directly asking readers to complete what he has begun. Like the printer's irony in the preface, which allowed understanders to demonstrate their own worthiness, Donne's satires – especially these incomplete ones – require his audience's knowledge and caring. Only understanding readers will see beyond the satires' narratives and discover Donne's sometimes subversive meanings. When Donne writes in the final lines of *Satyre IIII* that "some wise man shall, / I hope, esteeme my writs Canonicall" (lines 243–44/Yy1r), he seems to acknowledge how much he depends on understanders, both to unlock his poems' irony and, more broadly, to interpret the 1633 volume. As opposed to the courtier's knowledge "Of triviall houshold trash" (line 98/Xx2v), Donne needs wise, active readers who, by comprehending his satiric tone, may be motivated to reform the court and, he hopes, establish his canonical status.

Ultimately, in 1633, the audience for Donne's *Poems* is being invited to help transfer the author's works from manuscript to print. In the previous chapter, we saw how Ben Jonson in his 1616 Folio emerged as a poet of transition – an author trying to feel at home in both the court and printing house. Seventeen years later, Donne in *Poems, By J. D.* is similarly pulled

---

[55] H. R. Woudhuysen, *Sir Philip Sidney and the Circulation of Manuscripts 1558–1640* (Oxford, 1996), p. 20.

in two directions. His imperfect verses recall the mutability of scribal publication, while their specific presentation still depended on the stationers
who designed and printed the book. In like manner, the censor's interventions foreground the author's lack of control in the process of material
production, while the satires' dashes leave open the possibility that readers
will track down the poet's manuscript copies and thus reinforce his authority. The overall design of *Poems* – reflecting not only this shift from
manuscript to print, but also, perhaps, a deliberate marketing strategy –
repeatedly presents readers with these near paradoxes. Their cumulative
effect preserves the absent J. D. as a manuscript poet still writing for an
exclusive group of understanders, while the evocations of his ongoing presence ironically cast him as a Jonsonian author, overseeing this collection
and speaking to us personally through his printed book.

Among Jonson's most notable observations about Donne, William
Drummond reports that, "he esteemeth John Done [*sic*] the first poet in the
World in some things."[56] Presumably Jonson was describing Donne's poetic
accomplishments, but with the publication of the posthumous *Poems,*
Donne, like Jonson – and Sidney, Herrick, and Milton – was being constructed as one of the first autonomous English authors. If Jonson also truly
believed that Donne "for not being understood, would perish," then the
1633 *Poems,* specifically targeted to reach the most discerning understanders,
helped to prove him wrong.[57]

---

[56] Jonson, *Conversations with William Drummond,* in Herford and Simpson, 1: 135. Mark Bland has
argued that Donne and Jonson, "linked in manuscript after manuscript," had a "deep and enduring
friendship." See Bland, "Jonson, *Biathanatos* and the Interpretation of Manuscript Evidence," *Studies
in Bibliography* 51 (1998): 154–82.
[57] Jonson, *Conversations with William Drummond,* in Herford and Simpson, 1: 138.

CHAPTER 5

Herrick unbound

Non scribit, cuius carmina nemo legit.
– Martial[1]

In its configuration of the author and reader's relative authority, Robert Herrick's *Hesperides* (1648) falls somewhere between Jonson's 1616 Folio, on the one side, and Sidney's *Arcadia* and Donne's 1633 *Poems*, on the other. Like his poetic "Father," Jonson (R1r/H-575), Herrick uses omissions to assert his control over his texts in *Hesperides*, but, like Donne's and Sidney's publications, Herrick's collection emphasizes the reader's role in filling his poems' blanks.[2] The ultimate omission for Herrick remains his unwritten, poetic future, and the missing pieces in two of his poems, we will see, exemplify the process that he wants future readers to undertake with his larger body of work.

From the start, *Hesperides* showcases Herrick's self-consciousness; the volume contains more than fifty-five separate poems in which the poet addresses himself, his book, or his readers. All of the opening ten verses are so directed. In the first poem, Herrick dedicates the collection "TO THE MOST ILLUSTRIOUS, AND Most Hopefull PRINCE, CHARLES, Prince of *Wales*" (A3); with the second verse, he requests that the reader should "*Condemne the Printer . . . and not me*" for the book's "*Tares*" and "*Transgressions*" (A4r). Then – before we come across even one of Herrick's

---

[1] "No one writes, whose poems no one reads." Martial, *Epigrams*, ed. and trans. D. R. Shackleton Bailey, 3 vols. (Cambridge, MA, 1993), book III, epigram 9 (1: 206–7).
[2] This and all subsequent references to Herrick's text are taken from *Hesperides: Or, The Works Both Humane & Divine of Robert Herrick Esq.* (London, 1648; Wing H1596) held at the Harry Ransom Humanities Research Center at the University of Texas in Austin (Pforz 468). Printed as a double book with *His Noble Numbers: Or, His Pious Pieces*, the book consists of 244 leaves and collates 8°: A⁴B-Z⁸Aa-Cc⁸ ²Aa-Ee⁸ [$4 signed (-A1, A2, A3, A4, B4)]. P4 is mis-signed as Y4, and C7, M8, and O8 are cancels. *Hesperides*, the first collection, appears on B1r–Cc7v; *Noble Numbers* is printed on ²Aa1r–Ee8r (verso blank) with a separate title page (Cc8r, verso blank) dividing the two collections. For the reader's convenience in locating specific poems, I include parenthetically the numeration of individual verses from *The Complete Poetry of Robert Herrick*, ed. J. Max Patrick (New York, 1963), preceded by the corresponding signatures from the 1648 text.

150

famous nervelets, lawns, or lilies – we encounter "The Argument of his Book," "To his Muse," "To his Booke," "Another," "Another," "To the Soure Reader," "To his Booke," and "When he Would Have his Verses Read" (B1r–B2r). The remaining self-conscious poems are broadcast throughout the collection – a wide poetic net spread out to ensnare anyone who attempts to duck past the book's opening sally.

All of these quasi-autobiographical gestures invite readers to approach *Hesperides* as the expression of a single individual. Herrick appears, like Donne, to speak to his audience directly, and, like Jonson, to have overseen his publication and arranged the texts deliberately. *Hesperides'* title page (figure 5a), resembling the design of Jonson's 1616 Folio, also emphasizes Herrick's authorship, "THE WORKS | BOTH | HUMANE & DIVINE | OF | Robert Herrick *Efq.*" (A2r); the separate title page for *Hesperides'* companion collection similarly stresses the poet's proprietary rights to the text, "HIS | NOBLE NUMBERS: | *OR,* | HIS PIOUS PIECES" (Cc8r). Whereas the perception of Donne's presence in his 1633 *Poems* paradoxically required his absence from the book's material production, Herrick's volume presents no such problems. The collection concludes with a second set of poems in which the poet addresses himself, his book, and his lasting reputation. "Tho Kingdoms fal," Herrick presciently forecasts in the penultimate verse, he will survive through his book, a pillar of fame to "stand for ever by his owne / Firme and well fixt foundation" (Cc7v/H-1129).

In this chapter I want to examine the relationship between Herrick and his readers in terms of such lofty aspirations. While *Hesperides* surely foregrounds the poet's presence, it also emphasizes his dependence on other people – during both the book's material production and its reception among unpredictable readers. Showing first how the physical text demonstrates the author's lack of autonomy, I then turn to Herrick's comments about the importance of audience participation as a means of overcoming the limitations of print. *Hesperides'* two incomplete poems – "The Apparition of his Mistresse Calling him to Elizium" (Q8v–R1r/H-575) and "The Country Life, to the Honoured M. End. Porter" (S7r–S8r/H-662) – most dramatically enact this reciprocal relationship between poet and readers. While demonstrating Herrick's exquisite authority, these fragments simultaneously demand a cooperative audience. In this way, Herrick's two poems reflect the author's increasing status during the middle of the seventeenth century: Herrick's personality may dominate his book – as the personalities of Donne, Jonson, and Sidney dominate their publications – but only with readers' help, Herrick again and again insists, can he write successful poetry and achieve lasting fame.

HESPERIDES:

OR,

THE WORKS

BOTH

HUMANE & DIVINE

OF

ROBERT HERRICK *Esq.*

OVID.

Effugient avidos Carmina nostra Rogos.

LONDON,

Printed for *John Williams,* and *Francis Eglesfield,*
and are to be fold at the Crown and Marygold
in Saint *Pauls* Church-yard. 1648.

Figure 5a. Title page of Robert Herrick's *Hesperides* (1648).

DELIGHT IN DISORDER

Although *Hesperides'* introductory and concluding verses have a clear order – John L. Kimmey describes the two clusters of personal poems as a "prologue" and "epilogue"[3] – critics disagree about the volume's overarching cohesion. Herrick seems to accept, as Gordon Braden observes, the "likelihood of spot-reading," for at least one of the opening verses, "To the Soure Reader" (B2r/H-6), begins with the conditional clause, "If thou dislik'st the Piece thou light'st on first."[4] Any collection comprising 1,402 brief poems necessarily "exhausts the attention, both of reader and of writer . . . one is always starting over again, only to go not very far."[5] Randall Ingram has similarly empowered Herrick's readers by suggesting that many of *Hesperides'* poems defy a single organizational strategy. He proposes that the book "might rather be described as multiply coherent, permitting multiple readers to participate in the making of multiple patterns."[6]

Most recent critics, however, have followed Kimmey in attempting to show that Herrick put together the collection "with a firm plan and purpose in mind."[7] As Roger Rollin argues, *Hesperides* "is not a book meant for browsing" but should instead "be read from beginning to end, in sequence, as one might follow a garden path."[8] At stake for these critics is Herrick's status as a major or minor poet: if Herrick oversaw the book's design and crafted so many precise, intertextual relationships, then surely he deserves entry into the pantheon of major Renaissance writers.[9] Thus Ann Baynes Coiro specifically locates the volume's "integrating structure" within the tradition of Renaissance epigram books. Like Kimmey and Rollin, she argues that Herrick himself "gathered together the work of his lifetime into one polished, self-presented and self-presenting volume."[10]

---

[3] John L. Kimmey, "Order and Form in Herrick's *Hesperides*," *Journal of English and Germanic Philology* 70 (1971): 255–68, this quotation, p. 256.

[4] Gordon Braden, *The Classics and English Renaissance Poetry: Three Case Studies* (New Haven, 1978), p. 182.

[5] Braden, *The Classics and English Renaissance Poetry*, p. 181.

[6] Randall Ingram, "Robert Herrick and the Makings of *Hesperides*," *Studies in English Literature, 1500–1900* 38 (1998): 127–47, this quotation, p. 144.

[7] Kimmey, "Order and Form in Herrick's *Hesperides*," p. 268.

[8] Roger B. Rollin, "Witty by Design: Robert Herrick's *Hesperides*," in *The Wit of Seventeenth-Century Poetry*, ed. Claude J. Summers and Ted-Larry Pebworth (Columbia, MO, 1995), pp. 135–50, this quotation, p. 141.

[9] T. S. Eliot first relegated Herrick to the status of a minor poet because "there is no . . . continuous conscious *purpose* about Herrick's poems." See Eliot, "What Is Minor Poetry?" *The Sewanee Review* 54 (1946): 1–18, this quotation, p. 10.

[10] Ann Baynes Coiro, *Robert Herrick's* Hesperides *and the Epigram Book Tradition* (Baltimore, 1988), pp. 3, 4.

I would suggest instead that *Hesperides* reflects a more collaborative provenance, an origin that would have prevented the poet from dictating his poems' exact sequence. The question is not whether Herrick intended to have *Hesperides* printed in a particular order but how much real control the author had over his book's design and printing. In practical terms, that any seventeenth-century poet would have been able to insist on a precise organization for printing over 1,000 separate poems seems unlikely; that the mostly unproven Herrick could have dictated the conditions for this specific volume seems even less plausible.[11]

A brief, bibliographical analysis reveals Herrick's limited role in the book's production. Although critics have interpreted the errata list in *Hesperides* as proof that the poet was a "meticulous . . . craftsman,"[12] other books published and/or sold by Francis Eglesfield and John Williams frequently included errata. In Henry Jeanes' *The Works of Heaven upon Earth* (1649), for example, the publishers use a pronouncement above the errata that echoes *Hesperides'* similarly placed warning about the book's "*Tares*" and "*Transgressions*" (A4r). Jeanes asks his "*Gentle Reader . . . to amend with thy pen, these grossest escapes of the Printer: for they are such as spoyle the sense . . .*"[13]

More importantly, because the sixteen items in *Hesperides'* errata almost exclusively correct typical printing errors, they could have been made by a member of the printing house instead of Herrick. Here readers are invited to repair misspellings ("*Gotiere*" to replace "*Coteire*" D5r/H-111; "*Lachrimae*" to replace "*Lacrime*" M3v/H-371); substitutions ("*ʃoft*" to replace "foft" G2r/H-193; "*having drunk*" to replace "havink drunk" Q3v/H-554); misreadings ("*onely one*" to replace "Onely our" F11r/H-157; "*such fears*" to replace "such Heates" G6r/H-204); omissions of letters ("*Rods*" to replace "*rod*" D11r/H-97); and omissions of words ("*to thee the*" to replace "*To thee*" K4v/H-293A; "*the flowrie*" to replace "flowrie" G4v/H-201).[14]

The two corrections that most substantially alter the meaning of Herrick's poems also seem slight enough to be plausibly made by a member of the

---

[11] Whereas L. C. Martin argued that Herrick's contemporary reputation probably peaked some twenty years before the publication of *Hesperides*, J. Max Patrick has challenged the assertion that Herrick was "well-known" at any time before 1648. See Martin, ed., *The Poetical Works of Robert Herrick* (Oxford, 1956), p. xvii; and Patrick, "'Poetry Perpetuates the Poet': Richard James and the Growth of Herrick's Reputation," in *"Trust to Good Verses": Herrick Tercentenary Essays*, ed. Roger B. Rollin and J. Max Patrick (Pittsburgh, 1978), pp. 221–34.

[12] George Walton Scott, *Robert Herrick, 1591–1674* (New York, 1974), p. 89.

[13] Henry Jeanes, *The Works of Heaven upon Earth* (London, 1649; Wing J513), A2v.

[14] The remaining items in the errata are exclusively substitutions ("*let chast*" to replace "yet chaste" O5r/H-465; "*a wife as*" to replace "a wise as" Y8r/H-885); and misreadings ("*washt or's*" to replace "Washt o're" L6r/H-336; "*thy brest*" to replace "thy bed" N4r/H-417; and "*to rise*" to replace "to kisse" S2v/H-634).

printing house who compared the text with the author's copy. The errata instruct readers to change "*when He sees*" to "*where so ere he sees*" (²Bb3v/ H-71) and to repair the line "Ah! woe woe woe woe woe is me" so that it instead reads "*Ah woe is me, woe, woe is me*" (N3r/H-412). The first of these changes corrects such a conspicuously incomplete line of pentameter, "God crowns our goodnesse, when He sees," that the printer probably misread the author's copy, confusing "where" for "when" and leaving out the miss-ing iamb. The second correction also likely occurred when the compositor glanced away from the manuscript: misremembering which words were repeated, he duplicated "woe woe" instead of repeating "is me." Because the author's copy would have contained the correct readings for both these errors, neither item demonstrates that Herrick continued to fine-tune his poems during the final stages of publishing. Even Herrick's warning printed above the errata (A̲4r), while it helps to establish his presence at the start of the volume, does not suggest that the poet oversaw the book's creation but instead reveals his dependence on readers and stationers. Wittily appro-priating Martial's similar disclaimer from his *Epigrammata*, Herrick asks readers to help complete his poems and explains that he produced "*good Grain*" but could not prevent the printers from having "*sow'd these Tares throughout my Book*" (A̲4r).[15]

Hesperides's variants also provide little evidence that Herrick participated actively in the publication process. A. W. Pollard has identified variants in seven different formes: L(o), Q(o), X(i), Cc(i), ²Dd(i), ²Dd(o), and ²Ee(i).[16] Although we need to qualify our conclusions until a more thorough comparison of surviving copies can be conducted, most of these changes appear to be minor stop-press corrections, some of which a corrector could have identified without reference to the copy. Presumably, the different states exist because the gatherer took sheets from formes in both their corrected and uncorrected states when gathering them into a complete copy of the book. Pollard notes, for example, that while some copies misnumber all of the pages on one side of sheet X, other copies paginate these leaves correctly; in like manner, some copies contain the misprint "compulsine" (Cc2r), while other copies contain the bungled correction, "compulsinve."

Hesperides' other stop-press corrections include minor changes in orthog-raphy and punctuation that suggest a member of the printing house proof-read with the copy or, at least, with attention to the content of the poems.

---

[15] *Cf.* Martial, *Epigrams*, 2.8, lines 1–4 (1: 140–41).
[16] A. W. Pollard, "A List of Variations in Three Copies of the Original Edition of Herrick's *Hesperides* and *Noble Numbers*," *The Library*, new series, 4 (1903): 206–12, with an addendum, pp. 328–31. This article mistakenly identifies sheet Cc as sheet Dd.

The printer has inserted or deleted a comma (^{2}Ee5v), moved a parenthesis (^{2}Dd1v), added a space between words (Cc6r), and added or moved a final "s" (L1r, Cc7v, ^{2}Dd6v). In theory, Herrick could have been behind some of these small improvements; we ultimately do not know why the printer would have troubled with such time-consuming repairs of such minor details – at the poet's request, say, or according to the printer's own standard of correctness. Some of the changes probably occurred when the printer attempted to correct an obvious mistake elsewhere in the same forme. That some copies print "Demon" and others read "Dæmon" (L4v), for example, does not represent a change for which a printer would likely bother to stop the press, but was presumably made when the egregious error "jestn ithis" (L3r) was repaired to read "jest in this" on the same side of sheet L.

In this context, the single substantive change, "played" *versus* "started" in Q(o), looks less like an authorial revision and more like the result of another printing blunder.[17] Granted, the effect in "Upon her Feet" may represent a subtle improvement:

> Her pretty feet
> Like snailes did creep
> A little out, and then,
> As if they played at Bo-peep,
> Did soon draw in agen.
>
> (Q1r/H-525)

Just as the poem's successive feet mimic the movement of the beloved's flirtatious toes – first creeping leftward on the page (lines 3–4), then drawing back (line 5) – the specific revision of "played" to "started" would improve the line's meter while conveying both a heightened sense of expectation (As if they "began") and a more abrupt motion (As if they "leapt out").[18] Although Herrick could have been reviewing the sheet and insisted on tinkering with this one word, we also need to acknowledge the likelihood

---

[17] Leah S. Marcus has suggested that the parenthetical insertion of "almost" in "Dean-bourn" (C7r/ line 12) supports her argument that Herrick participated in *Hesperides'* publication and continued to fine-tune some of his verses. She may be right. But the omission of this word, which occurs in only one known copy of *Hesperides*, more likely represents an oversight that a corrector repaired soon after the print-run had begun. Because the insertion of "almost" is needed to sustain the poem's otherwise regular pentameter, Herrick probably included it in his original manuscript. See Marcus, "Robert Herrick," in *The Cambridge Companion to English Poetry: Donne to Marvell*, ed. Thomas N. Corns (Cambridge, 1993), pp. 171–82, especially p. 174; *The Poetical Works of Robert Herrick*, ed. L. C. Martin (Oxford, 1956), pp. xxiii, 29; and Pollard, "A List of Variations," p. 208.

[18] We do not know for certain, however, whether "played" was changed to "started," or "started" changed to "played." L. C. Martin records that six copies he examined read "started" and fifteen read "played." See *The Poetical Works of Robert Herrick*, ed. Martin, p. 194.

that the compositor had difficulty reading the author's copy. As anyone who has attempted to decipher Elizabethan handwriting can attest, the confusion of "pl" and "st" would not even require an especially messy manuscript. One typical form of the miniscule "s" resembles some forms of "p," while the commonly looped Elizabethan "t" may also have a foot like an "l."[19] A corrector could have then caught the mistake by consulting Herrick's copy and, without the poet's assistance, accurately re-interpreted this word.

During the seventeenth century, the traditional procedures for proof-reading remained relatively thorough. In *Mechanick Exercises of the Whole Art of Printing (1683–1684)*, Joseph Moxon describes how the corrector would "carefully and vigilantly" examine and mark up a first proof, some-times working with an assistant who read the copy aloud. The compositor would then repair in the forme the faults that the corrector detected:

> Then he carries the *Form* to the *Press* and lays it on the [*Correcting-*]*Stone* for a *Second Proof*, and sometimes for a *Third Proof*, which having *Corrected*, he at last brings the *Form* to the *Press*, and again lays it on the *Stone* . . . After all this *Correcting* a *Revise* is made, and if any *Faults* are found in any *Quarter* of it, or in all the *Quarters*, he calls to the *Press-man* to *Unlock* that *Quarter*, or the whole *Form*, that he may *Correct* those *Faults*.[20]

Moxon does not entirely exclude authors from this correcting process, but he suggests that they rarely played an important role. He advises the writer of a manuscript

> *to deliver his* Copy *perfect . . . For by no means he ought to hope to mend it in the* Proof, *the* Compositor *not being obliged to it: And it cannot reasonably be expected he should be so good Natured to take so much pains to mend such Alterations as the second Dictates of an Author may make, unless he be very well paid for it over and above what he agreed for with the* Master Printer.[21]

Nothing in *Hesperides* that we have seen so far suggests that the book's creators deviated from this standard arrangement. Nor did Herrick, recently expelled from his vicarage in Devonshire, likely have the resources to make

[19] See R. B. McKerrow, *An Introduction to Bibliography*, 2nd edn. (Oxford, 1928), pp. 222–30; and Philip Gaskell, *A New Introduction to Bibliography* (Oxford, 1972), pp. 361–67. For a telling sample of Herrick's handwriting, see the facsimile of one of his letters in F. W. Moorman, *Robert Herrick: A Biographical and Critical Study* (New York, 1962), pp. 134–35.

[20] Joseph Moxon, *Mechanick Exercises of the Whole Art of Printing (1683–1684)*, ed. Herbert Davies and Harry Carter, 2nd edn. (London, 1962), pp. 238–39, 247. As D. F. McKenzie also notes, Moxon's description of proof-reading corresponds to the available evidence gleaned from analyzing Elizabethan texts. See McKenzie, "Printers of the Mind: Some Notes on Bibliographical Theories and Printing-House Practices," *Studies in Bibliography* 22 (1969): 1–76.

[21] Moxon, *Mechanick Exercises of the Whole Art of Printing*, pp. 250–51.

sure the compositor was "very well paid" for any additional labor that last-minute changes would have required. In fact, we do not know whether the poet was residing in London in 1647 when the book first went to press.[22]

But if Herrick had been living nearby when his collection was printed, the insertion of three cancel leaves in *Hesperides*, C7, M8, and O8, further supports his absence from the printing house. Although one of these cancels appears to correct a less significant error – "lively-food" is replaced with "lively-hood" in "To his Peculiar Friend Sir Edward Fish" (M8v)[23] – the two other cancels correct substantive mistakes: one repairs an inverted stanza in "Kissing Usurie" (C7v), and the other restores the omitted eleventh stanza to "The Wassaile" (O8v). Had Herrick overseen his book's printing and regularly perused advance sheets, he would presumably have had these errors corrected during an earlier stage of proof-reading. The survival of so many copies of *Hesperides* without the replacement leaves suggests that all these corrections were made especially late: the printer, as was common during this period, repaired the text after some imperfect copies had already been sold.[24] L. C. Martin notes that corrected and uncorrected copies survive in almost even proportion; out of the twenty-one copies he examined, twelve contained all the replacement leaves, but nine still contained at least one of the cancellanda.[25]

---

[22] According to Anthony à Wood, Herrick spent at least part of the Commonwealth period in "S. Ann's Parish in Westminster," but no London parish by that name existed during the seventeenth century. Scott suggests that Herrick "most probably" returned to London immediately after his expulsion and speculates that Wood meant St Anne's Street in St Margaret's parish. See Wood, *Athenae Oxonienses*, 4 vols. (New York, 1967), 3: 250–52; and Scott, *Robert Herrick, 1591–1674*, pp. 94, 185.

   We also need to remember that, although *Hesperides* reads "1648," the book's printing probably began in 1647. The title page of *Noble Numbers* reads "1647," and the later date on the title page of *Hesperides* – printed with the book's other preliminaries, *after* the title page for *Noble Numbers* – could indicate when the printers completed their work, or it could reflect the common practice of dating books with the subsequent year so as to make their title pages look more current. According to Thomas N. Corns' analysis of *Hesperides'* contemporary references, Herrick probably finished assembling his poems in autumn 1647, and the book was printed in early 1648. See Corns, Appendix A, in *Uncloistered Virtue: English Political Literature, 1640–1660* (Oxford, 1992), pp. 307–8. The latest poem that we can confidently date from *Hesperides* remains Herrick's song "To the King, Upon his Welcome to Hampton-Court" (Aa2v/H-961), commemorating an event from 24 August 1647.

[23] This slight change resembles the equally minor mistakes corrected by cancels in other early modern books. See R. W. Chapman, *Cancels* (London and New York, 1930), p. 7.

[24] Apparently, all the cancel leaves were not inserted at the same time, for the cancel of M8 occurs with less frequency than the cancels of C7 and O8. If the need for cancels had been discovered before the printers finished work on the book, the extra cancel leaves could have been set in the last sheet along with the preliminary matter. From my examination of the paper's chain lines in the copies held at the British Library and the Harry Ransom Humanities Research Center, I could not determine whether the same sheet had been used for the cancels and introductory materials.

[25] Martin, ed., *The Poetical Works of Robert Herrick*, p. xxii.

Even the quality of *Hesperides'* cancels suggests the author's limited role in the printing, for he does not seem to have read proofs of the replacement leaves; in at least one surviving copy, the printers did not take sufficient care, and the cancel of O8 has been inserted the wrong way round.[26] Herrick almost certainly did not take this opportunity to polish his poems. The substantive change of "watry" for "warty" to describe "incivility" in "Dean-bourn" (C7r/H-86), for example, could merely be a transposition, especially since more egregious errors are introduced in the same replacement leaf. The verso misprints "Between thy Breasts" as "Between thy Breast" in "To Julia" (C7v/H-88), and "A sacred" is misprinted as "Asacred" in "To Laurels" (C7v/H-89).

To help establish that Herrick did oversee the design of *Hesperides*, critics have sometimes emphasized his epigram to the diplomat and courtier Michael Oldisworth (Cc3v–Cc4r/H-1092). Here the poet claims that "Fames rear'd Pillar" will appear "In the next sheet" (lines 5, 6), an apparent allusion to "The Pillar of Fame" (H-1129), the collection's penultimate poem. As Ann Baynes Coiro explains,

"The pillar of Fame" does indeed follow "To the most accomplish Gentleman Master Michael Oulsworth" on the next sheet of the gathering as it would have appeared before being folded, bound, and cut. It is therefore a reference to the actual printing process, and the epigram is presumably one of the very last poems Herrick wrote for publication.[27]

While Coiro's attention to the book's material production is laudable, Herrick's epigram to Michael Oldisworth actually illustrates the poet's lack of control over his book's printing process. The poem contains another of the "*Transgressions*" that we were warned about in the couplet above the errata (A4r). "The Pillar of Fame" does not, as Herrick seems to indicate, appear "in the next sheet." It is printed on the same sheet, 2C – on the same side of the same sheet 2C(i). Herrick may have expected "The Pillar of Fame" to be printed on the next sheet, or perhaps this line originally referred to a lost manuscript collection that positioned the two poems differently. But if Herrick in 1648 was thinking about his works in relation to each other, his epigram to Oldisworth reveals that he could not ultimately guarantee a precise ordering for his poems.

---

[26] These pages introduce so many minor changes in spelling, spacing, hyphenation, and punctuation that they look hurriedly composed or, perhaps, composed according to printing-house conventions rather than with the author's manuscript. The incorrect insertion of O8 occurs in a copy of *Hesperides* that I examined at the British Library, shelfmark E.1090.

[27] Coiro, *Robert Herrick's* Hesperides *and the Epigram Book Tradition*, p. 142. See also Braden, *The Classics and English Renaissance Poetry*, p. 182.

The errors in *Hesperides'* catchwords also raise doubts about the publishers' observing a firm plan in organizing Herrick's volume. The practice of printing the first word from the following page at the end of each page's direction line was supposed to aid the compositor in properly ordering a text. But on eight pages in *Hesperides* the catchwords do not correspond to the first word on the following page. Although one of these disagreements could have arisen because the compositor misread the next line of poetry – in this case, "*You*" instead of the correct "*Yet*" (D7r) – the other errors suggest that the compositor sometimes deviated from the manuscript for some reason. On H8r, for example, the catchword reads "*His*" while the first word on the verso actually reads "To," in the title "To the High and Noble Prince, George" (H8v). Perhaps an entirely different page should have followed H8r, or, because the second and only other poem on the verso is "His Recantation," we may wonder whether the catchword "*His*" was initially correct and Herrick or a member of the printing house intended to reverse these poems' positions.

The same kind of mistake occurs on one of the leaves in *Noble Numbers*: the catchword reads "*His*" instead of the correct "*God*." That the third poem on the verso is titled "His Creed" (²Bb4r) again raises the possibility that the order of the poems was suddenly altered. L. C. Martin explains two other incorrect catchwords by speculating that a short poem about "Selfe love" was mistakenly omitted from the top of N1r.[28] This explanation not only accounts for the erroneous catchword, "Selfe," at the bottom of the preceding page (M8v) but it also rectifies the catchword "She" on N1r: adding a brief poem about self-love would bring N1r up short, in the midst of "The Dreame"; the next page would then begin correctly with the line "She told me too" (line 5). While all the errors in *Hesperides'* catchwords could reflect Herrick's re-shuffling his book at the last minute, these mistakes also suggest that members of the printing house – perhaps unintentionally – helped to determine the poems' ordering. For whatever reason, the collection's organization during the production process at least seems to have been subject to change.[29]

[28] Martin, ed., *The Poetical Works of Robert Herrick*, p. xxii.
[29] The errors in some of *Hesperides'* other catchwords suggest the misordering of stanzas within individual poems, a mistake, as we have already seen, that one of the cancelled leaves attempted to repair. The catchword on L6r reads "Then," for example, while the new stanza on the verso begins "Thus." This mistake could represent another misreading, but, because the subsequent two stanzas in this verse to John Weeks both start with "Then" (H-336), we may suspect that the compositor inadvertently switched the stanzas' order within the poem. Both alignments make sense: the poet lists the various verses and memories that will comfort him in his old age, and could either first "call to mind things half forgot" (line 114) or first ask his son "(If a wild Apple can be had) / To crown the Hearth" (lines 122–23).

Renaissance poets in general, we need to remember, traditionally had limited practical control over their works' printing. While authors continued to become more visible during the seventeenth century, and, as we saw in the introduction, their legal and economic authority gradually increased, we should not presume that they tried painstakingly to control the design of their books. Even the most assertive writers had to work with printers and booksellers who typically made the essential decisions for transforming authors' ideas into their printed, public forms.[30] Having put up the capital for a book, a stationer could choose the format, design the title page, and oversee the proof-reading – all elements that potentially influenced the book's meaning. Writers concerned about the printed form of their works could finance their books' publication themselves or try to negotiate with specific stationers. But often printers, obtaining a marketable manuscript, did not even seek an author's approval. As the bookseller Humphrey Moseley announces in Abraham Cowley's *The Mistresse* (1647; Wing C6674), "It is not my good fortune to bee acquainted with the Authour any farther then his fame"; Moseley decided to publish the poet's work because, he claims, a copy "[fell] into my hands" (A2r–v). He justifies this same type of poetic license in his unauthorized edition of Henry Vaughan's *Olar Iscanus* (1651; Wing V123), "I have not the Author's Approbation . . . but I have Law on my Side" (A6r).

The portrait of the poet opposite *Hesperides'* title page (figure 5b) prepares us, ironically, for Herrick's lack of practical authority over his book's material creation. Beginning a text with the author's engraved image should establish his identity as the organizing principle for classifying and interpreting the contents. As Roger Chartier has argued, such portraits reinforce "the notion that the writing is the expression of an individuality that gives authenticity to the work."[31] But in the case of *Hesperides*, the frontispiece does not specifically announce itself as an image of Herrick. Because no contemporary portraits of the author survive, we cannot know whether the engraver, William Marshall, was attempting to depict Robert Herrick or trying to represent an ideal Roman poet.[32] Perhaps the figure's exaggerated

---

[30] See Dobranski, *Milton, Authorship and the Book Trade* (Cambridge, 1999), especially pp. 20–26.

[31] Roger Chartier, *The Order of Books*, trans. Lydia G. Cochrane (Stanford, 1994), p. 52.

[32] I am not entirely convinced by the argument that *Hesperides'* "engraving contains a genuine portrait" because Marshall's other engravings demonstrate a "close attention to the idiosyncratic features of individual faces." See Norman K. Farmer, Jr., "Herrick's Hesperidean Garden: *ut pictura poesis* Applied," in *"Trust to Good Verses": Herrick Tercentenary Essays*, pp. 15–51, these quotations, p. 28. On the relationship between the mimetic and ideal in Renaissance art, see Harry Berger, Jr., "Second-World Prosthetics: Supplying Deficiencies of Nature in Renaissance Italy," in *Early Modern Visual Culture: Representation, Race, and Empire in Renaissance England*, ed. Peter Erickson and Clark Hulse (Philadelphia, 2000), pp. 98–147.

Figure 5b. Portrait frontispiece from Robert Herrick's *Hesperides* (1648).

Roman nose was even meant punningly to recall Publius Ovidius Naso. Within the collection, Herrick describes himself, like the poet on the frontispiece, as having curly hair (Cc7v/H-1128), but he also refers to "my Beard" (F3v/H-170), a detail noticeably lacking from the opening portrait.

We may question, too, whether such a self-conscious author, a poet who so frequently writes about himself and his book, would have missed an opportunity to mock Marshall's caricature. As Leah Marcus has observed, a "long line" of English frontispiece verses "all assert, through one device or another, the inadequacy of the visual by comparison with the verbal."[33] Perhaps most famously, Jonson in the beginning of Shakespeare's Folio instructs readers to "looke / Not on his Picture, but his Booke," and Milton caustically tells readers of his own 1645 *Poems* to "Laugh at the botching artist's mis-attempt."[34] In *Hesperides*, though, Herrick remains uncharacteristically silent. Writing the frontispiece's Latin epigraph, John Harmar avoids all mention of the book's portrait: "Phoebus except, all else thou dost outvie / In style, and beauty, and capacity."[35]

The frontispiece in *Hesperides*, which evokes a sense of the author's abiding presence at the start of the collection, thus also implies Herrick's lack of power in his book's material production. We begin the volume with a Roman caricature designed by William Marshall and an epigram signed by John Harmar of the College of Westminster. And the poet Herrick remains at least twice removed: the picture portrays not an author but his bust. This memorial image teases us with possibility that the depicted poet, whoever he is, has already died.[36]

TRUST TO GOOD READERS

This tension between Herrick's authorial presence and his dependent status also finds expression in the collection's quasi-autobiographical poems, but

---

[33] Leah S. Marcus, "Milton as Historical Subject," *Milton Quarterly* 25 (1991): 120–27, this quotation, p. 123; and see her similar argument in *Unediting the Renaissance: Shakespeare, Marlowe, Milton* (London, 1996), p. 221. Marcus writes, however, that the specific portrait on *Hesperides*' frontispiece is "presumably of the author" (*Unediting the Renaissance*, p. 183).

[34] Jonson, "To the Reader," in Shakespeare, *Comedies, Histories, & Tragedies* (London, 1623; STC 22273), A1v; for this translation of Milton's Greek epigraph, I am relying on David Masson, *The Life of John Milton*, 7 vols. (1874–81; New York, 1946), 3: 459.

[35] I am using J. Max Patrick's translation of the Latin in *The Complete Poetry of Robert Herrick*, p. 8.

[36] Most portraits in seventeenth-century books served as memorials of deceased authors. Exceptions occurred in some folio editions, such as Michael Drayton's *Poems* (1619) and James I's *Workes* (1616), as well as a few editions in smaller formats: Robert Armin's *The Two Maids of Moreclake* (1609) and Milton's *Poems* (1645), *The History of Britain* (1670), and *Artis Logicae* (1672). The earliest portrait that I have found is a woodcut of the author John Heywood in his allegory *The Spider and the Flie* (1556).

with these works, as we will see in this section, the poet actively seeks readers' intervention to stave off the debasement that could come with taking his poetry to press. Herrick not only invites readers to correct the printer's "*Transgressions*" (A4r); he also calls upon his audience to look after his printed book after he has died. Thus the opening dedication to Prince Charles posits the book's most prestigious audience member as both *Hesperides'* origin and destination. Proclaiming the prince as "my Works *Creator*, and alone / The *Flame* of it, and the *Expansion*" (A3r), Herrick announces that Prince Charles controls his past, present, and future: the prince inspired the poet's little stars (lines 7–8), ushers his book into the world (line 2), and will give these poems immortal life (line 10).

Perhaps more obviously, *Hesperides'* dedication, along with the verses above the errata, also functions as a rhetorical defense mechanism. By allying the collection with Prince Charles and disavowing responsibility for the poems' various "*Tares*" (A4r), the author is looking in part to deflect the criticism of ungenerous readers. If, as the couplets about the errata hint, Herrick's audience is to play such an important role in the text, he wants to make sure that they – like the "Understanders" in Donne's *Poems* – fully appreciate his works. In "When He Would Have his Verses Read," for example, Herrick requests that readers peruse his poetry after they "have both well drunke, and fed" (B2r/H-8). He wants to safeguard his book's future by having readers approach his poems not only with an open mind but also in a good humor.

Herrick even jokes about reducing the book's circulation so as to avoid possible censure. Playfully adopting the pastoral mode, he instructs his muse to stay within "The poore and private *Cottages*" and avoid "Courts and Citties" because there "Contempts" dwell (B1r–v/H-2). Herrick here is addressing the scope of his poetry – his muse inspires a "meaner Minstralsie" (B1r/H-2) than the lofty rhyme that John Milton, for example, aspired to build – but his exaggerated diction also suggests that he wants to target his book to a select audience. In one of the collection's many verses entitled "To his Booke," the poet instructs his lines to "go not neere / Those faces (sower as Vineger)" (Y5v/H-868); in another, he tells the collection, "Come thou not neere those men, who are like *Bread* / O're-leven'd; or like *Cheese* o're-renetted" (B2r/H-7). This kind of gesture, as we saw in chapter 1, occurred commonly in prefaces and introductory epistles during the seventeenth century, and even such an ambitious poet as Milton accepted that his fit readers might be few. But in *Hesperides* Herrick sounds especially apprehensive: he does not want his book even to "go . . . neere" a hostile audience. Whereas we saw Jonson in his *Epigrammes* and the printer in

Donne's *Poems* telling their respective readers to take care, Herrick tells his book to do so and makes few direct attempts to persuade readers of his poetry's merits.

Instead, Herrick casts himself as a protective parent, jealously guarding his child's virtue. "Deerely I lov'd thee; as my first-borne child," Herrick affectionately tells his volume, "While thou didst keep thy *Candor* unde-fil'd" (B1v/H-3). His poems have since fallen out of favor because they lost that "*Candor*" and became widely read:

> But when I saw thee wantonly to roame
> From house to house, and never stay at home;
> I brake my bonds of Love, and bad thee goe,
> Regardlesse whether well thou sped'st, or no.
>
> (B1v/H-3)

While the immediate subtext for this verse is Jesus' words to his followers – he instructs them to stay with their laboring hosts and "Go not from house to house" (Luke 11: 7) – Herrick's specific choice of "wantonly" and "undefil'd" evokes sexual impropriety.[37] The poet wants his book to remain humble like Christ's followers but he also associates his poems' popularity with infidelity: if his book were to reach a wide audience, it would be behaving promiscuously; only if it accepts a small readership can it then remain pure. This passage reflects in part the standard, seventeenth-century prohibition against a gentleman poet descending to print.[38] Jonson in "To My Booke-seller" thus permits his Folio to be sold but refuses to have it "offered, as it made sute to be bought."[39] In like manner, Herrick realizes that by having his poems printed he may compromise the integrity of his poetry and become, in Jonson's terms, a mere verser, wantonly degrading his talent in order to please more readers and thus sell more books.

This anxiety resurfaces in a later poem as Herrick again bids his book to go forth – but suddenly calls it back to offer a last piece of advice:

---

[37] With "undefil'd," Herrick may have had another biblical passage in mind, specifically Psalm 119: 1, "Blessed are the undefiled in the way, who walk in the law of the Lord." See *The Complete Poetry of Robert Herrick*, ed. Patrick, p. 13.

[38] On the sexual politics of Renaissance printing and the use of gender to express anxiety about the press, see Wendy Wall, *The Imprint of Gender: Authorship and Publication in the English Renaissance* (Ithaca, NY, 1993), pp. 15–16, 219–20, 346–47.

[39] Jonson, "To My Booke-seller," line 6, in *The Workes of Benjamin Jonson* (London, 1616; STC 14751), Ttt1r–v. For the currency of this sentiment during the Renaissance, see J. W. Saunders, *The Profession of English Letters* (London, 1964), and Steven May, "Tudor Aristocrats and the 'Stigma of Print,'" *Renaissance Papers* (1980): 11–18.

> Go with thy Faults and Fate; yet stay
> And take this sentence, then away;
> Whom one belov'd will not suffice,
> She'l runne to all adulteries.
>
> (Z2r/H-899)

The enjambment of "stay / And," emphasized by the preceding caesura, suggests the poet's urgency as he tells his book not to leave and then must improvise a reason for it to linger. The rhymed terms "stay" and "away" neatly capture the poet's conflicting desires, while the absence of rhyme in the final lines points up the harsh consequences of a wide circulation. Here again Herrick playfully suggests that his book should under-achieve and only reach a small readership: like a father trying to preserve his child's repu-tation, he fears that too many suitors/readers will somehow defile his poetic offspring. That Herrick continues to describe his book's popularity in terms of sexual misconduct also implies the intimate relationship he conjures for readers and his book. While he does not want numerous readers opening up and paging through his volume, a single, good reader can become the book's "belov'd," tenderly looking after the author's work after he has let it go.[40]

We may detect, too, a Platonic theory of immortality behind Herrick's concern for his poetry's possible defilement. In the *Phaedo*, Socrates argues that a soul's fate depends on the type of life it leads: "if it departs pure, dragging with it nothing of the body," then it enters "into the invisible, divine, immortal, and wise," and "lives in truth through all after time with the gods." If, on the other hand, the soul departs when "it is defiled and impure," then it "is dragged back into the visible world" and "flits about the monuments and the tombs."[41] As Herrick takes *Hesperides* to press, he may be worrying that the book's material form will compromise his poems' lasting value, especially since a printed (*versus* manuscript) book would more likely reach the wider audience that the poet wants to shun. Will ungenerous readers adulterate his book and drag it "back into the visible world," or will they help his works live "through all after time"? In this context, Herrick's sexual metaphors suggest how much power he thinks *Hesperides'* readers possess: they not only determine his book's reputation but also control its ultimate fate.

At times, as we saw in *Hesperides'* dedication to Prince Charles, Herrick sounds assured about his poetry's future after his own death. Compared

---

[40] Compare Shakespeare's similar phrasing in *Troilus and Cressida*, ed. David Bevington ([Nashville, TN], 1998), as Ulysses angrily describes coquettish women as "encounterers" who "wide unclasp the tables of their thoughts / To every tickling reader!" (4.5.59–62).

[41] Plato, *Phaedo*, trans. Harold North Fowler (Cambridge, MA, 1947), 80E–81B, 81D (pp. 279–83).

to such popular ballads as "the *farting Tanner*" or "the *dancing Frier*," his book, he presciently predicts, will continue to find "new life" (N2r/H-405, Bb2v/H-1019). In "The Pillar of Fame," he similarly boasts that

> What we up-rear,
> Tho Kingdoms fal,
> This   pillar   never   shall
> Decline   or   waste   at   all.
> (Cc7v/H-1129)

Herrick here treats his book's material form as contributing to – not hindering – his verses' immortality. Just as this shape poem relies on its physical appearance to reveal its meaning, Herrick implies that his works will find lasting value through the "pillar" that his book signifies. In "His Request to Julia," Herrick even more forcefully equates his poetry's publication with its completion: "If I chance to die / Ere I print my Poetry," he instructs Julia, then she should burn his book because he does not want it "to live not perfected" (C2r/H-59). The act of binding *Hesperides* accordingly marks his poetry's – and, by extension, Herrick's – boundless future: "The bound (almost) now of my book I see, / But yet no end of those therein or me" (Bb2v/H-1019).

Simultaneously, though, despite these confident predictions, Herrick realizes that he cannot alone control his publication's fate. As he reflects on his own mortality, he wonders who will look after his printed volume: "What will ye (my poor Orphans) do / When I must leave the World (and you)" (R8v/H-626). Concerned about the consequences of a wider, print distribution, the poet calls on readers to help preserve his poetic offspring after he has died. Again, he compares himself to a protective parent, worrying about leaving his "Babes . . . fatherless" and repeatedly searching for "fost'ring fathers" (R8v/H-626), a "friendly Patron" (Y2v/H-844), or "a kinsman, or a friend, / That may harbour thee, when I / With my fates neglected lye" (Cc7r/H-1125). If Herrick sounds more confident in the dedication to Prince Charles, he there draws strength from his monarch's heir, whom he casts as the collection's ultimate protector. Even in "The Pillar of Fame" the poet admits that his accomplishment depends on someone else: Herrick refers to "*his owne* / Firme and well fixt foundation" but he is appropriating this conceit from Petrarch's *Canzoniere*, and he openly portrays the pillar's construction as a collaborative endeavor, "What *we* up-rear" and something that "*we* set" (my emphasis).[42]

---

[42] See Petrarch, *The Canzoniere*, trans. Mark Mulsa (Bloomington, 1996), no. 10 (pp. 10–11) and no. 269 (pp. 384–85). Whereas Petrarch – and subsequently in England, Sir Thomas Wyatt – used the

Most often Herrick expresses his concern about readers in terms of his book's physical form:

> I see thee lye
> Torn for the use of Pasterie:
> Or see thy injur'd Leaves serve well,
> To make loose Gownes for Mackarell:
> Or see the Grocers in a trice,
> Make hoods of thee to serve out Spice.
>
> (Y2v/H-844)

The book's detractors in this passage do not just attack the poet's wit or disrespect his artistry; instead, Herrick portrays misunderstanding his poetry as physically misusing his book's leaves. While he may have fretted about readers who would literally tear apart his book, Herrick was also borrowing an Elizabethan commonplace rooted in the works of Horace, Martial, and Catullus. And like Martial, who frequently envisioned his epigrams within a real, material *liber*, Herrick conceives his *Hesperides* first and foremost as something physical.[43] He focuses attention on the publication as the poems' originative moment – "Before the Press scarce one co'd see / A little-peeping-part of thee" (Z2r/H-899) – and correspondingly describes the neglect of his work as its material destruction. Herrick's depiction of *Hesperides*' physical mistreatment points to the risk that he believes he undertakes by printing his poems: has he degraded his starry verse into a mere commodity, only suitable for wrapping fish or funneling spices?[44]

Perhaps because the answer for Herrick lies with his readers he lashes out at anyone who might prove unhelpful. A reader may "dislik'st" just one verse, and Herrick offers reassurance: "Thinke that of All, that I have writ, the worst" (B2r/H-6). He implies that readers need only leaf through the collection to find something better. We may even interpret the size of Herrick's *Hesperides* as another defensive gesture: such a large body of work presumably prevents readers from claiming that they can find nothing of

---

image of a broken pillar to signify a poet's dependence on a patron, Herrick here seems to lean on readers of his printed book. Compare Wyatt, "The pillar perished," in *The Complete Poems*, ed. R. A. Rebholz (New Haven, 1978), p. 86.

[43] I am here indebted to Braden's comparison of Martial and Herrick in *The Classics and English Renaissance Poetry*, pp. 181–82.

[44] We may also find in Herrick's conception of letter and spirit a parallel to his support for the value of ceremony in religious worship: just as Herrick accepts the interconnection of his book's form and meaning, he followed Laudian ideology in believing that the outward aspects of worship could support inward devotion. For a discussion of the latter idea, see Achsah Guibbory, *Ceremony and Community from Herbert to Milton* (Cambridge, 1998), pp. 79–118.

value. By offering over 1,000 poems from which readers can choose, the author takes much of the pressure off the success of any individual verse.

More often, though, Herrick seeks retaliation against his book's ungenerous readers and devises appropriate corporeal punishments for their crimes against his text. When Herrick imagines coming across his book lying on the ground, "*Absyrtus*-like all torne confusedly" (Aa2r/H-960), his allusion to Medea's dismembered brother allies his star-inspired volume with Absyrtus' fitting sobriquet, "Phaëton" or "Shining One." But Absyrtus' murder, more than the obvious choice of Orpheus' dismemberment, also conveys the treachery that Herrick attributes to his ungenerous readers and the hardship that he hopes such readers will, like Jason and Medea, eventually suffer. If readers use his book as waste paper, Herrick hopes that "every Ill, that bites, or smarts, / Perplexe him in his hinder parts" (B2r/H-5). And for readers who claim that "All disgustfull be," Herrick curses them with a fittingly disgusting illness: "The Extreame Scabbe take thee, and thine, for me" (B2r/H-6). He also wants to harm the reader who dislikes his poems and with a "long-black-Thumb-nail marks 'em out for ill"; he hopes the hand of such a reader will develop painful inflammations, "for to unslate, or to untile that thumb!" (F4v/H-173).

Herrick's Old Testament sense of justice corresponds to the reciprocal relationship that he forecasts between his readers and his book. He wants to believe that readers need *Hesperides* as much as his book needs them. As he jeeringly tells his "Criticks," his poems provide them with a "means to live"; without Herrick's book, "The Cause," their critiques "wo'd die" and lose all "effect" (D1r/H-96). When, in like manner, Herrick answers his "Ill Reader," he explains that those who find his "lines are hard" must blame themselves: his poems "are both hard, and marr'd, / If thou not read'st them well" (L8r/H-344). Here the poet suggests that he wrote good verses and anyone who disagrees does "not read'st . . . well." But Herrick's diction simultaneously betrays readers' power to re-define his poems: if readers deem his poems difficult to understand, then his works are diminished; they become "both hard, and marr'd" by the readers' poor abilities, despite the poet's efforts.

Herrick describes the "Generous Reader," in contrast, as someone who can "See, and not see," who will appreciate his poetry and "Wink at small faults, the greater, ne'rthlesse / Hide" (C8v/H-95). The use of the plural in this same poem – "Let's doe our best, our Watch and Ward to keep" – also indicates that Herrick wants the book's audience to work with him; for his book to be great, both we and he must "doe our best." He accordingly attributes the success of his poem "To Master Laurence Swetnaham" to

Swetnaham himself: "if there be / A fault, tis hid, if it be voic't by thee. / Thy mouth will make the sourest numbers please" (Cc3r/H-1089). Although Herrick is addressing a specific, single reader, he again implies that his poetry needs just the right audience. Swetnaham serves as both the verse's subject and a necessary collaborator who perfects Herrick's work by giving voice to it.

Only verses by classical authors, Herrick seems to claim in "To Live Merrily, and to Trust to Good Verses" (G5v/H-201), can live forever without anyone's help. He lifts his cup to some of his favorite ancient poets and recalls Ovid's description that even Tibullus' great talent was reduced to a small urn:

> Trust to good Verses then;
>   They onely will aspire,
> When Pyramids, as men,
>   Are lost, i'th'funerall fire.
>
> And when all Bodies meet
>   In *Lethe* to be drown'd;
> Then onely Numbers sweet,
>   With endless life are crown'd.
>   (lines 45–52)

Here Herrick momentarily juxtaposes letter and spirit. "Good Verses" and "Numbers sweet" achieve "endless life," whereas "Pyramids, as men, / Are lost" and "all Bodies" will ultimately die. Yet this poem, too, illustrates the need for an attentive audience: Herrick himself represents the consummate Renaissance reader, using and preserving these other authors and their works within his own writings. If he is trying in *Hesperides* to persuade himself of the lasting accomplishment of his own poetic endeavors, he demonstrates again and again that all "good Verses" – including those by Virgil, Ovid, and Catullus – must trust to good readers for them to "superlast all times" (N2r/H-405).

O HAPPY LIFE!

The omissions in Herrick's *Hesperides* enhance the tension, as we will see in this section, between the poet's lasting renown and his audience's participation. Understanding his limited authority, Herrick attempts to direct readers' reactions by providing specific points of entry into his texts. Like the dedication to Prince Charles, or the couplets preceding the book's errata, the unfinished verses in *Hesperides* appear to be part of a larger strategy to safeguard both the poet's reputation and his book.

In the unfinished poem "The Apparition of his Mistresse Calling him to Elizium" (Q8v–R1r/H-575), for example, Herrick briefly turns the tables on his classical predecessors: they become readers of him. As the poet's ghostly companion takes him on a tour of the Elysian fields, she points out the local flora (for example, "fragrant Apples," "shrubs, with sparkling spangles," lines 10, 11) and some of Elysium's most celebrated residents (for example, Homer, Horace, and Lucan, as well as Jonson, Beaumont, and Fletcher). She then pauses at the Greek poet Anacreon:

> Ile bring thee *Herrick* to *Anacreon*,
> Quaffing his full-crown'd bowles of burning Wine,
> And in his Raptures speaking Lines of Thine,
> Like to His subject; and as his Frantick-
> Looks, shew him truly *Bacchanalian* like,
> Besmear'd with Grapes; welcome he shall thee thither,
> Where both may rage, both drink and dance together.
>
> (lines 32–38)

This specific scene reveals more than Herrick's desire to attain immortality through verse; the poem's heavenly setting allows the poet to create an ideal community of great writers who enjoy each other's company and respect one another's work. Just as Herrick reads and writes about these classical authors, they read and write about Herrick, for, as his mistress explains, poets in Elysium "sing the stories of our love" (line 24). That Anacreon in the above passage is specifically "speaking Lines of Thine, / Like to His subject" suggests that he has committed some of Herrick's poems to memory and appreciates how much he and Herrick share.[45] At last, Herrick, a student of Anacreontic verse, has found his poetry's ideal reader – Anacreon himself – the "one belov'd" whom he had fearfully sought among *Hesperides'* earth-bound audience (Z2r/H-899).

Such an audacious image of mutual admiration again suggests Herrick's sense of dependence: he conceives a life after death that emphasizes camaraderie and reciprocity more than individual merit; with this one scene, he combines his debt to ancient writers and his desire to find admiring readers. Yet, because "The Apparition of his Mistresse" apparently remains unfinished – it begins with the Latin tag "*Desunt nonnulla*——" ("Some things are missing") – we also may doubt Herrick's confidence in this heavenly vision. Given the author's repeated apprehensions about his book's

---

[45] On Herrick's relationship to the Anacreontea, see Braden, *The Classics and English Renaissance Poetry*, pp. 196–232. As Braden observes, it is fitting that Anacreon recites Herrick's poetry in "The Apparition of his Mistresse" because, "in a way that does not hold for Herrick's relation to the other classical poets, these two write the same kind of poem" (p. 214).

physical form and his concerns about dying before his poetry is "perfected" (C2r/H-59), any incomplete work in *Hesperides* would seem to under-mine his own aspirations to write for "All times" and achieve immor-tality through verse. As opposed to the "Firme and well fixt foundation" (Cc7v/H-1129) that Herrick had hoped to construct with his readers' assis-tance, this poem's missing pieces evoke the "torne" body of Absyrtus into which, Herrick had feared, ungenerous readers would rend his printed book (Aa2r/H-960).

Hesperides in fact contains two incomplete poems; the other is "The Country Life, to the Honoured M. End. Porter, Groome of the Bed-Chamber to His Maj." (S7r–S8r/H-662). While we cannot know how many seventeenth-century readers would have overlooked or found dis-tinctive two fragments among the volume's more than 1,000 poems, the incompletion of two verses at least enhanced the collection's apparently dis-ordered inclusiveness: paging through *Hesperides*, readers could alight on various types of poems, elegant or coarse, brief or long, dramatic or didactic, pastoral or erotic, finished or unfinished. The printing of so many poems, including two that Herrick never completed, may have even misled readers into thinking that *Hesperides* contained the author's entire body of work.

"The Country Life" and "The Apparition of his Mistresse," however, rep-resent more than just two poems that Herrick happened to leave unfinished. In contrast to Donne's genuinely unfinished "Resurrection, imperfect" and "To the Countesse of Bedford," *Hesperides'* incomplete poems resemble Jonson's verse epistle to the Countess of Rutland: Herrick's works, we will see, become more meaningful by announcing that they are missing some parts. Nothing in the spacing on these pages indicates that the compositor abbreviated the verses himself, and, while the book's catchwords suggest that the publishers influenced the collection's ordering, it is difficult to imagine that a member of the printing house chose on his own to label these particular poems "unfinished." Whereas the provenance of Donne's tags and titles remains doubtful, the tags and titles in *Hesperides* – like those in Jonson's 1616 Folio – are almost certainly authorial.[46] Herrick may not have controlled his book's material creation, but only he had the authority to single out such apparently complete texts as somehow deficient.

Except for the concluding announcement, "*Caetera desunt*," Herrick's "The Country Life" surely looks finished. One of four poems in *Hesperides*

---

[46] The titles of some poems in *Hesperides* cast the author in the third person, as if someone other than Herrick were introducing them: "The Argument of his Book" (B1r), "His Protestation to Perilla" (E8v), and "The End of his Worke" (Cc7r). But other, more personal titles suggest the poet's status as the works' creator, "To my Ill Reader" (L8r/H-344) and "To my Dearest Sister" (X7r/H-818).

addressed to Endymion Porter, a high-ranking official in Charles I's house-hold, this poem offers a conventional image of a happy, bucolic existence: "May-poles . . . with Garlands grac't" (line 53) and "great-ey'd Kine" with breath as "Sweet as the blossomes of the Vine" (lines 33–34).[47] We do not know Herrick's specific motive for dedicating this poem to Porter, but the effect of the title is to associate these images of tranquil contentment with "His Maj." The poem thus depicts the rituals of a "Sweet Country life" (line 1) and, more subtly, the country's sweet life during the reign of Charles I. This allusion, in conjunction with the pronouncement that "The Kingdoms portion *is the Plow*" (line 28), must have had a special reso-nance when the book went to press in 1647 – a period, as Thomas N. Corns describes it, "poised between past horrors and the uncertainties of imminent conflict."[48] In November 1647, the king had fled from the Army's custody to the Isle of Wight, and although 1647 and 1648 were marked by flickering hopes of renewal, past defeats left the future of Stuart England in serious doubt. Porter himself had been in exile since 1645, first in France, then in The Netherlands, and would not return home until shortly before his death in 1649.

While modern critics have uncovered a complex and nuanced expres-sion of allegiance to the king and his supporters within *Hesperides'* various poems, "The Country Life" offers a gentle lament for life under Charles I.[49] As Leah S. Marcus has observed, Herrick uses pastoral ceremonialism in both *Hesperides* and *Noble Numbers* to represent "an ideal prototype reced-ing alarmingly under Puritan attack with each passing year."[50] Herrick augments such royalist intonations in "The Country Life" by casting Endymion Porter elsewhere in the collection as the king of poets: "before thy Threshold, we'll lay downe / Our Thyrse, for Scepter; and our Baies for Crown" (D6r/H-117). A patron and friend of Herrick as well as Ben Jonson,

---

[47] Herrick addresses three other poems to Porter, H-117, H-185, and H-1071. *Hesperides* also contains a fifth poem in which Porter himself speaks, "An Eclogue, or Pastorall between Endimion [*sic*] Porter and Lycidas Herrick, set and sung" (H-492).

[48] Corns, *Uncloistered Virtue: English Political Literature, 1640–1660*, p. 95.

[49] Whereas critics once discussed Herrick's poetry in the context of Laudian ideology and Stuart loyalism (see, for example, works by Corns, Peter Stallybrass, and Claude J. Summers), attention has shifted more recently to the apparently dissonant moments in his texts. Some critics have even questioned whether the poet was in fact committed to Laudianism and a Stuart monarchy (see, for example, select articles in *Robert Herrick*, special edition of *George Herbert Journal*, ed. Ann Baynes Coiro 14.1–2 [1990–1991]). While many of these latter discussions provide valuable insight into individual poems, efforts to soft-pedal or down-play Herrick as a supporter of Laudianism tend to misrepresent his poetry, and, as Achsah Guibbory notes, wrongly imply "that only the Laudian ideology was repressive – that the puritan one was liberating." See Guibbory, *Ceremony and Community from Herbert to Milton*, pp. 79–118, this quotation, p. 80.

[50] Marcus, *Childhood and Cultural Despair* (Pittsburgh, 1978), pp. 134–35.

Robert Davenport, and Thomas Dekker, the beneficent Porter represents the poets' "chiefe Preserver" (F8r/H-185), a close acquaintance who "do'st give / Not onley subject-matter for our wit" but also "Oyle of Maintenance to it" (D6r/H-117). Here we glimpse another aspect of Herrick's dependence, for he claims to need Porter, both practically and poetically, to write his works. In "An Ode to Master Endymion Porter, upon his Brothers Death" (F8r/H-185), Herrick conflates these two types of assistance, as Porter both comforts the grieving author ("*Porter*, while thou keepst alive, / [even] In death I thrive," lines 15–16) and inspires his new verses ("Thanks to the gen'rous Vine; / Invites fresh Grapes to fill his Presse with Wine," lines 26–27). That this poem could be describing the death of either Porter's or Herrick's brother reveals how closely Herrick related to his friend and patron; the verse contains two voices that bleed together, with Porter most likely speaking in the first two stanzas and Herrick replying in stanzas three and four.[51] In "An Eclogue, or Pastorall between Endimion [*sic*] Porter and Lycidas Herrick, , [*sic*] set and sung", [*sic*] (P2v–P3r/H-492), the two friends again combine their voices in a dialogue. When Porter prepares to leave his pastoral companion, Herrick stops writing poetry: without Porter's assistance, Herrick's "whilome merry Oate" lies "neglected . . . / And never purls a Note" (lines 2–4).

As with the reciprocal relationship that Herrick posits between book and readers, he wants to believe that patron and poet are also mutually dependent. The use of chiasmus, "We are Thy *Prophets Porter; Thou our King*" (Cc1r/H-1071), suggests such a balance of power: Porter needs guidance from his *vates*, according to Herrick, and they look to him for their subsistence. This *quid pro quo* also corresponds to the symbiosis of King and farmer that Herrick depicts in "The Country Life." Just as "The Kingdoms portion *is the Plow*" (line 28), so the patron in the title needs the poet's encomiums if he wishes to become famous after death; and just as dethroning Charles I presumably threatens the country's pastoral paradise, so eliminating the patron's endowment would threaten the poet's livelihood.

This theme of mutual dependence is first suggested by the poem's full title, which calls attention to both Herrick's service to Porter and Porter's duty to the king: "The Country Life, to the Honoured M. End. Porter, Groome of the Bed-Chamber to His Maj." Herrick then begins the poem by asserting that those "Whose lives are others, not their own" cannot

---

[51] Claude J. Summers has come to the same conclusion about the ode's two speakers. See Summers, "Herrick's Sequence of Grief and Comfort," *ANQ*, new series 2 (July 1989): 104–9.

appreciate the "Sweet Country life" that he will describe (lines 1–2). Presumably, he meant to praise Porter as someone who could enjoy country pleasures, but the poem's title has already reminded us that Porter's life was not entirely his own, for he had served the king as "Groome of the Bed-Chamber." Herrick concludes the poem on a similar note, explaining that husbandmen have such a "Happy life" because they "all the day themselves doe please" (lines 70, 72). Husbandmen, in other words, should find happiness because they do not need to please anyone else – unlike poets such as Herrick, who writes this poem to Porter, and unlike men in great places such as Porter, who works for Charles I. If we were looking for a dissonant moment in the text, we need not search beyond this framing device. Although the poet addresses Porter directly throughout the poem, Porter would ironically seem to qualify as someone divorced from this pastoral existence, someone "serving Courts" who, according to Herrick, must "be / Less happy" than a common husbandman (lines 3–4).

The poem's opening and title also initiate a larger pattern of negation that quietly anticipates the final tag, "*Caetera desunt*―――." Herrick first announces that rustic pleasures remain "unknown" to those "Whose lives are . . . not their own" (lines 1–2); he then describes various things that are *not* a part of a countryman's life away from courts and cities: "Thou never Plow'st the Oceans foame," for example, "Nor to the Eastern Ind dost rove" (lines 5, 7). Herrick punningly adds that Porter, feeling "content" with his land's "sweet content," is "Not envying others larger grounds" (lines 16, 18). In the country, Porter has modest needs: his "Ambition's Master-piece / Flies no thought higher then a fleece" (lines 11–12). Concluding the poem with a list of traditional pastimes, Herrick uses another negating gesture to note that "no man payes too deare" for "Russet wit" and "Nut-browne mirth" (lines 60–61).

All these negations look forward to the poem's ultimate omission. While it is tempting to speculate that the poem lacks an ironic envoi such as the last triplet in "The Hock-Cart" (I1r–I2r/H-250), which rhymes "raine," "paine," and "againe" to hint that the "Lords of Wine and Oile" exploit the "Sons of Summer," Herrick's use of "*Caetera desunt*―――" in "The Country Life" may itself be a subtle, subversive gesture. Like the poem's negations, which repeatedly describe what is not, this Latin tag encourages readers to notice what the poem – and, by extension, the country – currently wants. The penultimate negation, that Porter hunts "Birds, not Men" (line 69) and experiences "nought t'affright / Sweet sleep" (lines 74–75), points up the cruel reality that in 1648 men were actually being hunted, and frightful events were probably disturbing the sleep of the king, Porter,

Herrick, and many of *Hesperides'* readers. In this context, the Latin tag, "*Caetera desunt———*," serves as an epitaph for a negated golden age. As the poem's pastoral scene stands for the country's sweet life, Herrick's poem becomes an elegy for both a threatened world order and a soon-to-be-deposed monarch.

The poem also contains another, more precise omission that reinforces such a political interpretation. When Herrick writes "O happy life! if that their good / The Husbandmen but understood!" (lines 70–71), he alludes to a passage from Virgil's *Georgics*: "*O fortunatos nimium, sua si bona norint, / agricolas!*" Herrick, however, has severed Virgil's sentence in mid-verse and omitted the reason that Virgil offers for the farmers' good fortune:

> *O fortunatos nimium, sua si bona norint,*
> *agricolas! quibus ipsa, procul discordibus armis,*
> *fundit humo facilem victum iustissima tellus.*

[O happy husbandmen! Too happy, should they come to know their blessings! for whom, far from the clash of arms, most righteous Earth, unbidden, pours forth from her soil an easy sustenance.][52]

By abbreviating this allusion to the *Georgics* and omitting "the clash of arms," Herrick fleetingly blocks out England's own war but paradoxically emphasizes its importance. The rest of the Virgilian allusion is missing, Herrick's most astute readers could infer, because in 1648 England was no longer "far from the clash of arms."

Such an omission empowers Herrick's readers while simultaneously confirming the author's own authority. On the one hand, the apparent imperfection of "The Country Life" makes it a more inductive, open-ended poem; on the other hand, Herrick appears to have implied a specific missing piece that he wanted readers to detect. That the poet elsewhere praises Porter as an especially adept man of letters suggests that even if he had doubts about the book's broader audience he at least expected Porter to notice what was left out. Perhaps Herrick added the Latin tag just in case. Porter had served as "Groome of the Bed-Chamber" in the 1620s, and we may even speculate that Herrick, having composed this poem twenty years earlier, updated it for *Hesperides* by enhancing the poem's various negations and tacking on the final Latin tag. Reading over this pastoral scene in 1647, the poet could have chosen "*Caetera desunt*" to stress that the country's golden days had since been lost.

---

[52] Virgil, *Georgics*, in *Virgil*, trans. H. Rushton Fairclough, rev. edn., 2 vols. (Cambridge, MA, 1986), book II, lines 458–60 (1: 148–49).

Like the image of Anacreon in "The Apparition of his Mistresse," the omission in "The Country Life" further demonstrates Herrick's sense of dependence: he reaches back to one of his classical predecessors and looks expectantly to his country's readers; the tag "*Caetera desunt*" borrows Virgil's Latin language even as it describes an uncertain future for the country's life and the poem itself. To defeat the silence that "*Caetera desunt*————" conveys would require that readers of both parties end England's "clash of arms" so that the Virgilian allusion could be truthfully restored. The incompletion of "The Country Life" symbolizes, moreover, Herrick's personal stake in England's ongoing conflict. If, as he indicates elsewhere in the collection, he needs both his audience and patron to write good verses, then without their assistance the country's sweet life will be cancelled and he, too, will be silenced – the poet's speech cut off apparently in mid-verse.

THE DEATH OF THE AUTHOR

Hesperides' other apparently unfinished poem, "The Apparition of his Mistresse Calling him to Elizium" allows Herrick to meditate more fully on the uncertainty of both his work's reception and his lasting fame. This omission, as we have already seen, gently undermines the author's aspiration to perfect his poetry and share Homer, Jonson, and Horace's posthumous fate. The poem remains an unanswered invitation, a mere "glim'ring of a fancie" (line 55), as the poet's ghostly mistress prematurely flits away.

Unlike the layout of "The Country Life," though, "The Apparition" calls attention to its incompletion at the start. Printed as a headnote, "*Desunt nonnulla*————" ("Some things are missing") necessarily informs how readers approach the text; it alerts us right away to the poem's missing parts. Most likely we would look for signs of missing lines or words, but we might also question, for example, whom has the poet has left out of Elysium? Is the poet acknowledging his own absence from this dreamscape? Is the poet signaling that the following apparition is limited and faint?

One solution would have readers turn to the alternate version of "The Apparition" published eight years earlier in *Poems: Written by Wil. Shakespeare* (1640). Herrick's poem appears in a separate section, "Excellent Poems . . . By other Gentlemen," without the Latin tag announcing an omission and with the different title "His Mistris Shade."[53] A brief comparison of the two versions reveals numerous, small differences – the

---

[53] Shakespeare, *Poems* (London, 1640; STC 22344), L5r–L6r. Quotations from the poem are taken from this edition and cited parenthetically.

transposition of "handsome striplings, naked younglings" (line 17), for example – as well as some, more substantive changes – the substitution of "*Beumont* and *Fletcher*" (line 51) for "*Shakespeare* and *Beamond*" (line 53), and the revision that in Elysium "*Iohnson* shall be plac'd" (line 59) to "*Johnson* now is plac't" (line 57).[54] Reading the two versions side by side also reveals that the verse in *Hesperides* omits a couplet from the 1640 text. In the earlier version Herrick specifies the type of crowns worn by Elysium's youth: "So soone as each his dangling locks hath crown'd / With Rosie Chaplets, Lillies, Pansies red, / Soft Saffron Circles to perfume the head" (lines 20–22). In *Hesperides*, by comparison, Herrick simply notes that the "younglings" are "with endlesse Roses crown'd" (line 20) – and he leaves out the lilies, pansies, and saffron.

Although the omission of this list of flowers would alone justify *Hesperides'* opening announcement, "*Desunt nonnulla———*," these two missing lines are probably not what the poet wanted readers to notice with the introductory Latin tag. The revision of the crowns' description seems too deliberate; the change from "dangling locks hath crown'd" to "with endlesse Roses crown'd" (line 20) supersedes the brief catalogue of flowers used in the earlier text. Having polished this poem in the intervening years, Herrick would have had no reason to notify readers of the earlier, slightly longer text.

More likely, if we interpret the Latin tag literally, we should look to the poem's last two lines. While the rest of the poem is written in pentameter, these lines are each missing an iamb: "I vanish; more I had to say; / But Night determines here, Away" (lines 65–66). The final couplet's two silent feet evoke the mistress' departing steps or, perhaps, the poet's own soundless tread which can not yet be heard in Elysium. That the mistress disappears while she still has "more . . . to say" also justifies the poem's Latin headnote. Like Orpheus' half-regained Eurydice or Aeneas' unembraceable Creusa, Herrick's mistress joins a long list of elusive women who escape their lovers' grasps. These suggestions of incompletion at least warrant the opening announcement that "Some things are missing"; perhaps Herrick wanted readers to notice that his vision of Elysium, like his desire for the mistress, comes up short.

But whereas Orpheus wanted to rescue Eurydice from death, and poets traditionally offer to immortalize their mistresses in verse, Herrick inverts this topos in "The Apparition": here his mistress calls him to join her among

[54] This change, as J. Max Patrick has suggested, may indicate that Herrick first wrote the poem before Jonson's death. See *The Complete Poetry of Robert Herrick*, ed. Patrick, p. 275.

Elysium's favoured souls. Herrick has written an almost suicidal seduction poem. As the title of the 1640 version suggests, the speaker is "His Mistris Shade," which denotes the ghost or spirit of his mistress calling him to join her in Elysium. In contrast to some of *Hesperides'* most famous verses, "Corinna's Going a Maying" (F5v–F6v/H-178), for example, or "To the Virgins, to Make Much of Time" (G7r/H-208), Herrick has here written an anti-*carpe diem* poem. In "Corinna's Going a Maying" the poet specifically argues that "All love, all liking, all delight / Lies drown'd with us in endlesse night" (lines 66–67), but in the unfinished "The Apparition" he associates death with both poetic and erotic fulfillment. Instead of wanting to seize the day and pursue earthly pleasures, he entertains the possibility of dying so that he and his mistress can together enjoy an "eternall May" and "perpetuall Day" in Elysium's "green Meddowes" (lines 12, 13, 14).

The mistress's untimely exit and the poem's abrupt conclusion imply that the poet at least temporarily eschews her offer. If the opening tag indicates that Herrick doubts his worthiness to live among Elysium's blessed residents, it also suggests that he is not yet ready to "Trust to Good Verses" and give up his earthly life. Like the mistress at the end of "The Apparition," Herrick still has "more . . . to say" before he finally departs (line 65). Readers may be reminded, too, of Herrick's other stunted, erotic fantasies in such poems as "The Vine" (B7v/H-41) and "The Vision" (E3v/H-142). In the former work, the poet is awakened prematurely by the intensity of his fantasy's "fleeting pleasures"; in the latter, the "sprightly *Spartanesse*" chides Herrick as he tries to kiss her thigh. The incompletion of "The Apparition" fits Herrick's characteristically thwarted sexuality, for the mistress's departure coincides with the poem's most evocative sexual language:[55]

> But harke, I heare the Cock,
> (The Bell-man of the night) proclaime the clock
> Of late struck one; and now I see the prime
> Of Day break from the pregnant East, 'tis time
> I vanish.   (lines 61–65)

The urgency of this final passage, combined with its erotically charged diction ("pregnant" and "Cock"), suggests that the dead mistress's midnight beckoning may represent an invitation to the little death of orgasm. Rather than replying, Herrick leaves the poem unfinished, balking at such a seductive offer and shooing away his mistress.

[55] On the "defensive and regressive" quality in Herrick's erotic poetry, see William Kerrigan, "Kiss Fancies in Robert Herrick," in *Robert Herrick*, special edition of *George Herbert Journal*, ed. Ann Baynes Coiro 14.1–2 (1990–91): 155–71.

That the poem only depicts a fleeting apparition of a mistress escorting Herrick through Elysium's landscape also suggests that the poet's own imagination cannot sustain him in the afterlife. He needs more than one of his fancied beloveds – a Julia, Lucia, or Corinna – to establish his poetic reputation. Without a reader such as Anacreon who memorizes and celebrates Herrick's verse, the poet cannot aspire to live with his literary heroes. Herrick's vision of Elysium accordingly emphasizes the poet in relationship to an attentive audience: in addition to Anacreon "speaking Lines of Thine" (line 34), Herrick glimpses Jonson holding forth in a "capacious roome" (line 56), Homer reading the *Odyssey* to a "crowd of Poets" (line 29), and Beaumont and Fletcher reciting one of their plays to "all ears" (line 51). Herrick's hesitancy to finish the poem and join these other writers suggests his ongoing pursuit of his own ideal audience. The poem's introductory announcement, "*Desunt nonnulla*———," focuses attention from the start on readers' active participation, not only to complete this one work imaginatively but also, by extension, to fulfill Herrick's aspirations. Instead of the gods granting the poet a place in this eternal dwelling – as they do for mortals in works by Homer, Pindar, and Hesiod – Herrick must hope that his readers favor him with immortality by providing this poem with a happy ending and, as we have seen in his other self-conscious works, by nominating him to the rank of these other writers.

Both "The Country Life" and "The Apparition of his Mistresse," then, use omission to signify an uncertain future – for, respectively, the country and the poet himself. But whereas "The Country Life" omits a specific allusion that Herrick implies, "The Apparition," even in the plural phrasing of its Latin headnote, seems to allow for readers' multiple responses as they identify and fill in the poem's blanks. Incongruously, when Herrick turns his attention to his own eternal soul, his readers seem to play a larger role in the text.

At times in *Hesperides*, Herrick sounds optimistic about his lasting renown. In one of the collection's many poems entitled "On Himselfe" (R3v/H-592), he boasts that he shall "Live by the Muse," whereas other people will "die / Leaving no Fame to long Posterity." Glancing at contemporary events, he adds that, "When Monarchies trans-shifted are, and gone; / Here shall endure thy vast Dominion." Herrick is reassuring himself that the demise of a Stuart monarchy need not undermine his own claim "to long posterity"; this particular "Here" presumably refers to the poem itself, and/or the page on which it was printed in the 1648 volume.

Yet, in another, later poem, also entitled "On Himselfe," Herrick offers a much gloomier image of his imminent demise:

Lost to the world; lost to my selfe; alone
Here now I rest under this Marble stone:
In depth of silence, heard, and seene of none.
                                      (Aa1r/H-954)

The poet has gone from predicting he will endure to bemoaning an almost
certain oblivion, from aspiring to "Live by the Muse" to envisioning himself
"Lost to the world; lost to my selfe." Such a dramatic mood swing suggests
Herrick's unsettled opinion about the future; he may be adopting multiple
personae in these works, reflecting the broader uncertainty of the Civil
War period, and/or charting his own "trans-shifted" perspective on fame.
Another poem entitled "On Himselfe" on the same page invites readers
to "weepe for" Herrick after he dies; the poet wants readers to "mourne,
or make a Marble Verse for me, / Who writ for many. *Benedicite*." (Aa1r/
H-952). Herrick, in other words, wants his readers to do unto him what he
has done unto so many others. He looks to his readers not just to improve
his poems and care for his book after he has died; he wants readers to bless
him and ultimately to take up their own pens.

If we return to the likelihood discussed at the beginning of this chapter –
that Herrick did not insist on a precise order for the volume – the inconsis-
tency of his quasi-autobiographical verses further indicates readers' control.
Where we drop into the collection will change our perception of Herrick;
we have the ability to piece together various versions of the poet, just as
we have the authority to devise various supplements to complete "The
Country Life" and "The Apparition of his Mistresse." The two Latin tags
in *Hesperides* represent only the most dramatic instances where readers can
intervene in the text. As with the ambiguous portrait on the frontispiece,
Herrick's final fate remains in readers' hands: they can either identify the
poet as Herrick and put him on this pedestal, or, by insisting on the image's
anonymity, deny him his pillar of fame.

In the next chapter we will see that John Milton more forcefully determines how readers fill in his book's blanks. Like Herrick, Milton uses omission to respond to England's contemporary political conflict, but whereas
Herrick in 1648 laments a lost golden age and meditates on an uncertain
future, Milton, writing after the Restoration, encourages readers of *Paradise
Regain'd . . . Samson Agonistes* to realize – and rectify – the lost opportunity of the Civil War. Part of the interpretive work that Milton sets out
for his book's readers requires that they bridge the gap between his two
religious works, a brief epic about Christ and a tragedy about a Hebrew
hero. Herrick's *Hesperides* ultimately invites a similar type of intervention.

As with the omissions in "The Country Life" and "The Apparition of his Mistresse," the blank spaces between his book's more than 1,000 poems signify that "some things are missing": readers must discover on their own the poems' intertextual relationships. Herrick has put his trust, finally, in his good verses and in us, his future good readers; only by attending to his collection's silences can we supply for the volume still new connecting narratives and themes.

CHAPTER 6

Milton's missing links

Omissions are not accidents.
– Marianne Moore[1]

Thus far I have argued that Renaissance omissions established authors' authority while encouraging active readers – regardless of whether the omission was created by the author himself (as with Jonson's and Herrick's texts), an anonymous respondent (as with Sidney's), or members of the printing house (as with Donne's). Writing after the Restoration, John Milton appears to have benefited from the gains in authorial authority reflected in all these incomplete publications: in *Paradise Regain'd . . . Samson Agonistes* (1671; Wing M2152), Milton stages perhaps the period's most elaborate textual omission.[2] What Milton perceived as the urgent need for political action also likely influenced his decision to leave out part of these poems; he may have boldly manipulated his two texts, but he did so in an effort, we will see, to empower the poems' audience. Characteristically seeking active readers throughout his career, Milton in *Paradise Regain'd . . . Samson Agonistes* uses omission to help readers discover both the need for their participation and the relationship between his poems and the new political climate of post-Restoration England.

Most discussions of Milton's readers begin with his famous formulation of *Paradise Lost*'s readership as a "fit audience . . . though few."[3] Casting the

---

[1] Marianne Moore, Author's Note, *The Complete Poems of Marianne Moore* (New York, 1967), p. vii.
[2] Although critics generally agree that Milton composed *Paradise Regain'd* between 1665 and 1670, various dates have been offered for the composition of *Samson Agonistes*: 1640–41, 1647–53, 1660–62, and 1667–70. Blair Worden has examined the poem in the context of writings by regicides in the 1660s and confirmed that Milton composed *Samson* after the Restoration, although, Worden cautions, "we could not properly argue that the poem must have been written immediately or shortly after the events which are so forcefully present in it." See Worden, "Milton, *Samson Agonistes*, and the Restoration," in *Culture and Society in the Stuart Restoration*, ed. Gerald MacLean (Cambridge, 1995), pp. 111–36, this quotation, p. 136, n.133. A helpful overview of this debate occurs in John Carey, ed., *John Milton: Complete Shorter Poems*, 2nd edn. (London, 1997), pp. 349–50.
[3] Milton, *Paradise Lost*, ed. Alastair Fowler, 2nd edn. (London, 1998), book VII, line 31. All subsequent quotations from *Paradise Lost* are taken from this edition and cited parenthetically in the text.

epic's readers as auditors, Milton here stresses his poetry's aural qualities and recalls his university training with its emphasis on rhetoric and public speaking. But that the term "audience" during the seventeenth century commonly referred to a judicial hearing or formal assembly (rather than a group of play-goers) also hints at the strenuousness and seriousness of reading Milton's epic.[4] "Fit," too, suggests that Milton was challenging his readers, for its meaning was influenced by the now obsolete adjective "feat"; a "fit audience" during the seventeenth century would thus signify a well-suited group of readers, as well as one that was adroit and intelligent.[5] The added concession, "though few," both conveys Milton's high standards – he is willing to sacrifice his audience's size for its understanding – and provides an incentive for his readers' efforts: they can join a small, special group, elect above the rest.

We find similarly descriptive passages in many of Milton's other poems and pamphlets. With his earliest works – *Arcades, A Mask, Lycidas*, and the Hobson verses – Milton would have known his audiences personally or at least well enough to anticipate their assumptions and abilities. But as more of his works went to press, he began to posit an ideal audience in his texts and incorporate sometimes subtle guidelines for readers to follow. These texts reveal a demanding poet but also one who wanted his audience to cooperate with him, who recognized how much he depended on readers to help establish both the value of his works and his own lasting reputation.[6] In the case of *The Doctrine and Discipline of Divorce* (1643, 1644), for example, Milton regretted that even after the second edition, no one had "vouchsaft a friendly conference with the author, who would be glad and thankful to be shewn an error, either by privat dispute, or public answer" (*CP* 2: 437). Surely this gesture is at least in part rhetorical: Milton

---

4   *OED* s.v. "audience" I.3, I.4.
5   *OED* s.v. "fit" 1.a, and "feat" A.1, A.2.
6   In *Surprised by Sin: The Reader in* Paradise Lost, 2nd edn. (1967; Cambridge, MA, 1997), Stanley Fish posits instead an antagonistic relationship between Milton and his readers. Fish describes how the poet repeatedly ensnares, then rebukes *Paradise Lost*'s fallen audience: "we are . . . accused, taunted by an imperious voice . . . with no consideration of our feelings" (p. 9). Fish would later back-track from his initial assertion that he is describing the experience of reading Milton's epic; he has since argued that his own account of "the Reader in *Paradise Lost*" is a recommended way to read the poem "within the assumption that the poem's method is to involve you in its plot by confronting you with interpretive crises" (p. xiv). I share this assumption as it applies to various works by Milton, but I disagree with Fish's image of Milton as a finger-wagging pedant and suggest that the poet presents readers with real, sometimes strenuous, interpretive choices. For a cogent refutation of Fish's argument, see John P. Rumrich, *Milton Unbound* (Cambridge, 1996). Some excellent discussions of Milton's readers include Sharon Achinstein, *Milton and the Revolutionary Reader* (Princeton, 1994); Joseph Wittreich, *Feminist Milton* (Ithaca, NY, 1987); and Nicholas von Maltzahn, "The First Reception of *Paradise Lost* (1667)," *Review of English Studies* 47 (1996): 479–99.

suggests that his detractors have been unreasonable and uncivil, and he implies that no one has "shewn [him] an error" because his argument did not contain any. Simultaneously, though, Milton casts writing as a social activity, one that benefits from a "friendly conference" between readers and writers. We may be reminded of his similar description of authorship from *Areopagitica*: "When a man writes to the world, . . . he searches, meditats, is industrious, and likely consults and conferrs with his judicious friends" (*CP* 2: 532). Milton's extended metaphor comparing the search for truth with building God's Temple also implies a collaborative effort, "some cutting, some squaring the marble, others hewing the cedars" (*CP* 2: 555). To arrive at truth, Milton insists, "there of necessity will be much arguing, much writing, many opinions; for opinion in good men is but knowledge in the making" (*CP* 2: 554).[7]

In this final chapter I examine how Milton uses omission to guide readers' active participation in *Paradise Regain'd* and *Samson Agonistes*. Throughout the 1671 volume Milton is appealing to a perceptive, learned audience, "not unacquainted with *Aeschulus*, *Sophocles*, and *Euripides*" (I3r), as he explains in a note preceding *Samson*.[8] The first part of this chapter discusses how the physical text invites readers to experience *Paradise Regain'd* and *Samson Agonistes* as a unified structure; the second part addresses an omission that especially calls attention to the two poems' interdependence and the reader's necessary involvement.[9] Although most modern editions fail even to mention that this passage, labeled *Omissa*, originally appeared at the end of the 1671 volume, a bibliographical examination reveals that the missing text is not the result of a compositor's error.[10] In fact, the *Omissa* represents an

---

[7] For a fuller discussion of Milton's notion of authorship in *Areopagitica*, see Dobranski, *Milton, Authorship and the Book Trade* (Cambridge, 1999), pp. 104–24.

[8] This and all subsequent references to the poems are taken from the copy of *Paradise Regain'd. A Poem. In IV Books. To which is added Samson Agonistes* (London, 1671), held in the Stark Collection at the Harry Ransom Humanities Research Center at the University of Texas in Austin (Stark 6302). References to specific signatures appear parenthetically in the text; the number following the virgule refers to standard, modern line numbers.

[9] I previously discussed the *Omissa* in "Samson and the *Omissa*," *Studies in English Literature, 1500–1900* 36 (1996): 149–69, and chapter two of Dobranski, *Milton, Authorship and the Book Trade*. I borrow from both of these works in the first part of this chapter.

[10] In ten out of the twelve modern editions of the poem that I examined, the editors do not mention that they have inserted the text. Only Frank Allen Patterson remarks, but without explanation, that "Lines 1527–1535 and line 1537 were added in 1671 at the end of the book under *Omissa*," and John Carey similarly notes that "In *1671* ll. 1527–35 and 1537 were omitted, but supplied in the *Omissa*. Thus in the uncorrected state of *1671* l. 1536 was given to the chorus, not Manoa." See Patterson, ed., *The Works of John Milton*, 18 vols. (New York, 1931–38), 1: 330–99, 599–605; and Carey, ed., *John Milton: Complete Shorter Poems*, p. 406. All quotations of Milton's shorter poems are taken from Carey's edition and cited by line number within the text.

important authorial addendum. These ten lines threaten to alter the outcome of Samson's fate and, when read at the back of the book, retroactively
evoke the status of miracles in *Paradise Regain'd*. Holding out the promise
of Samson's restored sight and perfect victory, the omitted passage points
up the actual consequences of his final act; requiring readers' intervention
to restore the text, the *Omissa* also emphasizes the need for the type of
active obedience that Jesus embodies.

THE 1671 TEXT

Even a cursory, bibliographical examination of *Paradise Regain'd* and *Samson
Agonistes* indicates that the two poems were designed to be published
together in 1671. The title page of the first edition refers to both works
(*Paradise Regain'd . . . To which is added Samson Agonistes*, A1r; see figure 6a)
and the penultimate page lists "Errata in the former Poem" and "Errata in
the latter Poem" (P4r). That the book's leaves are signed consecutively also
suggests that the conjunction of these poems was intentional: the text of
Paradise Regain'd is printed on B1r through H8r (verso blank), and the text
of *Samson Agonistes* follows on I2r through P3r with a separate title page
dividing the two poems on I1r (verso blank) (see figure 6b).[11]

The more complicated consideration remains whether Milton conceived
Paradise Regain'd and *Samson Agonistes* as a cohesive whole – and in this
particular order – or whether their combined publication was decided at the
printing house. Although neither poem explicitly refers to the other, the two
seem to share a precise, intertextual relationship that exceeds the typology
of their New and Old Testament sources. Balachandra Rajan was among the
first to suggest that Milton strategically juxtaposed Jesus' perfection with
Samson's fallibility so as to emphasize the relationship "between the clarity
of the completed understanding and the darkness through which the design

[11] *Paradise Regain'd . . . To which is added Samson Agonistes* (1671) is an octavo of 110 leaves, which
collates A²B–O⁸P⁴[$4 signed (-A1, A2, E3, P3, P4)]. The pagination is as follows: 110 leaves (pp. *i–iv*,
1–111 *112*; *1–2* 3–7 *8* 9–101 *102–104*). The collation suggests that the compositor may have imposed
the final gathering P with the preliminaries, A1 and A2, which would account for six of the eight
leaves in this sheet. Presumably, the printer could have used the two remaining leaves for cancels
to correct, for example, the omission of the ten lines on O5r. However, only one cancelled leaf
has been discovered to date: in most copies N3 is integral and correctly paginated, but in several
copies it is a cancel. The only difference between the integral and canceled leaf that has been
discovered is that the inserted page incorrectly reads "79" instead of "70" for the page number on
N3v. See K. A. Coleridge, *A Descriptive Catalogue of the Milton Collection in the Alexander Turnbull
Library, Wellington, New Zealand* (Oxford, 1980), p. 217. Presumably, the text on the integral leaf
is the result of a stop-press correction, with the inserted cancel replacing an earlier, uncorrected
reading.

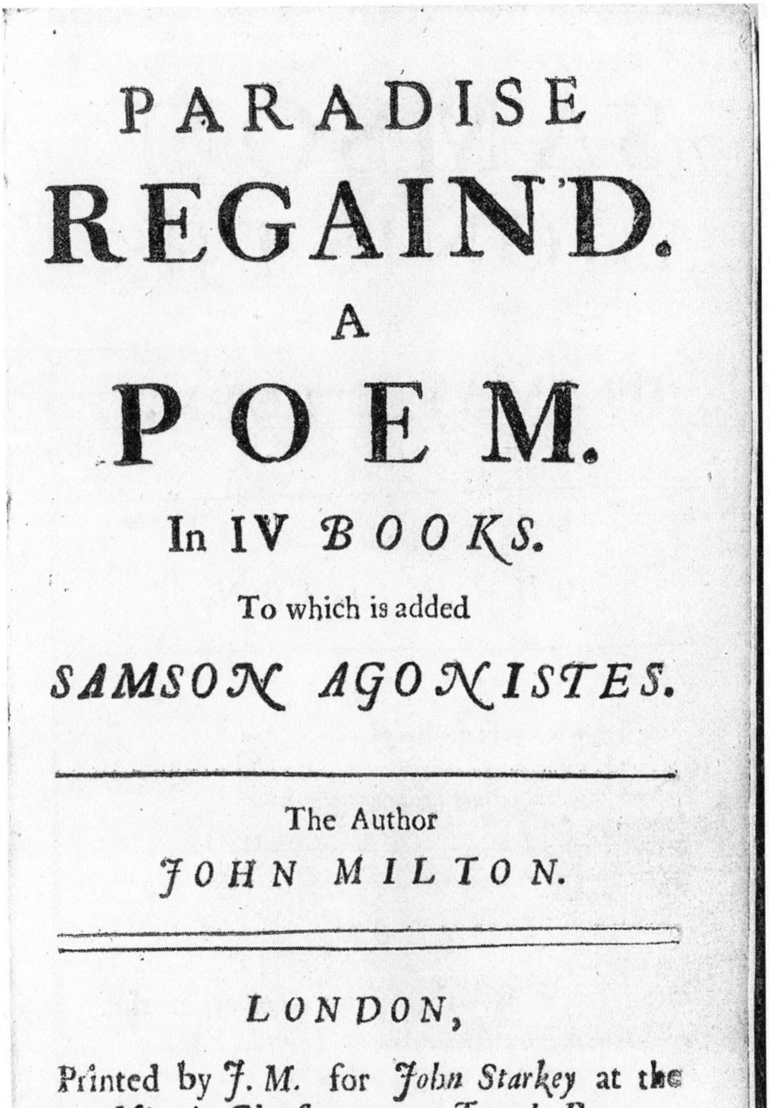

PARADISE REGAIN'D.

A
POEM.

In IV *BOOKS*.

To which is added

SAMSON AGONISTES.

The Author

JOHN MILTON.

LONDON,

Printed by *J. M.* for *John Starkey* at the
Mitre in *Fleetstreet*, near *Temple-Bar*.
MDCLXXI.

Figure 6a. Title page of John Milton's *Paradise Regain'd . . . Samson Agonistes* (1671).

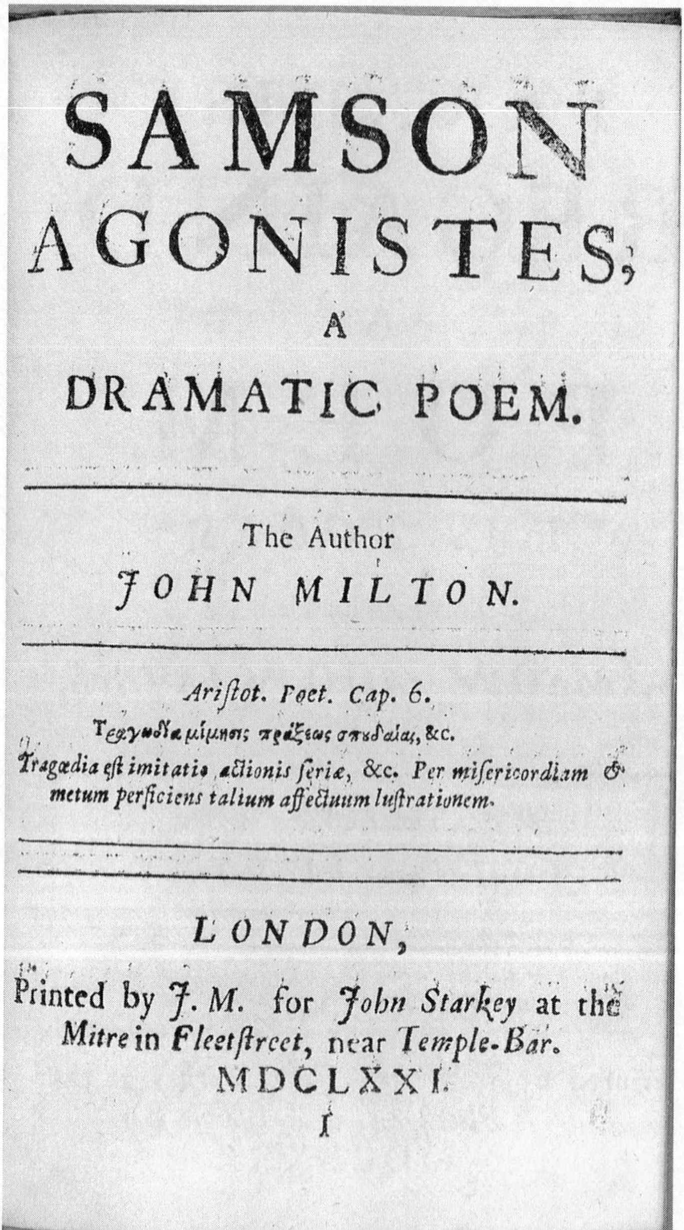

SAMSON AGONISTES,

A

DRAMATIC POEM.

The Author
J O H N M I L T O N.

Ariſtot. Poet. Cap. 6.

Τεϱγωδία μίμησις πϱάξεως σπυδαίας, &c.

Tragœdia eſt imitatio actionis ſeriæ, &c. *Per miſericordiam &
metum perficiens talium affectuum luſtrationem.*

L O N D O N,

Printed by *J. M.* for *John Starkey* at the
Mitre in *Fleetſtreet*, near *Temple-Bar.*
MDCLXXI.
I

Figure 6b. Separate title page of *Samson Agonistes* in John Milton's *Paradise Regain'd . . .
Samson Agonistes* (1671), sig. I1r.

is seen in fragments."[12] Later, Mary Ann Radzinowicz, John Shawcross, and Joseph Wittreich discussed elaborate interrelationships of genre, allusion, and what Wittreich identified as a complex "system of echoing."[13] Wittreich argues that the two poems, through their "dialectical interplay," make "a single poetic statement" about "staying the course and . . . how and why that matters."[14]

Double books such as *Paradise Regain'd . . . Samson Agonistes* occurred frequently during the seventeenth century. Not only does Robert Herrick's *Hesperides* precede his *Noble Numbers* (1648), as we saw in the previous chapter, but Bacon's *Sylva Sylvarum* was printed with *New Atlantis* (1627), Michael Drayton's collected *Poems* is often found bound with *The Battaile of Agincourt* (1627), and some copies of Suckling's *Last Remains* (1659) were sold with *Fragmenta Aurea* (1658). Among Milton's publications, *Justa Edovardo King* (1638), the Cambridge collection that includes *Lycidas*, is divided into two halves, the English and Latin poems; and both Milton's 1645 and 1673 *Poems* are double books, separating the English (and Italian) poems from the Latin (and Greek) verses. We also know that Milton envisioned individual poems in relationship to each other, most notably *L'Allegro* and *Il Penseroso*, but also his two poems about the mail-carrier Hobson, the two sonnets on his divorce tracts, the four poems on the Gunpowder Plot, and the two poems about the Roman singer Leonora. In *Pro populo anglicano defensio secunda*, Milton suggests, if only in retrospect, that he commonly conceived his prose works as companion pieces: he explains that he had planned to write about the three types of liberty – ecclesiastical, civil, and domestic – and neatly divides this last category into marriage, education, and freedom of expression, claiming that he has gathered his early tracts around these three topics (*CP* 4: 624).

Rather than attributing the dual publication of *Paradise Regain'd* and *Samson* entirely to Milton, however, we need to remember that the stationer probably helped to shape the text. In addition to choosing the format and determining the layout, publishers might request that book-binders stitch together more than one text for marketing purposes – without bothering to seek the authors' approval.[15] Henry Wotton recalled coming across Milton's

---

[12] Balachandra Rajan, "'To Which Is Added *Samson Agonistes* –,'" in *The Prison and the Pinnacle*, ed. Balachandra Rajan (Toronto, 1973), pp. 82–110, this quotation, p. 98.

[13] See Mary Ann Radzinowicz, *Toward* Samson Agonistes: *The Growth of Milton's Mind* (Princeton, 1978), pp. 227–60; John T. Shawcross, Paradise Regain'd: *Worthy T'Have Not Remain'd So Long Unsung* (Pittsburgh, 1988), pp. 102–15; and Joseph Wittreich, *Interpreting* Samson Agonistes (Princeton, 1986), pp. 329–85, this quotation, p. 349.

[14] Wittreich, *Interpreting* Samson Agonistes, pp. 332, 344, 337.

[15] Whereas some types of books – for example, bibles, prayer books, and schools books – were typically sold bound, pamphlets and individual plays and sermons were mostly sold stitched. For

A Mask Presented at Ludlow Castle "in the very close of the late *R*'s Poems, Printed at *Oxford*," and Milton complained to the printer Adrian Vlacq that *Pro populo anglicano defensio* was "bound in with" a work by Alexander More, "against my will, even under the very same covers" (*CP* 4: 719).[16] The printer of Milton's *Epistolarum familiarium* chose instead to consult his author to make his book marketable. Finding Milton's personal correspondence "somewhat too few to form a volume of reasonable size," he inquired whether Milton had another "small work" that he "might chance to have kept by him, to fill up the space and compensate for the paucity of the letters."[17]

Such financial considerations may have especially influenced John Starkey's decision in 1671 to have *Paradise Regain'd* and *Samson Agonistes* printed together. The title page's wording, "To which is added *Samson Agonistes*," implies that the latter poem was intended as a supplement to the main text, if not meant as a mere afterthought. While we do not know whether Starkey decided on this specific diction, he retained the same wording on the title page of the second edition (1680), published six years after Milton's death. The fact that the advertisements in Starkey's book catalogue and *The Term Catalogues* borrow this phrasing also suggests that he at least approved of the title page's content.[18] Surely the publisher would not have depended on a blind poet to determine the page that advertised the poems in the "Windows also, and the *Balcone's*" where books were "set to sale" (*CP* 2: 524). As the person financing the book's production, Starkey would have naturally wanted a title page that emphasized *Paradise Regain'd* and "The Author *JOHN MILTON*": in 1671 he was hoping to profit from the popularity of *Paradise Lost* and exploit the notoriety of his regicide author.

We can only speculate whether the desire to present the book as a sequel to Milton's earlier epic also influenced Starkey and Milton to position *Paradise Regain'd* first, followed by the less potentially lucrative title, *Samson Agonistes*. The former is printed without any prefatory matter, but the latter includes a summary "Argument" (I3v) and a defense "Of that sort of

more expensive books, customers would purchase the sheets unbound or stitched, and then make arrangements with their own binders. See Philip Gaskell, *A New Introduction to Bibliography* (Oxford, 1972), pp. 146–47.

[16] For Wotton's complete letter, see *The Works of John Milton*, ed. Patterson, 12: 476.

[17] See "Typographus lectori," in *Epistolarum familiarium* (London, 1674), sig. A3r–A3v. I am borrowing this translation of the Latin by Phyllis B. Tillyard in *Milton: Private Correspondence and Academic Exercises*, ed. E. M. W. Tillyard (Cambridge, 1932), p. 3.

[18] See Edward Arber, ed., *The Term Catalogues*, 3 vols. (London, 1903), 1: 56. A similar entry occurs in "*A Catalogue of Books Printed for* John Starkey *Bookseller, at the* Miter *in* Fleetstreet *near* Temple-Bar" (A1r–A6r), dated 10 April 1671 and held in the British Library, London (shelfmark 1606/2015). The entry reads "*Paradise regain'd*, a Poem in four books, to which is added *Samson Agonistes*. The Author, *John Milton*, price bound 2 *s.* 6 *d.*" (A4r).

Dramatic Poem which is call'd Tragedy" (I2r–I3r). Did Starkey and/or Milton believe that *Paradise Regain'd* required no introduction but *Samson Agonistes* needed some explaining "to vindicate Tragedy" from "infamy" (I2v)? Publishing the volume eleven years after the Restoration, perhaps Milton preferred having *Paradise Regain'd* first so as to provide readers with a Christian context for understanding Samson's choices. Or the arrangement of the two poems may have reflected Milton's less sanguine perspective in 1671: rather than concluding with the hope manifested in Jesus' victory on the pinnacle, the author may have purposefully reversed the conventional order of his biblical sources so as to emphasize *Samson's* sense of loss and upheaval.[19]

Although we cannot pinpoint all of Milton's and Starkey's respective contributions to the 1671 edition, the financial and interpretive implications of its design suggest that the book would have suited both its author and publisher. *Paradise Regain'd . . . Samson Agonistes* manifests the type of ordinary, collaborative production that characterizes much seventeenth-century publishing. Its many errors in pointing and orthography, for example, are consistent with the efforts of a blind, elderly author who was relying on various agents in writing, proofing, and printing his later works. The nature of the book's variants and errata also suggest that Milton cooperated with members of the printing house. That the variants and errata correct unsystematically minor printing mistakes implies that careful correcting occurred before the run was underway.[20] If a printer made time-consuming stop-press alterations to correct minor errors, he would likely have insisted on following traditional procedures in the early stages of correction so as to avoid major errors that would greatly delay production.[21] The traditional procedure for proof-reading included up to four stages of correction, as we saw in the previous chapter, and entailed the press operator making "a *Proof* so oft as occasion requires."[22] In other words, after working to eliminate any major mistakes, printers had only to correct the kind of minor errors that appear in the variants and errata.

[19] Both Wittreich, *Interpreting* Samson Agonistes, chapter seven, and Shawcross, Paradise Regain'd: *Worthy T'Have Not Remain'd So Long Unsung*, pp. 107–11, discuss the interpretive implications of the volume's ordering.

[20] Only one of the book's variants seems to derive directly from Milton's orthography: four copies read "their fiery darts" (H2v/*Paradise Regain'd* 4.424), but fifty-six prefer Milton's characteristic spelling, "thir." This single change hardly indicates that Milton supervised the printing. For a complete list of variants and errata, see vol. 4 of Harris Francis Fletcher, ed., *John Milton's Complete Poetical Works Reproduced in Photographic Facsimile*, 4 vols. (Urbana, 1943–48).

[21] D. F. McKenzie, "Printers of the Mind: Some Notes on Bibliographical Theories and Printing-House Practices," *Studies in Bibliography* 22 (1969): 1–76.

[22] See Joseph Moxon, *Mechanick Exercises of the Whole Art of Printing (1683–4)*, ed. Herbert Davies and Harry Carter, 2nd edn. (Oxford, 1962), pp. 302–3, 238–39, and also quoted in McKenzie, "Printers of the Mind."

Certainly, the most prominent error and most distinctive bibliographical feature of *Paradise Regain'd . . . Samson Agonistes* is the *Omissa* (figure 6c). Analyzing these ten lines lends further insight into Milton's and Starkey's respective roles in the printing process. On the penultimate leaf (P3v) appear the following instructions and text:

> *Omissa.*
> Page 89 [O5r] after verse 537. which ends,
> *Not much to fear*, insert these.

> What if his eye-sight (for to *Israels* God
> Nothing is hard) by miracle restor'd,
> He now be dealing dole among his foes,
> And over heaps of slaughter'd walk his way?
>   *Man.* That were a joy presumptuous to be thought.
>   *Chor.* Yet God hath wrought things as incredible
> For his people of old; what hinders now?
>   *Man.* He can I know, but doubt to think he will;
> Yet Hope would fain subscribe, and tempts Belief.

> After the next verse which begins, *A little stay*,
>   insert this.

>   *Chor.* Of good or bad so great, of bad the sooner;

> Then follows in order, *For evil news*, &c.

Turning to page 89, we discover that the scene to be revised occurs in *Samson Agonistes* as Manoa and the Chorus react to the noise of Samson, offstage, performing for the Philistines. Manoa is concerned that the Philistines "have slain my Son" and wonders if he "should stay here or run and see" (O5r/1516, 1520). The Chorus tries to reassure him:

>   *Chor.* Best keep together here, lest running thither
> We unawares run into dangers mouth.
> This evil on the *Philistines* is fall'n,
> From whom could else a general cry be heard?
> The sufferers then will scarce molest us here,
> From other hands we need not much to fear.
> A little stay will bring some notice hither,
> For evil news rides post, while good news baits.
> And to our wish I see one hither speeding,
> An *Ebrew*, as I guess, and of our Tribe.

>   (O5r/1521–40)

Without the *Omissa*, the poem still makes sense. Including the ten lines after "need not much to fear" simply delays the messenger's entrance,

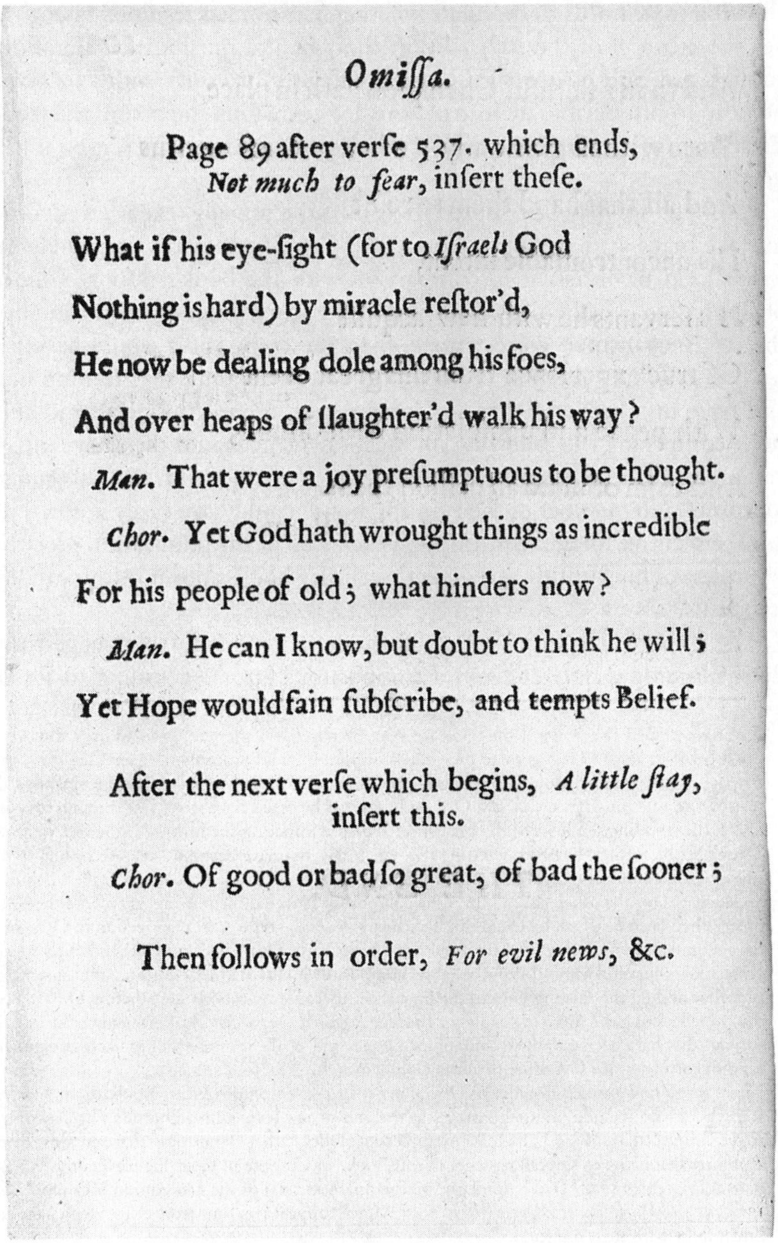

Omissa.

Page 89 after verse 537. which ends,
Not much to fear, insert these.

What if his eye-sight (for to *Israels* God

Nothing is hard) by miracle restor'd,

He now be dealing dole among his foes,

And over heaps of slaughter'd walk his way?

Man. That were a joy presumptuous to be thought.

Chor. Yet God hath wrought things as incredible

For his people of old; what hinders now?

Man. He can I know, but doubt to think he will;

Yet Hope would fain subscribe, and tempts Belief.

After the next verse which begins, *A little stay,*
insert this.

Chor. Of good or bad so great, of bad the sooner;

Then follows in order, *For evil news,* &c.

Figure 6c. *Omissa* from John Milton's *Paradise Regain'd . . . Samson Agonistes* (1671),
sig. P3v.

allowing the Chorus to speculate whether Samson has regained his sight.[23] Yet the creators of the 1671 edition thought the missing text significant enough not only to invent a discrete category of errors entitled *Omissa*, but also to offer elaborate instructions for correcting the poem: the reader must first insert nine lines on O5r; then, after the next line, insert a final one.[24]

Although we may be tempted to dismiss the missing text as just another mistake made at the printing house, the *Omissa* represents an entirely different kind of oversight in comparison with the book's minor instances of sloppiness.[25] If the copy from which the compositor worked contained the ten lines in their correct place, then the compositor would have first set fourteen lines of verse correctly on O5r (excluding the running head and page number) and then for some reason missed the next nine lines. After composing the following line accurately, he would then have missed yet another line of text before completing the page with the subsequent four lines. No member of the printing house could have easily ignored ten nonconsecutive lines of text through each step of the publication process – regardless of how untidy seventeenth-century books appear by our modern standards.

The printed line numbers along the left margins further suggest that the *Omissa* does not represent a compositor's error. According to Joseph

[23] As I have argued elsewhere, if the book were set by pages and the ten lines had been discovered missing before sheet O had gone to press, the compositor could probably have reset the type, page by page, without much trouble. Adding the ten lines to O5r, he could then have lengthened the text by two lines on O5v, O6r, O6v, O7r, and O7v. Or he could have re-set O5r through O8v and added the resulting ten lines to the final sheet P before imposing the formes. If the text were cast off and set by formes, however, resetting the type might not have been possible. According to this practice, the compositor set all the pages for one side of a sheet and sent them to the press before he set the pages for the other side. Thus, if the compositor detected the missing text after either O(o) or O(i) had been finished, he could not have easily re-set the type: such a correction to O5r would have required the re-setting of pages in both the inner (O5v, O6r, O7v, and O8r) and outer formes (O5r, O6v, O7r, and O8v). In this case, the compositor had two other choices, either inserting a cancel or adding the missing lines to the final sheet. Because no cancels in gathering O have been discovered among the surviving copies of *Paradise Regain'd . . . Samson Agonistes* and because all the variants that have been examined contain the *Omissa* on P3v, the printers did not likely attempt any kind of correction for O5r other than the *Omissa* in 1671.

[24] I have yet to find another instance of *Omissa* per se in a seventeenth-century publication; however, some books do include omitted passages at the end of the text. John Lilburne's *Englands Birth-Right Justified* (1645; Wing L2102), for example, concludes with a "Postscript" that contains "divers sentences belonging to severall passages of this Book, which were in their due places omitted, and here at last remembred" (F4v). Similarly, on the final leaf (H1) of the first edition of Milton's *The Doctrine and Discipline of Divorce* (1643; Wing M2108) appear two omitted passages with page and line numbers for their insertion.

[25] For a more detailed discussion of errors and stop-press corrections in the first edition, see Dobranski, "Samson and the *Omissa*," pp. 153–55, and chap. 2 of Dobranski, *Milton, Authorship and the Book Trade*.

Moxon's description of composing marginal notes, the line numbers were probably set separately and added during the imposition rather than in the galley.[26] While imposing the pages, the compositor could then have verified the alignment with the line-numbering in the manuscript, a procedure that would have presumably prevented him from missing ten nonconsecutive lines of text.

It is even less plausible that the *Omissa* represents an oversight if the manuscript were cast off before being set. "Casting off" refers to the procedure by which the master printer or a compositor estimates the number of lines in a manuscript so as to calculate the amount of paper needed for the printing and to parcel out work on the book. With poetry, however, a compositor would not need to estimate; he could simply count the lines of verse.[27] Thus, when casting off *Samson Agonistes*, the compositor would not likely have skipped nine lines, have counted a single line, and then missed a final one. Even if the compositor had missed ten lines elsewhere in the manuscript, the solution of omitting these ten nonconsecutive lines and inserting them as an *Omissa* seems unnecessarily complex.

More importantly, if the *Omissa* had been a printing error, the compositor also would need to have altered the final punctuation mark in the line, "A little stay will bring some notice hither" (O5r/1536). In the 1671 edition, a comma follows "hither" in the Chorus's speech; the comma and the coordinate conjunction "for" separate two independent clauses: "A little stay will bring some notice hither, / For evil news rides post, while good news baits." With the insertion of the *Omissa*, however, Manoa now says "A little stay will bring some notice hither"; the Chorus now replies, "Of good or bad so great, of bad the sooner; / For evil news rides post, while good news baits" (lines 1537–38). The revised passage would read as follows (I have underlined the *Omissa* to clarify where the inserted text occurs):

> *Chor.* Best keep together here, lest running thither
> We unawares run into dangers mouth.
> This evil on the *Philistines* is fall'n,
> From whom could else a general cry be heard?
> The sufferers then will scarce molest us here,

---

[26] Moxon explains that the "*Page* and *Notes* stand safer, being cloathed with the *Furniture*, than they do when they stand Naked in the *Galley.*" See *Mechanick Exercises of the Whole Art of Printing*, p. 218. I am grateful to D. F. McKenzie for drawing my attention to this point in private correspondence.

[27] For *Samson*'s prose preliminary matter, the compositor estimated generously, allotting four leaves with ample space to spare. The type for the title page is set on I1r (verso blank), the defense of tragedy on I2r through I3r, the "Argument" on I3v, and "The Persons" on I4r (verso blank).

From other hands we need not much to fear.
What if his eye-sight (for to *Israels* God
Nothing is hard) by miracle restor'd,
He now be dealing dole among his foes,
And over heaps of slaughter'd walk his way?
 Man. That were a joy presumptuous to be thought.
 Chor. Yet God hath wrought things as incredible
For his people of old; what hinders now?
 Man. He can I know, but doubt to think he will;
Yet Hope would fain subscribe, and tempts Belief.
A little stay will bring some notice hither,
 Chor. Of good or bad so great, of bad the sooner;
For evil news rides post, while good news baits.

(lines 1521–38)

The word "hither" (line 1536) thus becomes Manoa's last word, and a full stop is now needed.[28] All the modern editions of the poem that I examined conform to the 1680 text in placing a full stop after "hither"; as Frank Allen Patterson explains, "the comma in 1671 is naturally used since l. 1538 follows immediately after."[29] But the implication of this change in punctuation is significant: because the 1671 text uses a comma instead of a period, the ten lines in the *Omissa* were not left out accidentally. The compositor would have to alter the text willfully for it to fit the oversight of these ten lines.

THE IMPACT OF THE *OMISSA*

Based on both the improbability of a simple oversight and the change in punctuation, the *Omissa* does not suggest a mistake made in the printing house, but rather an authorial addendum, written during some stage of the text's creation.[30] That the ten lines in the *Omissa* make a single point and are clearly of a piece also decreases the likelihood that the compositor would happen to overlook this particular block of text.

The question then becomes why Milton would have bothered to make such a seemingly minor revision, and how does it affect our interpretation of *Paradise Regain'd* and *Samson Agonistes*. Most obviously, inserting the

[28] Each time a character speaks in *Samson Agonistes*, a full stop is used to mark the end of the speech.
[29] Patterson, ed., *The Works of John Milton*, 1: 604.
[30] According to the simplest explanation, while touching up *Paradise Regain'd . . . Samson Agonistes* before sending the manuscript to the printer, Milton made the ten-line revision in the margin or on a separate piece of paper that the compositor initially overlooked. In this case, the *Omissa* would still represent an authorial revision rather than ten lines that the compositor happened to omit.

Omissa modifies the dramatic structure of *Samson* by delaying the reader's learning what has occurred off-stage. Like the Messenger's long-winded explanation that follows, the exchange between Manoa and the Chorus heightens our suspense. Raising the possibility that Samson has regained his sight, the Chorus's teasing comments conclude with the abrupt revelation, "Then take the worst in brief, *Samson* is dead" (O6r/1570).

This slight modification also enhances the ambiguity of Samson's destroying the temple. In the original version, the Chorus sounds pessimistic as it tries to interpret the source of the off-stage noise: "A little stay will bring some notice hither, / For evil news rides post, while good news baits" (O5r/1536, 1538). The Chorus is claiming, in other words, that they will soon find out what has happened because it must be bad news, and bad news travels fast. By comparison, the Chorus in the revised version sounds hopeful, speculating that Samson's "eye-sight" may have been "by miracle restor'd" (P3v/1528). The *Omissa*, moreover, interrupts the causality of the Chorus's original logic: with the insertion of this passage, as we have seen, the line "A little stay will bring some notice hither" is no longer spoken by the Chorus and instead becomes Manoa's guarded response to the Chorus's encouraging conjecture. Manoa agrees that God could perform such a miracle, but he "doubt[s] to think he will" (P3v/1534) and concludes that they will soon find out, one way or the other. The Chorus now replies, "Of good or bad so great, of bad the sooner; / For evil news rides post, while good news baits" (lines 1537–38). No longer predicting bad news, the Chorus noncommittally observes that they will find out soon if the news is bad, later if the news is good.

By incorporating the *Omissa*, the usually reliable Chorus thus indulges in erroneous wishful-thinking; gone is the sense of foreboding created by the original form of the Chorus's aphorism. While Milton's contemporary readers would have been familiar with Samson's story from the Book of Judges, they could not have known for certain how the poet would depict the final catastrophe.[31] The *Omissa* supersedes the subtle foreshadowing of the Chorus's pessimistic prediction and momentarily distracts us with a potential outcome that differs from the poem's biblical source.

The inclusion of the *Omissa* in the double book also seems to highlight the different perspectives of the poems' two protagonists – Samson's defiance and destruction *versus* the Son's reason and renewal. Whereas

---

[31] For other treatments of Samson's story, see Watson Kirkconnell, ed., *That Invincible Samson: The Theme of* Samson Agonistes *in World Literature with Translations of the Major Analogues* (Toronto, 1964).

the Chorus envisions Samson ruthlessly "dealing dole among his foes" and traipsing "over heaps of slaughter'd" (P3v/1529–30), Satan in *Paradise Regain'd* describes Jesus as "addicted . . . / To contemplation" (G5r/4.213–14), and recalls how as a boy Jesus "went'st / Alone into the Temple" during the feast of Passover (G5r/4.216–17). In contrast to Samson, who topples Dagon's temple and dies, Jesus enters a Hebrew temple to teach "the gravest Rabbis" (G5r/4.218).[32]

But before concluding that Milton casts Samson as the Son's foil, we need to remember that the Chorus in the *Omissa* is wrong: Samson's sight has not been "by miracle restor'd" as he performs for the Philistines, and he never gets to walk "over heaps of slaughter'd" because by destroying Dagon's temple he destroys himself. Like Jesus' momentary temptation to "quell" violence and perform "victorious deeds" during his own visit to a temple (B6v/1.215, B7r/1.218), the *Omissa* teases readers with a fleeting image of Samson's sudden, perfect triumph. That we already know Samson's fate from the Book of Judges makes the possibility of such a miracle no less enticing. When Manoa advises, "That were a joy presumptuous to be thought," the Chorus reasonably insists, "God hath wrought things as incredible / For his people of old; what hinders now?" (P3v/1531–33).[33]

The image of Samson's victory that the *Omissa* conjures contrasts sharply with what really happens at the feast of Dagon. As opposed to the supernatural restoration of Samson's sight in the *Omissa*, Milton's hero actually

---

[32] Readers of the 1671 volume may have been initially confused by the *Omissa*'s hopeful sentiment. Because the pages of *Paradise Regain'd* and *Samson Agonistes* are numbered separately, the first edition contains two pages labeled "89." Coming across the directions at the back of the book, readers might try incorporating the missing text into either poem – especially if, according to convention, they were writing in the corrections before they began reading and could not immediately recognize the speech-prefixes, *Man.* and *Chor.* Whereas the errata are labeled "former Poem" and "latter Poem" (P4r), the *Omissa* does not announce to which poem it belongs. Contemporary readers would have quickly discovered that inserting the missing text on to page 89 of *Paradise Regain'd* does not work; the line numbers in *Paradise Regain'd* do not match the *Omissa*'s instructions, and that poem also contains no speech-prefixes. But, the temporary conjunction of these passages nevertheless reveals the difference between the two poems' protagonists. The *Omissa* is to be inserted on page 89 of *Samson Agonistes*, as the Chorus and Manoa react to the noise of Samson destroying the temple, and it is on page 89 of *Paradise Regain'd* that Satan describes Jesus as "addicted . . . / To contemplation" (G5r/4.213–14) and recalls how Jesus "went'st / Alone into the Temple" (G5r/4.216–17).

[33] Earlier Manoa – not the Chorus – had made a similar argument about Samson's restored sight:

> . . . God who caus'd a fountain at thy prayer
> From the dry ground to spring, thy thirst to allay
> After the brunt of battel, can as easie
> Cause light again within thy eies to spring.
> (L4r–L4v/581–84)

Manoa, too, optimistically predicted that "since his strength with eye-sight was not lost, / God will restore him eye-sight to his strength" (O4v/1502–3).

strikes out blindly – unable to see and, figuratively, struggling of his "own accord" to interpret God's providence (O8r/1643). In the *Omissa*, Samson only deals "dole among his foes" (P3v/1529), but, in fact, as Milton emphasizes, he murders

> all who sate beneath,
> Lords, Ladies, Captains, Councellors, or Priests,
> Thir choice nobility and flower, not only
> Of this but each *Philistian* City round.
>
> (O8r/1652–55)

Even the detail, not included in the Book of Judges, that "The vulgar only scap'd who stood without" (O8v/1659), calls attention to the scale of Samson's destruction. The Chorus and Manoa accordingly describe Samson's sighted restitution in the *Omissa* as "incredible," a "miracle," and a "joy" so "presumptuous" that it dare not be "thought" (P3v/1528, 1531, 1532). But their response to Samson's actual, self-destructive, final act necessarily sounds more equivocal. When Manoa first hears that Samson has died, he exclaims that "all my hope's defeated" and the "worst indeed" has occurred. "A dreadful way thou took'st to thy revenge," he tells his absent son (O6r–O6v/1571, 1591).

The difference between the *Omissa* and the conclusion that Milton writes for *Samson Agonistes* is the difference between miracle and tragedy, between revenge fantasy and real-world violence, between divine intervention and the struggle of a "wayfaring/"warfaring" Christian (*CP* 2: 515). Whereas we glimpse a miraculous vision of Samson's restitution in the *Omissa*, the poem instead concludes with a problematic image of his final act – suicidal, large-scale, "dearly-bought . . . , yet glorious!" (O8v/1660) – which, we know from the Book of Judges, ironically fails to effect a lasting political change for Israel. Uncovering deliberate patterns of uncertainty in *Samson Agonistes*, Stanley Fish has described Milton's depiction of Samson's climactic act as "radically indeterminate." As Fish neatly summarizes, "the only wisdom to be carried away from the play is that there is no wisdom to be carried away."[34] But knowing that Milton deliberately added the *Omissa* gives us license to emphasize the impact of these ten lines and helps us better understand how Milton portrays Samson's final destruction. If, like Samson, we resort to violence, Milton suggests through the contrastive imagery of the *Omissa*, we must do so blindly and at considerable cost.

---

[34] Stanley Fish, "Spectacle and Evidence in *Samson Agonistes*," *Critical Inquiry* 15 (1989): 556–86, these quotations, pp. 567, 586.

THE READER'S "STRENUOUS LIBERTY"

Within the context of the 1671 edition, the *Omissa* also echoes the type of miraculous intervention that Satan in *Paradise Regain'd* wants the Son to summon. When Satan tempts Jesus to "Command / That out of these hard stones be made thee bread" (C2r/1.342–43), Jesus refuses to call on such supernatural powers, needing only his faith, reason, and knowledge of Scripture to defeat Satan. Jesus boasts that he, like Satan, "can at will, . . . / Command a Table in this Wilderness, / And call swift flights of Angles ministrant" (D8v/2.383–85), but to make such a command, he argues, would be to "distrust" God (C2v/1.355). Even on the pinnacle when Satan derides Jesus and demands that he "Cast thy self down; safely if Son of God" (H6r/4.555), Jesus refuses, explaining that "it is written, / Tempt not the Lord thy God" (H6r/4.560–61). Rather than being rescued by angels, Jesus on his own stands fast, his physical posture symbolizing his conviction, the description of his "uneasie station" (H7r/4.584) implying that his position against Satan is nevertheless difficult.[35]

Each time that Satan tries to convince Jesus that he can only be rescued "By Miracle" (C2r/1.337), Jesus affirms his faith in God's plans. While we ought not to overemphasize the coincidence that the word "miracle" also occurs in the *Omissa* (P3v/1528), this repetition allies the Chorus's fantasy with Satan's temptations, and hints at the problem of a supernatural resolution for Samson and the Son. Milton used the word "miracle" or "miraculous" only seven times in his poetry, four of them in the 1671 volume. Manoa remembers that his son was "the miracle of men" (K6v/364), for example, and he finds it "Miraculous" (L4v/587) that Samson, though blinded, is still strong. The use of "miracle" in the *Omissa* most closely echoes Milton's use of the word in his translation of Psalm 136: just as God in that poem "doth the wrathful tyrants quell" with "miracles" that "make / Amazed heaven and earth to shake" (lines 10, 13–14), so the Chorus in the *Omissa* imagines God performing a miracle that allows Samson to quell

---

[35] A few critics have argued that Jesus in fact uses supernatural powers to defeat Satan on the pinnacle. Barbara K. Lewalski, *Milton's Brief Epic* (Providence, RI, 1966), for example, claims that Jesus is "the recipient of a miracle of divine protection" (pp. 316–17); and Hugh MacCallum, *Milton and the Sons of God: The Divine Image in Milton's Epic Poetry* (Toronto, 1986), has suggested that the description of Jesus's "uneasie station" merely signifies "the way the pinnacle appears to a human observer" (p. 258). But, as John Carey observes, Milton would probably not emphasize that Jesus's position was "uneasie" if the Son were rescued by a miracle. Responding to MacCallum, Carey reminds us that "station" in the seventeenth century could refer to both a position as well as a standing posture. Why would Milton mention that this position was difficult unless that information was relevant for Jesus in this scene? See Carey, ed., *John Milton: Complete Shorter Poems*, pp. 417–18, 510, as well as his *Milton* (New York, 1970), p. 128.

the wrathful Philistines. The function of miracles, Milton more generally explains in *De doctrina christiana*, "is to demonstrate divine power and strengthen our faith" and "to ensure a weightier condemnation for those who do not believe" (*CP* 6: 341, 342).[36] But, he adds, "Miracles are no more able to produce belief than, in itself, doctrine is: that is to say, they cannot produce it at all. It is God, in either case, who must give the right mind" (*CP* 6: 565).

Like Satan's quick-fix solutions for the Son, the *Omissa*'s miraculous image of revenge and regeneration is tempting – Samson regains his sight, conquers the Philistines, and walks away. And, as the Chorus and Manoa emphasize, God could perform such a miracle, "for to *Israels* God / Nothing is hard" (P3v/1527–28). But both poems suggest the limited value of miracles that Milton implies in *De doctrina*: to resist sin and defeat God's enemies we cannot passively await His special favor. Neither Samson nor Jesus is rescued by divine intervention because to do so would contradict God's express purposes. God sends his Son into the wilderness and exposes him to Satan's temptations because "I mean / To exercise him" (B5r/1.155–56) and "shew him worthy of his birth divine" (B4v/1.141). God similarly seems to be testing Samson's fortitude: "debas't / Lower then bondslave" (I6r/37–38), Samson must first own up to his past errors, then overcome them by applying the "gifts and graces" with which he has been "eminently adorn'd" (L7r/679).

As both Jesus and Samson experience, God's "liberty" is "strenuous" (K4r/271) because it requires obedience in the face of overwhelming temptation and despair. In *Paradise Lost*, God explains that he has made angels as well as humans "Sufficient to have stood, though free to fall"; if they were "Not free, what proof could they have given sincere / Of true allegiance, constant faith or love" (book III, lines 99, 103–4). For God suddenly to interfere in *Paradise Regain'd* or *Samson Agonistes* would deny Jesus and Samson the opportunity to prove their allegiance; a *deus ex machina* resolution to either poem would liberate both protagonists but paradoxically limit their free will.

Some critics, disturbed by Samson's large-scale destruction, have argued that, short of divine intervention, Milton at least ought to have more clearly indicated that God inspired Samson's decision to pull down Dagon's temple and murder "all who sate beneath" (O8r/1652). According to this way

---

[36] For a fuller discussion of Milton's ideas about miracles, see Maurice Kelley, "Milton and Miracles," *Modern Language Notes* 53 (1938): 170–72; and John Illo, "Miracle in Milton's Early Verse," *Costerus: Essays in English and American Language and Literature* 1 (1972): 133–37.

of thinking, the Son's passivity in *Paradise Regain'd* reflects Milton's own commitment to quietism following the failure of the Commonwealth.[37] By juxtaposing the Son's endurance with Samson's violence, Milton would then have been suggesting in the 1671 volume that humans fail to live up to Jesus' example – or, as Joseph Wittreich describes it, that "the prophetic promise of a new paradise may be dashed in the tragedy of history."[38] Wittreich has most fully articulated and developed this position that *Paradise Regain'd* and *Samson Agonistes* represent "how-to-live and how-*not*-to-live poems": Jesus exemplifies the New Testament image of a God "whose only law is love," and Samson personifies the Old Testament image of a God "whose law is vengeance."[39]

The scene described in the *Omissa* complicates this apparent dichotomy, however. Whereas the Messenger's second-hand report prevents us from knowing Samson's state of mind when he actually destroys Dagon's temple, God's intervention in the *Omissa* facilitates Samson's rampage. God miraculously restores Samson's sight, the Chorus implies, *so that* he can deal "dole among his foes" and traipse "over heaps of slaughter'd" (P3v/1529–30). That the *Omissa* contains one of the volume's most violent images suggests Milton did not reject the use of force on principle. Milton and the publisher Starkey thought this supernatural vision important enough to have it included at the end of the 1671 volume. The *Omissa* does not tempt readers with the hope of a peaceful resolution, but instead presents a fantasy of justice that is divine, swift, and bloody.

In response to critics such as Wittreich, Joan S. Bennett has turned to modern liberation theology as an "imaginative window" to help explain how seventeenth-century readers could have reconciled Samson's large-scale destruction with the Son's passivity.[40] Working in part from John 18:36 ("If my kingdom were of this world, then would my servants fight"), Bennett presents the liberationists' contention that free people are obligated

[37] See, for example, Andrew Milner, *John Milton and the English Revolution: A Study in the Sociology of Literature* (London, 1981), pp. 147, 175.
[38] Wittreich, *Interpreting* Samson Agonistes, p. 370. Noting that Milton "nowhere glorified slaughter," Irene Samuel was among the first to challenge the traditional view of Samson's final act as divinely inspired. See Samuel, "*Samson Agonistes* as Tragedy," in *Calm of Mind: Tercentenary Essays on Paradise Regained and Samson Agonistes in Honor of John S. Diekhoff*, ed. Joseph Anthony Wittreich (Cleveland, 1971), pp. 235–57, this quotation, p. 252. Also see Helen Damico, "Duality and Dramatic Vision: A Structural Analysis of *Samson Agonistes*," *Milton Studies* 12 (1978): 91–116.
[39] Wittreich, *Interpreting* Samson Agonistes, pp. 379, 350.
[40] Joan S. Bennett, "Asserting Eternal Providence: John Milton through the Window of Liberation Theology," in *Milton and Heresy*, ed. Stephen B. Dobranski and John P. Rumrich (Cambridge, 1998), pp. 219–43; and Bennett, *Reviving Liberty: Radical Christian Humanism in Milton's Great Poems* (Cambridge, MA, 1989).

to oppose "forcers of conscience" like the tyrannical Philistines. Although God wants us to love one another, "such love did not mean enduring passively until the apocalypse."[41] Jesus' repeated ability to resist temptation was not meant as a direct model of behavior, nor was it entirely passive: as Bennett observes, Christian readers can instead turn to the example of Jesus' obedience as "both the source and model" of their "own spiritual liberation and public action."[42]

More specifically, in *A Treatise of Civil Power* (1659), which Bennett also cites, Milton does not object to all violence: he insists that "the kingdom of Christ [is] not governd by outward force; as being none of this world, whose kingdoms are maintaind all by force onely." But, he avers, "a Christian commonwealth may defend it self against outward force in the cause of religion as well as in any other" (*CP* 7: 256–57). In *De doctrina christiana*, Milton culls various passages from scripture to illustrate that Jesus, too, "conquers and crushes his enemies" so as to fulfill his "kingly function" (*CP* 6: 435, 437). Christopher Hill has identified this latter view as part of a larger Protestant tradition that treated the hatred of God's enemies as a duty. Although such convictions may seem strange to modern readers, Hill demonstrates that Milton would have heard them early and often, the first time as a boy in the sermons of Richard Stock, his parish minister.[43]

Returning to *Paradise Regain'd . . . Samson Agonistes*, we discover that when Jesus considers quelling "Brute violence" (B7r/1.219), he never rules out the need for force. He instead resolves "At least to try" to "make perswasion do the work of fear" (B7r/1.223–24) and accepts that Satan's "projects deep / Of enemies, of aids, battels and leagues" remain "Plausible to the world, [though] to me worth naught" (F5v–F6r/3.391–93). According to the editors of the *OED*, "plausible" during the seventeenth century could mean either genuinely laudable or merely appearing so.[44] Jesus may be acknowledging that such "projects" sometimes deserve approval (although they are useless for him), or he may be implying that warfare sometimes seems worthwhile, but only when judged by worldly standards.

---

[41] Bennett, *Reviving Liberty*, p. 157.

[42] Bennett, *Reviving Liberty*, p. 169. As Peggy Samuels has also shown, Milton combines the Son's "utter calm" with "reforming vehemence." Rather than describing a spiritual retreat from the world in *Paradise Regain'd*, Milton suggests "a private realm in which one trains the judgment to rely on other tribunals besides the state and ecclesiastical authorities and uses that clarified judgment to speak severely to and attempt to reform others." See Samuels, "Labor in the Chambers: *Paradise Regained* and the Discourse of Quiet," *Milton Studies* 36 (1998): 153–76, these quotations, pp. 169, 172.

[43] Christopher Hill, "*Samson Agonistes* Again," *Literature and History*, 2nd series 1 (1990): 24–39.

[44] *OED* s.v. "plausible" A.1–2, A.3.a.

Less ambiguous is the Son's earlier concession, "the stubborn only to destroy" (B7r/1.226). This statement seems to validate unequivocally Samson's climactic action: he pulls down the pillars, in the words of the Messenger, "at once both to destroy and be destroy'd" (O6v/1587). Only after turning to the errata do we discover that "destroy" in *Paradise Regain'd* is to be replaced with "subdue", a change that substantially mitigates – without entirely eliminating – Jesus's threat of violence. In the corrected text, Jesus no longer will annihilate "proud Tyrannick pow'r" (B7r/1.219), but he still holds out the possibility of bringing such tyrants into subjection by intimidating or conquering them. Like the insertion of the *Omissa*, the change from "destroy" to "subdue" suggests a last-minute revision, perhaps as Milton was considering having *Paradise Regain'd* and *Samson Agonistes* published together. Because the text presents these changes as the readers' responsibility, we become collaborators in the 1671 volume. Revising Jesus's diction calls our attention to the question of violent action and forces us to examine how far Jesus warrants Samson's destruction.

Many of Milton's seventeenth-century readers, as Christopher Hill reminds us, would have approached Jesus's temptation and Samson's imprisonment specifically in terms of England's recent political upheaval.[45] After the Restoration, Puritan saints and commonwealthmen frequently turned to such biblical accounts to help understand contemporary experiences.[46] If, as Hill has argued, the character of Samson came to symbolize the revolution and, in particular, the revolutionary army, then seventeenth-century readers would have found the *Omissa* especially important: these ten added lines contain one of the poem's most urgent and violent images for the revitalization of the Good Old Cause.[47] We can imagine Milton, the disillusioned polemicist and statesman, adding the *Omissa* as he boldly entertained the possible "miracle" (P3v/1528) of a renewed revolt against monarchy. Milton uses the prospect of Samson's regained sight to recall that "to *Israels* God / Nothing is hard" (P3v/1527–28), not even, by implication, overthrowing Charles II and returning England to a republican government.

In the context of the 1671 volume, however, the possibility of the *Omissa* also serves as a warning. If Milton after the failure of the Civil War did not retreat to an inner paradise, he also no longer held any illusions about

---

[45] Hill, *Milton and the English Revolution* (London, 1977), p. 435; and Hill, *The Experience of Defeat: Milton and Some Contemporaries* (New York, 1984), pp. 312, 318.

[46] See Worden, "Milton, *Samson Agonistes*, and the Restoration," pp. 111–36.

[47] I discuss the passage's political implications more fully in Dobranski, "Samson and the *Omissa*," and chap. 2 of *Milton, Authorship and the Book Trade*.

political activism. The author of *Eikonoklastes* and former Secretary for Foreign Languages under the Commonwealth, Milton had gone into hiding after the Restoration, was briefly imprisoned, and witnessed the censure and execution of many of his friends and collaborators – "thir carkasses / To dogs and fowls a prey, or else captiv'd," as the Chorus tells Samson (L7r/693–94). Through *Paradise Regain'd . . . Samson Agonistes*, Milton cautions readers against "the urge for instant solutions," which Hill includes among the "temptations" that "led the English revolutionaries astray."[48] Following the failure of English republicanism, Milton's readers could not rely on God's miraculous intervention and had to reject the vain hope of acting without suffering. To regain paradise and defeat their enemies, readers must instead, according to the Son and Samson's examples, act of their "own accord" (O8r/1643) using their strength, faith, and reason.

Regardless of whether Milton wrote *Paradise Regain'd* and *Samson Agonistes* separately, he may have revised one or both of them sometime before publication so as to make the 1671 volume more cohesive.[49] Perhaps the *Omissa* represents such a revision: these ten lines help to unify the two poems by calling attention to the temptation of miracles and the strenuousness of God's liberty. Milton may have even intended that the ten lines of the *Omissa* appear at the end of the book to emphasize this suggestive exchange between the Chorus and Manoa.[50] Like the correction of "destroy" to "subdue" in the errata, the *Omissa*'s imagery highlights the question of violent action.

By having these ten lines printed as an omission, Milton was also demonstratively rejecting a *deus ex machina* resolution for his Christian protagonists. Although he frames *Samson Agonistes* as a tragedy "after the antient manner" of Aeschylus, Sophocles, and Euripides (I2v), he thus distinguishes his dramatic poem from the works of these particular classical authors. Instead, Milton's dismissal of *deus ex machina* may have been inspired by Aristotle's concept of tragedy in the *Poetics*.[51] Aristotle asserts that "the unraveling of the plot should spring from the plot itself, and not from

---

[48] Hill, *Milton and the English Revolution*, p. 421.

[49] On the date of the two poems' composition, see note 2.

[50] While the term *Omissa* may seem to imply negligence, we should note that Milton used various forms of "omission" in his other works to indicate a deliberate excision. In *The History of Britain* (1670), for example, Milton pledges to remove parts of existing Roman narratives as a means of enhancing them: "if ought by diligence may bee added, or omitted, or by other disposing may be more explain'd, or more express'd, I shall assay" (*CP* 5: 41).

[51] On the connection between *Samson Agonistes* and Aristotle's concept of tragedy, see Irene Samuel, "*Samson Agonistes* as Tragedy," and Derek N. C. Wood, "Aristotle, the Italian Commentators, and Some Aspects of Milton's Christian Tragedy," *Milton Studies* 29 (1992): 83–104.

deus ex machina." Plays ought not to include anything "unreasonable," but in exceptional cases when "there is something unreasonable, it should be outside the tragedy itself."[52] With the *Omissa*, Milton seems to have taken Aristotle's prescription literally, setting off this improbable turn of events from the rest of his tragedy. The placement of the *Omissa* suggests the implausibility of the miracle that it describes: God's special favor remains present but absent, isolated from the text and not something on which readers can rely.

MILTON AND HIS READERS

Modern editions that silently insert the *Omissa*, correct the errata, and disrupt the pairing of *Paradise Regain'd . . . Samson Agonistes* rob us of valuable information for interpreting the two poems. Aristotle's *Poetics*, for example, is quoted on *Samson*'s title page, another material element from the 1671 text that might assist our reading of the poems but that modern editions often eliminate (see figure 6b). When editors intervene in the book, they prevent us from fully participating in Milton's writing. This problem occurs with all early modern books, but *Paradise Regain'd . . . Samson Agonistes* especially illustrates the need for active readers. The first edition requires readers' participation in the text, just as Milton's two poems demonstrate the importance of Jesus and Samson's active faith and obedience. Milton's use of the Greek word *agonistes* describes not only Samson but also the poet's ideal audience: Milton subtly challenges his readers to become contestants in both the text and their world. Even Samson's opening request for help – "A Little onward lend thy guiding hand" (I5r/1) – whether addressed to God or a jailer, represents Milton's request at the start of the poem for each reader to lend a hand to the 1671 volume.

Throughout Milton's career, he would make similar requests of his audiences. Milton so often returns to the subject of active reading presumably because he thought the stakes were so high: books, he explains to Parliament in *Areopagitica*, serve as the "means . . . both to the triall of vertue, and the exercise of truth" (*CP* 2: 528). He accordingly presents readers with a series of choices in his writings, sometimes guiding his audience in a specific direction – as in the proem of *Paradise Lost* where he considers Sinai or Sion before concluding that his muse "dost prefer / Before all temples the upright

---

[52] *The Philosophy of Aristotle*, ed. Renford Bambrough, trans. J. L. Creed and A. E. Wardman (New York, 1963), p. 425 (15.1454b1–10).

heart and pure" (book I, lines 17–18)[53] – and at other times encouraging his audience's "exercise" by apparently withholding a definitive answer – as in the conclusion of *Samson Agonistes* where he foregrounds the reader's "strenuous liberty" by ambiguously portraying Samson's final act. If "the knowledge and survay of vice is in this world so necessary to the constituting of human vertue," Milton reasons in *Areopagitica*, then readers need to cultivate good reading habits: "how can we more safely, and with lesse danger scout into the regions of sin and falsity then by reading all manner of tractats, and hearing all manner of reason?" (*CP* 2: 516–17). Elsewhere Milton insists that "the ancient stories of the Church" need to be perused "diligently" so that readers can "marke how corruption, and *Apostacy* crept in by degrees, and to gather up, where ever wee find the remaining sparks of Originall truth" (*CP* 1: 650). Again, his diction – "marke," "gather up," and "find" – suggests that seventeenth-century readers had to engage critically and actively with their books.

Like many writers, Milton was not always successful in reaching a sympathetic audience – and was not always patient when he failed to do so. Consider his sonnets on the divorce tracts where he characterizes readers' hostile reactions as the "barbarous noise . . . / Of owls and cuckoos, asses, apes and dogs."[54] Deriding readers for failing to understand his argument, he imagines "some in file," standing around the bookseller's shop, gawking at the title page, and "spelling false" the tract's title.[55] The problem with the divorce tracts, he would later suggest, was that he should not have written in English, "for then I would not have met with vernacular readers, who are usually ignorant of their own good, and laugh at the misfortunes of others" (*CP* 4: 610).

Yet even after such disappointments – and, more devastatingly, the disappointment of the lost revolution – Milton continued writing and continued seeking an understanding audience. In the divorce sonnets, his frustration with readers grew from what he perceived as a lack of effort – the tract, he complains, is "now seldom *pored on*" (my emphasis)[56] – and was also influenced by the betrayal he felt from Presbyterians who not only misunderstood his argument but attacked him personally. Often, as with *The Doctrine and Discipline of Divorce* and *Eikonoklastes*, Milton added or enhanced his comments to readers in his works' second editions. If his audience failed to live up to his great expectations, he tried harder to

[53] James Hoyle, "'If Sion Hill Delight Thee More': The Muse's Choice in *Paradise Lost*," *English Language Notes* 12 (1974): 20–26; and Virginia R. Mollenkott, "Milton's Technique of Multiple Choice," *Milton Studies* 6 (1974): 101–11.
[54] Sonnet XII, lines 3–4.   [55] Sonnet XI, line 7.   [56] Sonnet XI, line 4.

map out the training and work he required of them.[57] Thus in a note added to a reprint of *Paradise Lost* Milton contrasts the poor tastes of "vulgar readers" with the refined appreciation of "all judicious ears." In part, he was responding angrily to impertinent readers who questioned why his epic did not rhyme. But these categories are also rhetorical: Milton invites readers to identify with the judicious and share his disdain for the vulgar.

We can never know how many Renaissance readers actually lived up to Milton's standards, how fit they were and how few.[58] As late as 1673 in *Of True Religion*, Milton was still urging his audience "to read duly and diligently the Holy Scriptures" (*CP* 8: 433) and still hoping they would prepare adequately and proceed thoughtfully: "Every member of the Church, at least of any breeding or capacity, so well ought to be grounded in spiritual knowledg, as . . . to examine their Teachers themselves" (*CP* 8: 435). Just as Jesus in *Paradise Regain'd* insists that readers must bring "A spirit and judgment equal or superior" to their books (G8r/4.324), Milton continues to appeal to a learned audience and have faith in the value of careful interpretation. When God in *Paradise Lost* wishes to emphasize that humans have free will and are accountable for their own decisions, He refers to them as "authors to themselves in all / Both what they judge and what they choose" (book III, lines 122–23). While "author" in the epic typically describes a solitary creator – so that Satan is "the author of all ill" (book II, line 381); God, the "author of all being" (book III, line 374) – Milton's diction here suggests the tremendous responsibility that he believed readers and writers share.[59] God may be articulating the Arminian concept of free will at the heart of Milton's theodicy, but the specific choice of "authors" hints at Milton's own dilation of "authorship" to include more than a text's composer. Instead of accepting the idea of textual predetermination, Milton empowers all individuals as potential authors or "creators" – writers and readers alike – who must judge and choose for themselves.

[57] Mary Ann Radzinowicz, "*Samson Agonistes* and Milton the Politician in Defeat," *Philological Quarterly* 44 (1965): 454–71, for example, addresses Milton's changing formulation of his audience in the first and second editions of *The Readie and Easie Way*.
[58] In the case of *Paradise Regain'd . . . Samson Agonistes*, according to Harris Francis Fletcher, "Many early readers of the two poems recorded their awareness of . . . weak lines, faulty spellings, awkward phrases, improper or misleading punctuation, by pen corrections, some examples of which seem to be very early, even nearly contemporary" (*John Milton's Complete Poetical Works Reproduced in Photographic Facsimile*, 4: 37). One of the copies I examined at the British Library, London (shelfmark C.14a12), for example, contains handwritten corrections of both the errata and *Omissa*.
[59] "Author" in *Paradise Lost* can also signify "father," as in the passages where Sin addresses Satan ("our great author," book X, line 236) or the poet describes Adam ("Our author," book V, line 397).

When "more is meant than meets the ear," as Milton writes in *Il Penseroso* (line 120), the more, he knew, writers and readers had to depend on each other. Whereas Stanley Fish in *Surprised by Sin* has posited a censorious author, successively trapping and berating his fallen readers in *Paradise Lost*, Milton's many comments about reading reveal a poet who again and again wanted his audience to collaborate with him. When in *Paradise Regain'd* . . . *Samson Agonistes* Milton's Samson bemoans that God has given him physical "strength without a double share / Of wisdom" (I6v/53–54), the double structure of the 1671 volume compensates for this insufficiency, specifically pairing Samson's power with both the Son's "wisdom" (B5v/1.175) and, Milton hoped, the readers' intelligence. Readers finishing the 1671 text would then have turned to the final pages and encountered both errata and *Omissa*. These categories of mistakes remind seventeenth-century readers of their role in Milton's volume, and perhaps more subtly, of their political responsibilities. Only through the efforts of diligent readers can things be set right, Milton suggests in 1671; only through readers' participation in the text can past errors be corrected and the promise that the *Omissa* holds ever be realized.

Postscript

> I look back over what I've written and I know it's wrong, not because
> of what I've set down, but because of what I've omitted. What isn't
> there has a presence, like the absence of light.
>
> – Margaret Atwood[1]

Given, then, the various types of omissions published during the
seventeenth century, we should not be surprised to learn that when John
Suckling's posthumous *Last Remains* was printed in 1659 it included his
unfinished tragedy, *The Sad One*.[2] Citing the precedent of Ben Jonson's
incomplete publications, the bookseller Humphrey Moseley explains that
he "thought it much better" to print Suckling's play "in the same state I
found it, without the least addition, then procure it supplied by any other
Pen; which had been not less preposterous then the finishing of *Venus*
Picture, so skillfully begun by *Apelles*, by some other hand" (a2).

That Moseley in this preface insists on the sanctity of Suckling's authorship reflects, once again, the newfound authority granted writers in early
modern England. Suckling's dramatic fragment is worth reading, Moseley
reasons, because it was written by such an "incomparable *Author*" (a2r).
In addition to the precedents of Jonson and the ancient painter Apelles,
the bookseller recalls that both Donne and Sidney had their unfinished
works printed: Moseley quotes Donne's defense of poetic fragments from
the preface to *Poems, By J. D.* (a3v) and notes the coincidence that Suckling's
book is dedicated to his sister, just "as the famous Arcadia was sent to that
excellent Lady, who was Sister to that great Author" (a1r).

But while Moseley assembles such a prestigious pedigree for Suckling and
The Sad One, the bookseller's direct appeal "To the Reader" indicates the
authority of Suckling's audience. Moseley may have sincerely believed that

---

[1] Margaret Atwood, *The Blind Assassin* (New York, 2001), p. 395.
[2] Sir John Suckling, *The Sad One*, in *The Last Remains of Sir John Suckling* (London, 1659; Wing
S6130), E1r–G8r. All subsequent quotations from this publication are taken from this edition and
cited parenthetically.

the poet's "most deficient Fragments" evince "a kind of Perfection" (a2r), but more important, he knew, was persuading readers to accept the author's excellence. Moseley even tampers with the evidence: the painting by Apelles that the bookseller cites was not left incomplete but had been finished and subsequently damaged.[3] Just that Moseley thought it necessary to defend the fragment's publication suggests, too, that the printing of unfinished works was not yet fully accepted in the 1650s. Moseley implies that some "other Pen" could supplement Suckling's text, the way Chapman tried to finish Marlowe's *Hero and Leander*, for example, or, as Moseley's audience must have known, various readers became writers and added to Sidney's *Arcadia*.[4]

With this emphasis on the reader's role and the poet's merit, Suckling's incomplete publication thus provides a fitting conclusion to both the poet's career and this book's case studies: the missing pieces in Suckling's text indicate the authority that authors and readers shared during the seventeenth century. While the play's inclusion in Suckling's posthumous *Last Remains* was designed to enhance the poet's stature – even his unfinished works, we are to infer, are worthy of printing – readers simultaneously were granted considerable responsibility, both to perceive the remaining fragment's value and to envision for themselves the narrative's outcome.

This balance of power between authors and readers reflects, as we have seen, the changing conditions of authorship in early modern England. Seventeenth-century writers were gaining new control over their texts – legally, economically, and, as in Suckling's case, symbolically – but Renaissance readers were also empowered: polemical traditions of learning, for example, and protocols of printed books encouraged readers to interact with authors' publications to make them meaningful, and, in some cases, readers appropriated a work in ways the author could not have imagined. It is this historical context that I have brought to bear on the omissions in the preceding case studies; through these texts' blank spaces we glimpse a reciprocal relationship between Renaissance writers and readers. Some works, like Suckling's *The Sad One*, are incomplete apparently because writers never happened to finish composing them. Yet such omissions still demonstrate

---

[3] Even Apelles, it seems, was unwilling to repair his damaged painting "and make it up againe as it was at first." Instead, the artist began a second picture of Venus, "which he minded should have surpassed the former," and it was this second painting that he died before completing. See Pliny, *The Historie of the World*, 2 vols., trans. P. Holland (London, 1601; STC 20029), [2]Zz6v (vol. 2, book 35, chap. 10).

[4] Suckling's unfinished play seems already to have benefited from an unknown reader's intervention: *The Sad One*'s act and scene divisions, as L. A. Beaurline observes, are uncharacteristic of Suckling and were probably added by someone other than the poet. See Beaurline, ed., *The Works of Sir John Suckling: The Plays* (Oxford, 1971), pp. 245–46.

the author's and readers' reciprocity, for the printing of Suckling's incomplete text, as with Sidney's unfinished *Arcadia* and Donne's posthumous fragments, is at once an honorific gesture and, as we have seen, an invitation for readers' active involvement. The other type of omission I have examined, where authors such as Jonson, Herrick, and Milton have deliberately left blank spaces in their works, depends on a similarly cooperative dynamic: readers could interpret these omissions by positing an autonomous author who purposefully left out information, and authors, in turn, could confidently omit parts of their works with the expectation that active readers would discover the omissions' significance.

In basing this argument on historical practices of reading and writing, I have not meant to imply that the omissions in these Renaissance texts chart a steady increase in the early modern author's authority, nor that they delineate a corresponding rise or decline in readers' activity. Instead, I have tried to show that our understanding of such imperfect texts can benefit from a comparative analysis; some omissions, as Moseley's preface to Suckling's *The Sad One* demonstrates, may even have been published in response to others.

But rather than attempting to plot each of these omissions within an overarching narrative, I would suggest that the development of the author and readers' relationship can be measured by contrasting the unintentional silences in Sidney's *Arcadia*, composed near the end of the sixteenth century, with the shrewd *Omissa* in Milton's *Paradise Regain'd . . . Samson Agonistes*, published almost one hundred years later. Whereas seventeenth-century readers exploited the unfinished state of Sidney's romance in freely adapting his *Arcadia* to the political culture of the Civil War period, the blank spaces in later publications such as Milton's seem designed to encourage as well as shape audience participation. Thus the omissions in Donne's 1633 *Poems* illustrate how stationers could invite readers to participate in constructing the author's authority; Herrick used omissions in *Hesperides* to appeal to readers in overcoming the limitations of print; and Jonson left out part of his "Epistle to Elizabeth Countesse of Rutland" both to safeguard himself against the material process of production and to undermine a courtly model of authorship.

These and other incomplete texts printed during the Renaissance may also be explained in the context of the period's tremendous social upheaval. In addition to those omissions that allude to the country's political conflict – in Herrick's and Milton's poems, as well as the anonymous poet's feigned omission to Sidney's *Arcadia* – the imperfect state of so many seventeenth-century publications suggests the larger sense of disappointment experienced by both sides during the Civil War period. The ellipses and broken dashes in the layout of those incomplete works, along with such evocative tags as "*The rest is lost*" or "*Caetera desunt*," formally convey the politically charged themes of fragmentation and lost opportunity.

And yet, as I mentioned at the start of this book, to make the case for the significance of Renaissance texts' missing pieces does not require that the publication of incomplete works was unique to the early modern period. While specific conventions and circumstances help to explain the origin, frequency, and meaning of Renaissance omissions, the cooperative model of reading and writing that such incomplete texts reveal has, I think, further-reaching implications.

Certainly various kinds of blank spaces occur in works written after the seventeenth century. When William Wordsworth and Samuel Taylor Coleridge published *Lyrical Ballads* in 1798, for example, they included without apology or explanation two poetic fragments, "The Foster-Mother's Tale" and "The Dungeon," both excerpted from Coleridge's tragedy *Osorio*; two years later in the collection's second edition, Wordsworth added two of his own incomplete works, "Nutting" and "A Fragment."[5] The blank spaces in these and many other Romantic poems – for example, *Kubla Kahn, The Recluse, The Triumph of Life, The Fall of Hyperion*, and *Don Juan* – presumably reflect this later period's prevailing consciousness; as Thomas McFarland has argued, "incompletion, fragmentation, and ruin occupy both the theory and the actuality of Romanticism."[6] I would add that such Romantic omissions also descend from Jonson's "Epistle to Elizabeth," Herrick's "The Country Life," and Donne's "Resurrection, imperfect." But unlike their Renaissance forebears, many of these incomplete Romantic works do not invite readers' participation; as Balachandra Rajan has shown, poems such as *The Triumph of Life* and *The Fall of Hyperion* contain "undecidable dissensions" and thus "ask not to be finished."[7]

During the Victorian period, a more collaborative relationship emerged between authors and readers in the blank spaces created by the serialization of novels. Each installment served as a temporary fragment: authors expected readers to remember what had previously transpired while teasing

[5] See Wordsworth and Coleridge, Lyrical Ballads: *The Text of the 1798 Edition with the Additional 1800 Poems and the Prefaces*, ed. R. L. Brett and A. R. Jones (London, 1963).
[6] Thomas McFarland, *Romanticism and the Forms of Ruin: Wordsworth, Coleridge, and the Modalities of Fragmentation* (Princeton, 1981), p. 13. See also Marjorie Levinson's excellent study of Romantic fragments, *The Romantic Fragment Poem: A Critique of a Form* (Chapel Hill, 1986).
[7] Balachandra Rajan, *The Form of the Unfinished: English Poetics from Spenser to Pound* (Princeton, 1985), pp. 14, 15.

them into conjecturing what might occur in later chapters. Nor were authors thought to be entirely in control of their works, for the novels' piecemeal publication prompted readers to appeal for the return of particular characters or the reassurance of a happy ending.[8] Not surprisingly, readers who had enjoyed the first six numbers of Charles Dickens' *The Mystery of Edwin Drood* thus attempted to compose their own continuations when Dickens died in 1870, leaving the novel unfinished.[9] Like the anonymous poet of "A Remedie for Love," who disguised himself as Sir Philip Sidney to respond to the *Arcadia*, some of *Edwin Drood*'s readers tried to pass themselves as Dickens to supplement his novel. Other readers, in what seems to indicate the evolving importance of name recognition, thought it advantageous to pretend that they were either Charles Dickens, Junior, or Dickens' friend and rival, Wilkie Collins.

While I am not attempting in this postscript to provide a thorough history of later literary omissions, even a brief survey illustrates the long-term legacy of the incomplete works published during the earliest stages of the English book trade. That both Victorian and Romantic authors and readers, despite their fundamentally different sensibilities, made use of such omissions also suggests the pliability of leaving out information from a literary work. And we could trace the legacy of Renaissance omissions further, to other types of blank spaces and to other genres and other media – the stripped down stage design of Thornton Wilder's *Our Town*, for example, or the spatial and temporal gaps elided by Godard's jump cuts in *Breathless*, or the diminution of detail across the eight lithographs of Picasso's "The Bull."

Among American writers, Ernest Hemingway most eloquently defined the collaborative implications of modern omissions:

> If a writer of prose knows enough about what he is writing about he may omit things that he knows and the reader, if the writer is writing truly enough, will have a feeling of those things as strongly as though the writer had stated them. The dignity of movement of an ice-berg is due to only one-eighth of it being above water. A writer who omits things because he does not know them only makes hollow places in his writing.[10]

For Hemingway, the benefit of removing information from a prose work exceeds an economy of language; it gives writing, according to his iceberg

---

[8] See Linda K. Hughes and Michael Lund, *The Victorian Serial* (Charlottesville, 1991), pp. 8–11; and J. Don Vann, *Victorian Novels in Serial* (New York, 1985), pp. 1–17.

[9] Margaret Cardwell, ed., *The Mystery of Edwin Drood*, by Charles Dickens (Oxford, 1972), pp. 253–55.

[10] Ernest Hemingway, *Death in the Afternoon* (New York, 1955), p. 192.

metaphor, dignity and power. Note, though, that in the above passage he juxtaposes the author's "knowledge" with the reader's "feeling." His diction suggests that an author's conscious choices affect readers intuitively; omitting things from a piece of writing adds to the overall effect by making the work more inductive, more experiential. In contrast to the demanding nature of Renaissance omissions, Hemingway's blank spaces do not seem to require readers' active labor. The novelist believed, as Susan Beegel explains, that all authorial omissions, good or bad, remain in a finished work for readers to apprehend, "like the ghosts of sensation where an amputated limb has been."[11] Beegel's own excellent metaphor conveys Hemingway's strong authorial bias while succinctly capturing the paradox of omission – absent and present, cut and cure, diminishment and betterment.

The fractured and stream of conscious style developed by other twentieth-century writers also depended largely on what was not said, but authors of these works provided few clues to help readers reconcile apparently unconnected utterances. T. S. Eliot's best-known poems, for example, comprise a series of fragments – scenes, images, and voices – that defy our and their protagonists' efforts to sort them adequately. When Eliot's Prufrock announces, "It is impossible to say just what I mean!" he offers both a lament and revelation, ironically articulating the poet's own struggle to communicate.[12] The theme recurs as Eliot contrasts the diminishing gaze of "eyes that fix you in a formulated phrase" (line 56) with the image of a withdrawn figure who avoids eye contact, only able to express discomfort and disappointment in nervous, miscellaneous gestures. This anonymous figure, identified merely as "one," remains misunderstood and virtually invisible, her single assertion an act of negation: "That is not it at all, / That is not what I meant at all" (lines 109–10). A distant relative of the often absent beloved in Renaissance seduction poems, Eliot's disconnected, hollow woman is symbol and symptom of a fragmented culture. This "one" gets to speak, but by definition she remains solitary and unidentifiable, receding from our sight even as she makes her revocatory pronouncement.

Such blank spaces as in "The Love Song of J. Alfred Prufrock" appear to differ from Renaissance omissions that fostered a collaborative relationship between authors and readers: the gaps that result from Eliot's missing

---

[11] Susan F. Beegel, *Hemingway's Craft of Omission: Four Manuscript Examples* (Ann Arbor, 1988), p. 92.

[12] T. S. Eliot, "The Love Song of J. Alfred Prufrock," in *The Complete Poems and Plays, 1909–1950* (New York, 1980), pp. 3–7, this quotation, line 104. All subsequent quotations from this poem are taken from this edition and cited parenthetically.

information seem designed to remain meaningfully empty. What we have here is not a failure to communicate, but an awareness of that failure as the author's and readers' starting point.

This sense of language's inadequacy also informs the omissions in late twentieth-century writings, whether the haunting emptiness and compressed style that characterize minimalist short stories, or the playful evasion and open-endedness of postmodern poetry and fiction. Thomas Pynchon's *The Crying of Lot 49*, for example, stops short, just before lot 49 is cried at auction, thus denying readers the answers that they, like the novel's protagonist, Oedipa Maas, have been anticipating. And that seems to be what the novelist wants readers to discover through omission: that answers always remain out of reach, that there are no absolute truths and each reader must fill in a text's blanks to create her own reality. Each reader, like the author himself, as Pynchon puts it, serves as "the projector at the planetarium" – that is, each of us projects our own universe onto the page and out into the world.[13]

We can also trace the indeterminacy of language to the deconstructionists' now familiar defense of absence as the basis for all communication. Language, according to this theory, depends on omission: because every word derives part of its meaning from the words that precede and follow it, language is never determined directly from the reality it attempts to describe. As Derrida writes, "the signified concept is never present in and of itself, in a sufficient presence that would refer only to itself."[14] To introduce a symbol, in other words, is to omit the thing that the symbol signifies and to produce unintended meanings through the play of other signifiers. As Lacan neatly summarized, "absence is evoked in presence, and presence in absence."[15] That is, words mark things that are absent, but words take on a reality of their own.

While the early modern writers I have examined in this book certainly appreciated the possible play of meaning created by poetic language, their use of omission is never only a sign of their limitations. On the contrary, instead of accepting that words mark things that are absent, these authors were incorporating blank spaces so as to mark especially significant moments in their texts. If some theorists see absence as a product of language's inherent limitations – all meaning would accordingly derive from

---

[13] Thomas Pynchon, *The Crying of Lot 49* (New York, 1982), p. 56.

[14] Jacques Derrida, "*Différance*," in *Margins of Philosophy*, trans. Alan Bass (Chicago, 1982), pp. 3–27, this quotation, p. 11.

[15] Lacan, *The Seminar of Jacques Lacan: Book I: Freud's Papers on Technique 1953–54*, ed. Jacques-Alain Miller, trans. John Forester (New York, 1988), p. 174.

the structure of language itself, as opposed to an author's intentions – the Renaissance omissions that I have examined are hyper-intentional sites of meaning, attempts by writers and stationers to use even absence as part of a linguistic system. In the silence of these blank spaces, we hear authors and readers straining to communicate across the distance imposed by the new medium of print.

Sometimes this strain may admittedly leave us wondering if what we are listening to is not an author's intentional utterance but the reverberations of our own practices of interpretation. As a teacher of early modern literature, I often work with students who doubt that Renaissance authors and readers were as canny or as subtle as some modern analyses imply. But Renaissance omissions, I have argued, are for this reason especially valuable: such blank spaces reveal the potency of both early modern writers and readers. By beginning each case study with a bibliographical analysis, we can establish whether an omission's provenance is authorial and then use the remaining fragments to examine contemporary conditions of reading and authorship.

In this last regard, more work needs to be done, and it seems only appropriate that, having written at length about omissions, I conclude by acknowledging some of my own book's missing parts. More should be said, for example, about the responses of individual readers during the Renaissance. Whereas I have focused attention on how seventeenth-century texts encode authors' utterances and expectations, the traces that contemporary readers have left of themselves – in marginalia, reading journals, and commonplace books – deserve further scrutiny.[16] More could be said as well about the role that the material conditions of authorship played in facilitating a collaborative relationship between early modern writers and readers. Members of the book trade represent especially important, liminal figures, occupying the subject position of both creator and audience: they are readers of a writer's work, but simultaneously they help to author the writer's printed text. And while my interest here has been exclusively in incomplete works that were printed during the Renaissance, provocative omissions survive in manuscripts from this period, perhaps most notably Milton's unfinished theological treatise, *De doctrina christiana*, but also, for example, Lucy Hutchinson's autobiographical fragment, or her translation

---

[16] For examples of this type of study, see D. R. Woolf, *Reading History in Early Modern England* (Cambridge, 2000), and John Morrill, "William Dowsing, the Bureaucratic Puritan," in *Public Duty and Private Conscience in Seventeenth-Century England*, ed. John Morrill, Paul Slack, and Daniel Woolf (Oxford, 1993), pp. 173–203.

of Lucretius' *De rerum natura* from which roughly 100 lines on *"The cause and effects of Love"* have been pointedly *"left out."*[17]

As we look beyond the seventeenth century, more work also remains to be done on the intersection of early modern and postmodern notions of authorship. With the advent of new literacy technologies, scholars have rightly heralded the dynamic fluidity of reading and writing with the aid of computers, but claims for the new technologies' democratic implications often understate the comparable impact that print had on Renaissance authors and their audiences. To argue, for example, that "the conceptual space of a printed book . . . is stable, monumental, and controlled exclusively by the author" whereas "the conceptual space of electronic writing . . . is characterized by fluidity and an interactive relationship between writer and reader" misrepresents the histories of reading and writing, especially as they evolved during the Renaissance.[18] As we strive to understand and predict the implications of computers for reading and writing in the twenty-first century, we need to begin with the various ways that these practices were already fluid and interactive in the 1600s – through such protocols as answer poems, commonplace books, errata lists, group-writings, and pamphlet wars.

To this list we can now add omissions. The suggestive power of silence provided early modern writers and readers not only a way to communicate but also a means to bolster their own and each other's status. As scholars continue to fill in the various "omissions" that survive in our understanding of the early modern period, we need to continue looking at how much authority authors claimed for themselves and what kinds of interpretive activity Renaissance readers undertook. The phenomenon of publishing incomplete works also can remind us more generally to expand our inquiries of even familiar texts into their gaps and fissures, to listen for an author's silences, and to consider, often for the first time, the relationship between what a text discloses and what it may meaningfully withhold.

[17] *Lucy Hutchinson's Translation of Lucretius*: De rerum natura, ed. Hugh de Quehen (London, 1996), p. 139.

[18] Jay David Bolter, *Writing Space: The Computer, Hypertext, and the History of Writing* (Hillsdale, NJ, 1991), p. 11. For the purposes of quotation, I am citing the first edition, but the second edition (Mahwah, NJ, 2001) contains similar language: whereas the reader of a printed book is "only a visitor in the author's cathedral," digital technology, according to Bolter, "seems to reduce the distance between author and reader by turning the reader into an author herself" (p. 4).

Index

219

Donne, John, Jr. 128
Dowsing, William 60–61
Drake, Francis 77
"Draught of Sir Phillip Sidney's
    Arcadia, A" 82–83, 86, 89
Drayton, Michael 58, 163, 189
drolleries 66, 88, 89–90
Drummond, William 47, 108, 115, 149
Drury, Elizabeth 137
Drury, Robert 137
Dunn, Kevin 36, 39, 122
Durfey, Thomas 38

education 42–43, 45–46, 47, 48
Eglesfield, Francis 154
Eikon Basilike 74–75
Eisenstein, Elizabeth 8, 30
Eliot, T. S. 153, 215
Elizabeth I 76–77, 108, 115, 134
Elstracke, Renold 69
emblems 33, 40, 41
Englands Sorrow Or, A Farewell to Essex 38
Ent, George 51
Erasmus 25, 27–28, 29, 31, 32, 46, 49
errata 39, 59–60; *see also titles of individual
    works*
Euripides 185, 205
Evelyn, John 47
exegesis, biblical 26–32, 33–34; *see also* readers
    and reading

Falco, Raphael 109
Falk, Ruth 136, 137
Fallon, Robert Thomas 133
Fallon, Stephen M. 17
Farmer, Norman K., Jr. 161
Feld, M. D. 7
Ferrand, Jacques 87
Feuillerat, Albert 64, 66
Field, Nathaniel 36
Fish, Stanley 10–11, 184, 199, 209
Fitzgerald, James, Earl of Desmond 115
Flesher (Fletcher), Miles 8, 9, 10–11, 120–21, 123,
    126, 127–31, 134–35, 138–39
Fletcher, Harris Francis 191, 208
Fletcher, John 62, 71, 104, 171, 178, 180
Florio, John 67
Forde, Emanuel 95
Fowler, Alastair 111
fragment poems 213
Frontain, Raymond-Jean 136, 137
"functional ambiguity" 16–17

Galen 51
Gants, David L. 101

Gardner, Helen 136
Garrison, James D. 110
Gascoigne, George 36, 43, 54
Gaskell, Philip 190
Gaywood, Richard 51
Godard, Jean-Luc 214
Goodyere, Henry 127, 130
Grafton, Anthony 21, 25, 32–33
Grazia, Margreta de 109
Green, Ian 48
Greene, Robert 39
Greg, W. W. 6
Greville, Fulke 67, 68, 80, 81
Grierson, Herbert J. C. 127, 134
Grund, Gary R. 73
Guibbory, Achsah 168, 173
Guillim, John 35, 39, 58
Gwinne, Matthew 67

Hale, J. R. 76
Hall, John 4
Hannay, Margaret P. 68
Harmar, John 163
Harrington, James 48
Harrington, John 68
Hart, E. F. 73
Harvey, Gabriel 21, 22, 40, 47
Harvey, William 49, 109
    Anatomical Exercitations 51, 52, 53
Haskin, Dayton 30, 32
Hawkins, Richard 62
Helgerson, Richard 8, 114
Heliodorus 69
Heminge, John 35, 37
Hemingway, Ernest 214–15
Henrietta Maria 77, 93
Herbert, George 39
Herbert, Henry 139
Herbert, Magdalen 130
Herbert, Mary, Countess of Pembroke 67–68,
    70
Herford, C. H. 100, 107, 113, 114
Herrick, Robert 17, 18, 58, 66, 149, 153, 154, 157,
    158, 165, 168, 171, 183
    Hesperides 2, 19–20, 39, 189
    and anxiety about print 164–72
    and authorial presence 150–51, 152, 162,
        161–63, 172, 177
    and readers 150–51, 154–55, 164–70, 171–72,
        174, 175, 176–82
    catchwords 160, 172
    collaborative creation of 151, 154–56, 160,
        163, 172
    date of 158
    errata 154–55, 159, 164, 170

Wilder, Thornton 214
Wilkins, John 40
Williams, Franklin B., Jr. 123
Williams, John 154
Williams, Raymond 12
Willis, Thomas 45
Wilson, Deirdre 13, 14–15
Wittreich, Joseph 184, 189, 191, 202
Wood, Anthony à 158
Woolf, D. R. 22, 34, 58, 217
Worden, A. B. 16
Worden, Blair 92, 183, 204

Wordsworth, William 213
works, unfinished *see* omissions *and titles of individual works*
Wotton, Henry 47–48, 124–26, 189
Woudhuysen, H. R. 148
Wroth, Mary
  Countess of Montgomeries Urania, The 4, 71
Wyatt, Thomas 167

Young, James 51

Zwicker, Steven 60